THE POLITICS OF ILLUSION

REPUBLICANISM AND SOCIALISM IN MODERN IRELAND

Henry Patterson

HUTCHINSON RADIUS
London   Sydney   Auckland   Johannesburg

Hutchinson Radius
An imprint of Century Hutchinson Ltd,
Brookmount House, 62–65 Chandos Place,
London WC2N 4NW

Century Hutchinson Australia (Pty) Ltd
89–91 Albion Street, Surry Hills, NSW 2010,
Australia

Century Hutchinson New Zealand Ltd
PO Box 40–086, Glenfield, Auckland 10, New Zealand

Century Hutchinson South Africa (Pty) Ltd
PO Box 337, Bergvlei, 2012 South Africa

First published by Hutchinson Radius 1989

© Henry Patterson 1989

British Library Cataloguing in Publication Data
Patterson, Henry
   The politics of illusion : republicanism and
   socialism in modern Ireland.
   1. Ireland. Revolutionary movements : Irish
   Republican Army History
   I. Title
   322.4′2′09415

ISBN 0 09 174259 5 (cased)
       0 09 174139 4 (paperback)

Set in Linotron Bembo by Speedset Ltd, Ellesmere Port
Printed and bound in Great Britain by
Mackays of Chatham PLC, Chatham, Kent

To Carmel and Sam

Contents

Preface

This is not a narrative history of the wider republican movement or of the IRA. Many individuals and incidents in that tradition do not figure here and those in search of them should look to the standard histories of Bowyer-Bell, Coogan, and Bishop and Mallie. *The Politics of Illusion* is concerned with the social and political dynamics of the republican movement, and this means that I pay much more attention to the relations between republicanism and the transformations of Irish society since partition in 1922 than is often the case in studies of the republican tradition.

The book could not have been written without the assistance of those who agreed to be interviewed – Gerry Adams, Jack Brady, Anthony Coughlan, Francie Donnelly, Jimmy Drumm, Sean Garland, Cathal Goulding, Eoghan Harris, Seamus Harrison, Roy Johnston, Seamus Lynch, Tomás MacGiolla, Paddy Joe McClean, Dessie O'Hagan, Eamonn Smullen, Kevin Smyth and Jim Sullivan. I also received assistance from Mary McMahon. Eric Byrne and Ellen Hazelkorn gave me valuable criticism of what I had written on Official Republicanism in Dublin in the mid-1970s. Richard Dunphy gave me access to his major work on the history of Fianna Fáil up to 1948. The book as a whole benefited from many conversations with Paul Bew, particularly on the nature of Sinn Féin's 'modernisation' since the mid-1970s. Carmel Roulston's work on the recent history of the Communist Party of Ireland was of great value, as were her detailed criticisms of the first draft of the book – which much improved it. Neil Belton has continued to be a source of support to the development of my work on Ireland and provided an intelligent and detailed editorial control.

None of the people I have mentioned has any responsibility for the positions and interpretations of the author.

I would like to acknowledge the assistance of the staffs of the National Library of Ireland; the State Paper Office, Dublin Castle; the Linenhall Library, Belfast; the Library, University of Ulster at Jordanstown and the British Library at Colindale. My research benefitted from grants and study leave given by the Research Sub-Committee of the Faculty of Humanities of the University of Ulster and from the assistance of Jennifer Irwin and Joan Philipson.

Henry Patterson.
Belfast, June 1989.

Introduction

The capacity of the current IRA to wage the longest sustained military campaign in the history of Anglo-Irish relations has been poorly reflected on by those who have written the main accounts of the republican movement. In part this is owing to the movement's own pronounced tendency to a monochrome remembrance of itself – as a principled and self-sacrificing minority who have challenged British rule down through the centuries despite and because of the apathy and 'materialism' of the majority of the Irish people. Histories of republicanism focusing largely on its violent activities to the exclusion of political and social context have done little to challenge such definitions.

More recently the level of reflection on republicanism has suffered from the rise of the academic 'terrorism industry', whose typologies have succeeded only in draining terrorism of any national or historical specificity. As Edward Said has written: '. . . the most striking thing about "terrorism", as a phenomenon of the public sphere of communication and representation in the West, is its isolation from any explanation or mitigating circumstances, and its isolation as well from representations of most other dysfunctions, symptoms and maladies of the contemporary world.'[1] The tendency to decontextualize current Irish terrorism is reinforced by the incongruity of a 'national liberation' struggle which, as its main non-violent nationalist critic has pointed out, has in the last twenty years killed twice as many Irish Catholics as the security forces of the 'occupying power'.[2] Nevertheless, to focus simply on the activities of Irish terrorists – whether their more newsworthy irruptions in Britain or Europe or the banally brutal killings of Irish Protestants in and out of uniform – is to limit ourselves to a moral outrage which is by now paper-thin and, ever more palpably, a diversion from serious thought about contemporary Ireland.

A key characteristic of the unproductive labelling of contemporary republicanism by its critics is that the terms used
tend to abstract the movement from those political and
ideological tendencies in the mainstream of Irish life which
have sustained the morale and ambitions of the Republican
leadership. Government ministers have referred to Sinn Féin
as a 'Marxist' organisation while in a speech to the annual
conference of his party in 1988 John Hume referred to them as
'Fascists';[3] but it is easy for Sinn Féin leaders like Gerry Adams
and Danny Morrison to point out that at various times in the
last twenty years they have had talks and negotiations with
leading British politicians and members of British governments, including Douglas Hurd, and that for seven months in
1988 they had a series of long discussions with Hume and
other leading members of the SDLP. Clearly, the very
ambiguities in the relations between the state and constitutional nationalism and republicanism reveal the existence of
a tendency which, despite the stridency of anti-terrorist
rhetoric, treats republicanism as a force not totally beyond
recognition.

While we need a more serious understanding of what
sustains republican violence, it is an evasion to conclude, with
the most recent history of the IRA, that 'the history of
republicanism since Wolfe Tone has shown that as long as
there is a British presence in Ireland it is an ineradicable
tradition.'[4] The real question is not whether a 'republican
tradition' exists; rather, it concerns the various transformations the tradition has undergone and the very variable degree
of popular support that has existed for it. The present
leadership of Sinn Féin admits that, as a result of a divisive and
demoralizing ceasefire negotiated between the then leadership
of the IRA and the Northern Ireland Office in 1975, 'a most
critical stage' was reached, and that 'if changes had not taken
place in a short time then the IRA would have been defeated.'[5]
These changes, which will be dealt with later, produced a very
different relationship between force and politics from that
established with the formation of the Provisional IRA in
1969–70. There is a parallel between the post-1975 changes
and those following the defeat of the IRA's military campaign

against the Northern Ireland state between 1956 and 1962. After 1962 there was a 'rethinking' which contributed to the split in the IRA and Sinn Féin in 1969. The participants in these developments tend to see them in a largely 'internalist' perspective. A central argument of this book, in contrast, is that the ability of physical force republicanism to resuscitate itself after its regular defeats, although partly to be explained by certain moral-existential characteristics of the 'republican personality', derives from the complex relation between the legacy of the 'incomplete' Irish national revolution of 1918–21 and a range of social, economic and communal grievances which republicanism can, more or less successfully, exploit.

Until the Treaty split and Civil war, the revolutionary nationalist movement of Sinn Féin, and the IRA, which had emerged in the aftermath of the Easter Rising of 1916, had strongly insisted on the trans-class and generally non-'sectional' nature of their project. However, in the wake of defeat, the opponents of the new order were forced to look to a range of hitherto neglected issues as a means of maintaining and expanding support. The conditions of small farmers and landless labourers; low wages, unemployment and bad housing in Dublin and the larger towns; the fears and resentments of the Catholic minority in the newly established Unionist regime in Northern Ireland: all would represent opportunities for republicans. Yet they would be severely inhibited by the ideological legacy of nationalist purism and by the organizational weight of a secretive militarism which maintained a deep distrust of 'politics'. In the inter-war period and again in the 1960s and 1970s, in reaction to the defeats of what came to be seen as an apolitical and purely militarist republicanism, there emerged what this book will call 'social republicanism': an effort to rally the masses to the 'anti-imperialist struggle' by taking up economic and social issues. This book is a study of social republicanism and its role in a number of crucial periods in modern Irish history. It will demonstrate the extreme difficulty that republicanism has experienced in managing the tensions that involvement in economic and social issues creates. These derive in part from the secretive nature of the tradition but also from the real danger that when such issues are taken seriously the central objective of republican struggle is put in question. From Peadar O'Donnell in the 1930s to Gerry Adams in the 1980s, the attractions of social republicanism are clear; but so are its dangers for those committed to the legitimacy of 'armed struggle'. Once republicanism takes up material issues – land annuities and rural depopulation in the 1920s and 1930s, or unemployment and poverty in the Catholic ghettoes of the 1980s – it risks marginalization through state-sponsored reform. Thus, another key factor bearing on the ability of the republican movement to maintain popular support is state response. The decline of the IRA in the 1930s is largely explicable by the absorptive capacity of De Valera's political and social programme; and by the same token no analysis of the current state of the IRA and Sinn Féin can avoid the issue of Thatcherism. There has been too much emphasis by historians on the 'republican tradition', taking us back through nine-teenth-century examples of Fenianism and 1848 to Wolfe Tone and the United Irishmen in the 1790s; such 'deep' history can blind us to the need to examine the very specific historical circumstances in which republicans operated, and which they were sometimes able to turn to their advantage. We need a more discontinuous, 'conjunctural' analysis that breaks with the fatalism of traditional approaches which, ironically, unconsciously mimic the self-serving certainties of the republican world view.

1

The Origins of
Social Republicanism

At the core of republican ideology since 1921 is the idea of the incomplete nature of the Irish national revolution of 1918–21. The pervasiveness and strength of this notion derive from its fusion of two crucial aspirations within Irish nationalism – for a 'sovereign' 32-county state, but also for a state that would be socially, economically and culturally different from Britain. It is to the Irish revolutionary of 1848, James Fintan Lalor, that we can look for the origin of the captivating idea that, since the 'Conquest' had been a double process of political and economic expropriation, the 'Reconquest' must necessarily be a dual process too. For Lalor, the core of the reconquest lay in the expropriation of the landlords and the reappropriation of land by the Irish peasantry.[1] For James Connolly and later Irish socialists and social republicans like Peadar O'Donnell, reconquest was a national revolution that was simultaneously a social revolution.

Connolly's influence was immense, given his double significance as a socialist of international stature and an executed leader of the 1916 Rising when he and his Irish Citizens' Army, an organizational embodiment of the fierce class battles of the 1913 Dublin Lockout, had participated in the revolutionary nationalist insurrection in Dublin. In one of his earliest articles he had written: 'If you remove the English army tomorrow and hoist the green flag over Dublin Castle, unless you set about the organisation of a Socialist Republic your efforts will be in vain. . . . Nationalism without social-ism – without a reorganisation of society – is only national recreancy.'[2] The dominant force in Irish nationalism from the 1880s to 1916 was the Irish Parliamentary Party. For Connolly this was a bourgeois leadership which endorsed not only

existing economic relations between Ireland and Britain but
the whole system of 'foreign' (i.e., capitalist) property
relations that British colonization had imposed on Ireland. A
merely political independence which left capitalist relations of
production intact was meaningless. Only the Irish working
class had an objective interest in Irish independence and he
therefore deduced that the only true national revolution would
be a socialist one. Connolly had created a powerful paradigm
linking the failure of the dominant political forces in nationalist Ireland to their class nature. The nationalist project of a 32-
county state independent of British influence was accepted;
only the capacity of the Irish bourgeoisie to realize it was
questioned. Thus, not only did Connolly seriously underestimate the capacity of the Protestants of Ulster, including
the majority of Belfast's working class, to frustrate the
aspiration for territorial unity, he also failed to anticipate the
space which existed in Catholic Ireland for a nationalism that
was not as obesely bourgeois as that of the Irish Parliamentary
Party and yet in no sense socialist – a space which the revivified
Sinn Féin organization would fill in the aftermath of 1916.
Connolly's lack of foresight is more understandable given the
original Sinn Féin ('Ourselves' or 'Our Own Thing').
Founded by Arthur Griffith in 1905, it was a small if energetic
alliance of Irish language and cultural revivalists, economic
nationalists and a smattering of representatives of the underground physical force tradition (the Irish Republican Brotherhood) which had made little political advance before 1916. It
had also been characterised, particularly in Griffith's writings,
by a fierce hostility to trade union militancy and socialism.
The post-1916 reconstruction of Sinn Féin into a broad
nationalist front capable of displacing the Irish Parliamentary
Party stemmed, in large part, from a transformation in the
attitudes of rural Ireland to separatist nationalism. Connolly's
essentially urban focus was unlikely to anticipate this decisive
shift.

   Connolly's own evaluation of the main social forces that
would make the Irish Revolution was fundamentally flawed
by his failure to come to grips with the nature of rural Ireland
and the central role within it of a rural bourgeoisie. That the
work of Ireland's only socialist of international standing has

had so little to say about rural Ireland would have serious debilitating effects on the subsequent history of Irish socialism. As Joe Lee has cogently argued, Connolly lacked a substantial grasp of the land question which so concerned the majority of the Irish population: 'Connolly's fatal tactical error was his reluctance to acknowledge the existence of rural Ireland.'[3] When he did deal with the countryside, it was to depict a peasantry which the British government's land legislation of the late nineteenth century had assisted into the stage of capitalist farming. However, it now faced inevitable impoverishment as Irish farming found itself in competition with the large-scale, mechanized farming of North America. Only social ownership of all the resources of Ireland and a protected economy could save the rural population from impoverishment. This catastrophist view of the future of Irish agriculture ignored, as Marx did earlier,[4] the economic and social weight of the Irish rural bourgeoisie, which was far from doomed to extinction. It led inevitably to the view that the only substantial bourgeoisie, in Catholic Ireland at least, was urban and comprador in nature, with a limited form of Home Rule as its ultimate political ambition. Thus Connolly was able to provide an optimistic prognosis for the coming Irish revolution, which would resolve the major contradictions between nationalism and socialism, and town and countryside. If the bourgeoisie was so integrated in the existing nexus of economic relations with Britain, any 'true' nationalist would see that real independence necessitated a social revolution. Town and countryside would be reconciled in a worker-peasant alliance brought about as impoverishment by international competition forced the peasants to see the limits of individual ownership and the necessity of a system of agricultural and manufacturing cooperatives.[5] The pleasing symmetry of these ideas may help to explain their continuing influence long after the War of Independence had demonstrated their profound inadequacy in grasping central economic and political realities. What actually happened was that a substantial section of the rural bourgeoisie showed itself willing to contemplate a much more radical form of settlement with Britain than Home Rule, and to support an armed

campaign to obtain it. There would prove to be a space for a
revolutionary nationalism with a conservative social content.

Social Forces and the Irish Revolution

The rural order from which nationalists drew their support
was socially divided between a large peasant class involved in
small and medium-scale farming and a growing stratum of
rich cattle graziers, with holdings of at least 200 acres and more
usually between 400 and 600 acres. These 'ranchers', as they
were popularly termed, were particularly concentrated in
three regions – the lowlands of north Leinster, the plains of
east Connaught and north Munster and the mountain pastures
and boglands of west Connaught.[6] The coexistence in the
west of ranches alongside peasants on small overcrowded
holdings was a source of often bitter tension and would create
problems for Sinn Féin during the War of Independence. It
would also cast a long shadow over republican radicalism in
the subsequent period.

In 1911 there were 328,743 Irish farmers of whom over
100,000 farmed less than 10 acres. There were, in addition,
450,000 workers in agriculture – farm labourers and the much
more substantial group of 'relatives assisting'. At the top of
the rural hierarchy were the 32,000 farmers with more than
100 acres.[7] There were thus two possible lines of fissure in the
Irish countryside: between rich farmers and labourers, and
particularly in the west, between the land-hungry smallholders and the ranchers in their midst. Such tensions were all
the more likely to erupt once the British land legislation
culminating in the Wyndham Act of 1903 removed the
landlord class as a unifying focus of resentment. An estimated
two-thirds to three-quarters of farmers had become owners of
their land by the outbreak of World War One. Nevertheless
significant agrarian grievances remained, particularly among
small farmers. The war slowed the process of land purchase
and also shut off the safety valve of emigration. One historian
has suggested of the 1916–21 period that 'it may indeed be that
the real dynamism which underlay the national movement
remained the pressure of population on the land. Land hunger,

exacerbated by the cessation of emigration, seems to have remained the only force which generated large scale popular action.'[8] The War of Independence had coincided with a major upsurge of rural social conflicts and trade union militancy. In the west of Ireland, which had a large concentration of the poorest land and smallest farms and where the Land Acts had done least to satisfy peasant land hunger, there was an upsurge of peasant activity aimed at forcing a radical redistribution of land. Such activity was described by the Unionist *Irish Times* as 'Agrarian Bolshevism' and was often regarded with little less hostility by Sinn Féin, which established arbitration courts to bring the land war under control. Dan Breen, one of the key guerrilla leaders in the War of Independence and later a militant opponent of the Treaty, subsequently told Peadar O'Donnell that if anyone had talked of dividing up estates in his area he would have had them shot.[9] As Paul Bew has pointed out: 'When, after 1916, Sinn Féin emerged as a new force in nationalist politics – sanctified by the "blood sacrifice" of the Easter Rising – it was able to outflank the Irish Party both on the left and on the right in agrarian matters according to convenience. In short, by 1918 Irish agrarian radicalism was, from the nationalist point of view, a profoundly ambiguous force.'[10]

Sinn Féin's first association with agrarian protest, in 1917 and early 1918, was short-lived and typically instrumental. In the words of one IRA man, 'I hadn't the slightest interest in the land agitation, but I had every interest in using it as a means to an end . . . to get these fellows into the Volunteers. . . . Up to that they were just an unorganised mob.'[11] Soon however, Sinn Féin and the IRA were concerned that social agitation was disrupting 'national' unity and scaring off potential supporters, and in February 1918 the standing committee of Sinn Féin expressed its opposition to unauthorized land-seizures and cattle drives.[12] In his path-breaking provincial study of the Irish Revolution, David Fitzpatrick shows how Sinn Féin organizers encouraged members who were small farmers and labourers to take part in agitation for the breaking up of the large grazing ranches of the west, in the early part of 1918 and again in early 1920 when the struggle was far more violent and widespread. However, although participation may have consolidated Sinn Féin support amongst the poorest sections of the Irish peasantry, it also fomented hostility in the larger farmers and the more comfortable members of the rural community whose support was a real political and material necessity for Sinn Féin: '. . . Republicanism itself had been tamed by the men of substance almost from the start. Like the Home Rule movement, which it so closely resembled, Sinn Féin was heavily dependent upon shopkeepers, employers and large farmers for income, and the Republican county councils for their rates . . . systematic intimidation might have alienated a substantial and articulate group of Irishmen from the Republican cause, thus breaching the underlying principle of consensus nationalism.'[13]

Sinn Féin's electoral triumph in 1918–73 Sinn Féiners as against 26 Unionists and 6 members of the old Irish Parliamentary Party – exaggerated both the size and the nature of its political victory. Irish Labour abstained from the elections and the Irish Parliamentary Party contested few seats. Also significant in the present context was the economic and social void at the centre of the Sinn Féin programme. Seán O'Faoláin drily summed it up: 'the policy of Sinn Féin has always been, since its foundation, that simple formula: Freedom first; other things after.' The author of the first scholarly account of the Civil War expands on this judgment: 'at whatever cost to ideological coherence, unity had to be preserved and divisive issues avoided.'[14] The electoral demise of the Irish Parliamentary Party owed more to their failure to deliver Home Rule due to Ulster Unionist resistance, and to Lloyd George's botched attempt to impose conscription on Ireland in 1918, than to positive popular support for the establishing of a republic. The Easter Rising and the execution by the British of its leaders had unleashed a tide of emotional nationalism which viewed the failures of the Parliamentary Party as terminal. The very success of the land legislation in making owners of a majority of Irish farmers removed any material interest they had in the continuation of the Union. It was precisely because the Irish programme on the land question had been largely met by the British parliament that an Irish constitutional party at Westminster became irrelevant. As a sympathizer of the defunct party noted in 1919: 'until Irish land purchase was peacefully completed the man who would suggest the withdrawal of the Irish party from London would make himself the laughing stock of Irish politics.'[15] Those who were most likely not to have been satisfied by the land legislation, who would have liked a much clearer commitment from Sinn Féin to the interests of small farmers and farm labourers, were disappointed as it made clear its overriding commitment to a pan-class appeal.

The result was a distinct lack of enthusiasm for the 'national struggle' in the province where smallholders had seen their agrarian struggles denounced by Sinn Féin and sometimes repressed by the IRA. Connaught, the most aggressively nationalist province in previous periods of agrarian agitation, was relatively restrained in the War of Independence, the central role passing to the province of Munster with its much more substantial medium-sized farmer class. In his pioneering analysis of the period, Rumpf relates the land question to participation in the War of Independence: 'The districts where the most violent agrarian unrest occurred during the period were not the centres of the national struggle. The social aspirations of the landless men were not primarily expressed in terms of hostility to the British administration. To a certain extent such aspirations were directly excluded from the national struggle, for the spirit which dominated the IRA leadership at all levels inculcated a deep suspicion of any attempt to mix social aims with the pure cause of the national struggle. The social condition of many areas of the west was not favourable to an active national fight. The main national resistance was concentrated in more prosperous districts, such as de Tocqueville noticed was the case in the French Revolution, and was also true of the German Peasants' Wars.'[16] A nationalism linked positively to the demands of the poorest and most marginal elements in the peasantry would have risked losing the support of the most powerful class in the Irish countryside and would have represented a substantially weaker challenge to the British state. Even if it had prosecuted the struggles of the smallholders against the 'ranchers', it would not have been creating the basis for a worker-peasant alliance: the aim of the land-hungry peasants was a comfortable holding, not the inauguration of some 'cooperative commonwealth'. It was symptomatic of Connolly's weakness in this area that he was forced onto the terrain of Gaelic revivalism in explaining supposed peasant openness to co-operation and alliance with workers by the invocation of a racial memory of 'the traditions . . . of the common owner-ship and common control of the land by their ancestors'.[17]

Sinn Féin's essential coolness or hostility to agrarian militancy was mirrored in its relation to the upsurge of trade union activity between 1917 and 1920. War-time inflation which ate into working-class living standards, an increased demand for labour which, by 1917, had combined with the introduction of compulsory tillage to cause a labour shortage in agriculture, and resentment at the unequal impact of war-time hardships: these were the key factors in a major growth in union membership. Between 1916 and 1920, the numbers represented by the Irish Labour Party and Trade Union Congress rose from 100,000 to 225,000 – a quarter of Irish wage-earners.[18] The Irish Transport and General Workers Union, established as a proto-syndicalist organization by James Larkin in 1909, grew massively from 5,000 in 1917 to 130,000 at the end of 1920.[19] Unionization spread into new areas and hitherto unorganized sectors of the working class. Most explosive was the organization of the most neglected stratum in the Irish countryside – the farm labourers. Although they constituted only 18% of the agricultural labour force in the 26-country area in the early 1920s, they were a regionally concentrated group: only 6% in Connaught but almost 33% in Leinster. In twelve Leinster and east Munster counties labourers represented about a third of the agricultural labour force.[20] They would contribute significantly to the growing number of strikes, strikers and strike days that Ireland saw between 1917 and the slump that set in at the end of 1920. Such strikes, especially when accompanied, as they often were, by well-organized picketing, sympathetic action and even active sabotage, and adopting the icono-graphy of 1917, with red flags and even detachments of 'Red Guards', helped in Fitzpatrick's words to 'strike fear into the heart of Republicans'.[21] In June 1920 the illegal Irish parlia-ment, Dáil Éireann, issued a proclamation clearly depicting such activities as sectional diversions: 'the present time when the Irish people are locked in a life and death struggle with their traditional enemy, is ill chosen for the stirring up of strife among our fellow countrymen.'[22]

In 1919 the Dáil had created arbitration courts and a Central Conciliation Board. Like the Sinn Féin courts of justice and the land courts, these institutions had the dual function of dislodging the British administration and defusing unrest. Emmet O'Connor provides an astringent summary of the role of such institutions, and of the Dáil's Department of Labour, headed as it was by the one Sinn Féin leader to proclaim herself a socialist, Constance Markievicz: 'These efforts had the practical effect of asserting Dáil Éireann's legitimacy to employers and employees, reducing strife and settling grievances, usually on the basis of precedents set out by [British] government machinery . . . . The Department also played a propagandist function being advertised by Sinn Féin as an illustration of its concern for trade unionists. However, nowhere is there any indication of structural reform appearing on the departmental agenda.'[23] When the post-war slump began to push up unemployment in early 1921, the republican government examined ways of dealing with it and put forward recommendations for increased tillage, extension of public works and the promotion of profit-sharing industries. However, it did not contemplate legislation in any of these areas, contenting itself with appeals to patriotism. It ignored a shrill memorandum from Markievicz, forecasting a violent revolution unless the Dáil moved to deal with 'disaffected workers'. Her proposals were hardly revolutionary: the establishment of food cooperatives, more road works, and the gimmicky idea of seizing and reopening a meat factory 'to show the workers we had their interests at heart'.[24]

The largely integrative approach of Sinn Féin and the Dáil to labour issues, their refusal to take sides with labour against capital, was viewed by many in the labour movement as a poor response to the positive role of the ILPTUC and individual unions in the War of Independence. In 1918 the labour movement, outside the predominantly Unionist parts of Ulster, had joined in the campaign against conscription and on 23 April had organized a 24-hour general strike against it. In December the ILPTUC abstained from the general election to allow Sinn Féin a straight fight against the Parliamentary Party. In April 1920 the ILPTUC staged a two-day general strike for the release of republican prisoners on hunger strike. Other important examples of labour contributions to the nationalist campaign were the nine-day total stoppage organized by the Limerick trades council against British militarism in April 1919, and the seven-month dockers' and railway workers' action against the handling and movement of munitions. For Sinn Féin this was little more than what would have been expected from any patriotic group of Irishmen. At the most it called for some show of listening to the voice of labour. Thus the labour leader Thomas Johnston was allowed to draw up a statement of social aims which the first Dáil would adopt as its 'Democratic Programme'. Considered too radical in its original form, the statement was amended by Seán T. O'Kelly and reduced to what O'Faoláin described as terms of 'a purely pious and general nature that committed nobody to anything in particular . . . '.[25] It typified the largely verbal and emollient concessions that mainstream republicanism was prepared to make to keep labour within the ambit of a political and military strategy firmly under republican control. Only after the Treaty split and the onset of civil war did some republicans begin to fashion a version of the War of Independence that depicted the source of the ultimate 'betrayal' as the IRA's predominating hostility to popular economic struggles.

The Civil War and the Emergence of Social Republicanism

Charles Townshend sums up the achievement of revolutionary nationalism by the time of the Treaty negotiations in December 1921 as follows: 'Physical force, whether or not as a result of its alliance with politically sophisticated Sinn Féin, had demonstrably worked. It had extracted from the British concessions which they had hitherto refused. It had prised open, in the more dramatic metaphor preferred by its adherents, England's grip on twenty-six out of the thirty-two counties of Ireland.'[26] Yet since physical force was incapable, in the words of the IRA's effective commander, Michael Collins, of 'beating the British out of Ireland militarily',[27] the militant nationalist aspiration for a republic was to be disappointed. The limit of British concession was to be dominion status within the British Empire and Commonwealth, and most offensive of all to the purer republicans was the provision for members of the parliament of the new Irish Free State to take an oath of allegiance to the British monarch as head of the Commonwealth.

The debate on the Treaty split Sinn Féin and the IRA and led to a bitter civil war between the 'Free State' forces who lost over 800 dead and the anti-treaty 'Republican' forces who lost many more. Casualties were far in excess of the numbers of Irish Volunteers killed in the 1916–21 period.[28] On the republican side in the Dáil the predominant concerns were issues like the Oath of Allegiance to the Crown, which symbolized the profound distance separating a 26-county British dominion from the Republic proclaimed in 1916. Many commentators since have attempted to explain what one Treaty supporter disparagingly referred to as the 'mystical, hysterical, neurotic worship of "The Republic".'[29] Part of the explanation must be sought in the necessary amorphousness of the political and social ideologies of the revolutionary elite. Predominantly petty-bourgeois professionals, journalists, and teachers, their origins lay disproportionately in the ascending class in post-Famine Ireland, the rural bourgeoisie. Their thinking about the economic and social dimensions of 'freedom' tended towards pieties about the need to avoid the extremes of capitalism and socialism and the massive industrial conurbation of Britain and other capitalist states, with their unhealthy polarization of classes brought about by too-great disparities of income. Thus even the paper of Arthur Griffith, the most vigorous advocate of tariff-based capitalist economic development, denounced the evils of the English factory system and 'dreamed in Wellsian terms of technological revolutions that would make such developments unnecessary in Ireland'.[30] Socialism and trade union militancy were often seen as twin examples of 'foreign' doctrines likely to divide the nation. Gaelic revivalism with its references to a 'pre-conquest' utopia of cooperative *gemeinschaft* reinforced this approach, as did the Catholic Church's

attitude to social questions, based on Pope Leo XIII's
encyclical *Rerum Novarum*, with its discussion of the twin evils
of socialist internationalism and the doctrine of the class
struggle.[31] Rejecting certain features of industrial capitalism
while leaving unquestioned the current economic realities in
Ireland, Sinn Féin was able to represent itself as a more
profound challenge to British rule than the 'bourgeois'
Parliamentary Party while not disturbing the equilibrium of
its wealthier supporters.

But precisely because the substance of Sinn Féin economic
and social philosophy was an accommodation with the main
lines of development of the post-Famine economic order, its
rhetoric of difference with the Parliamentary Party took on a
largely moralistic and 'principled' tone. This meant that it
would prove difficult and ultimately impossible for the Sinn
Féin elite to avoid a split when faced with such an impure
settlement as the Treaty. For of course the Treaty was a
compromise brought about by the realities of relative military
and economic power. For many of the Sinn Féin leadership,
just as the inspiring memory of a higher Gaelic civilization
would prove sufficient to insulate an independent Ireland from
the 'excesses' of capitalism, so another act of revolutionary
will would force the British finally to concede the unalloyed
Republic. Despite the overwhelmingly political and constitutional focus of the Treaty debates, there was a link between
the capacity of revolutionary nationalism to spiritualize real
social and economic antagonisms into a language of 'principles' and abstract freedom, and its profound difficulty in
adjusting to a situation where the criteria which had so often
been used to marginalize 'sectional' projects like that of labour
could now be turned against those who would settle for
something less than complete independence.

The anti-Treaty position was given major social sustenance
by the large reservoirs of agrarian dissatisfaction, particularly
in Connaught, which would prove much more active in the
Civil War than it had in the War of Independence. For many
small farmers and farm labourers, republican intransigence
was very clearly a function of perceived class interest. The
defeat of the republicans would be accompanied by the
simultaneous defeat of the remnants of agrarian radicalism: in

Meath, Clare and Waterford pro-Treaty forces physically repressed small farmers' and labourers' militancy.[32]

As his cause went down to defeat, a leading anti-Treatyite would produce in prison the few brief notes on which much of the subsequent vocation of social republicanism based itself. Liam Mellows wrote to Austin Stack, who before the Civil War had been successively Minister of Justice and Minister of Home Affairs, and was now a prominent anti-Treatyite. Mellows expressed his dissatisfaction with the republicans' apolitical approach, which 'could only judge of situations in terms of guns and men'.[33] He was influenced by an editorial in a recent edition of the *Workers' Republic*, the newspaper of the tiny Communist Party of Ireland, which had urged a social and economic programme capable of winning the masses to the support of the Republic. Mellows pressed the republican leadership to set up a government and to translate the Dáil's 1919 Democratic Programme into 'something definite. This is essential if the great body of workers are to be kept on the side of Independence.' A more specific social programme was justified by his interpretation of the Treaty split which showed that 'the commercial interest, so called, money and gombeen men are on the side of the Treaty. We are back to Tone . . . relying on "the men of no property". The "stake in the country" people were never with the Republic. . . . We should recognise that definitely now and base our appeals upon the understanding and needs of those who have always borne Ireland's fight.'

As the only radical document to be produced by a republican during the period, Mellows's *Jail Notes* were to become a major inspiration for leftist republicans – especially after his execution at the hands of the Free State government. Charles Townshend refers to him as 'the lone socialist within the leadership'.[34] This judgment at once inflates the socialist component of Mellows's outlook and encourages an under-estimation of his longer-term significance. Only 21 when he met Connolly in 1913, he was already well integrated into the physical force underground tradition through his membership first of the republican 'boy scout' movement Na Fianna Eireann and subsequently of the IRB. His horizons are well summed up in his declaration to his mother in 1913, 'I'm going to be another Robert Emmet.'[35] Emmet had led a confused and doomed insurrection in Dublin in 1803, gaining entry to the republican tradition largely through his florid speech from the dock and subsequent execution. Roy Foster's judgment on Mellows's hero is acerbic: 'His ideas were those of elite separatism: neither social idealism nor religious equality appear to have figured.'[36] A leader of the 1916 insurrection in Galway, Mellows then spent some time in the United States where he displayed signs of being influenced by Connolly's *Labour in Irish History* – though what took his attention was its assertion that capitalism was a foreign import and that pre-Conquest Ireland was a 'communistic clan' society.[37]

The real significance of Mellows becomes more apparent if certain dissonances in the *Notes* are acknowledged. Thus he suggested that the new social programme should follow the lines of the CPI's strategy which called for state control of industry, transport and the banks as well as the seizure and division of 'the lands of the aristocracy'.[38] At the same time, he claimed that such a programme 'does not require a change of outlook on the part of Republicans, or the adoption of a revolutionary programme as such'. Although the IRA Executive had begun to develop a more radical land policy, it was ingenuous at least to suggest that the sort of specifically radical programme that the CPI was demanding would have been welcome to the great majority of the anti-Treaty leaders. Their moralistic republicanism would have bitterly resisted any 'reduction' of their cause to a class movement.

More fundamentally the apparent radicalization of Mellows's republicanism simply served to provide another means of avoiding the realities of popular acceptance of the Treaty. The pro-Treaty position was conveniently ascribed to a rump of 'pro-imperialist' moneyed elements who, with the help of the British and the support of the Catholic Church and the 'unprincipled' leadership of the Labour movement, were hoodwinking the people. As a radical nationalist Mellows assumed the fundamental unity of the nation. Apart from the West British bourgeois excrescences, any divisions amongst the people were artificially fostered by 'Imperialism'. This conjured out of existence realities like the Ulster Unionists, and in the 26-county area it reduced the substantial support for the Irish Labour Party and Trade Union Congress (until 1930 the political and trade union wings of the Irish labour movement were organically linked), which had given de facto support to the Treaty, to the question of the supposed corruption of its leadership: 'the official Labour Movement has deserted the people for the fleshpots of the Empire.' In fact in the elections earlier in 1922 the ILPTUC had won almost as much support as the anti-Treatyites and had 17 of its 18 candidates elected.[39] That there was more to the question than a corrupt leadership was at least partly recognized when, in his letter to Stack, Mellows mentioned a visit made by leaders of the ILPTUC to the republicans occupying the Four Courts in Dublin (it would be the shelling of the Four Courts by the pro-Treaty supporters that signalled the beginning of the Civil War): 'they remarked that no effort had been made to put the Democratic Programme into execution.'[40] Mellows concluded therefore that the working class were 'naturally' for the Republic, but had been temporarily alienated by the inadequate policies of the republican movement. That for many workers the Treaty was a regrettable but necessary compromise that could be built on, while the anti-Treaty cause threatened only a barren, internecine and destructive conflict was not a thought which a republican like Mellows, no matter how radical some of his language, could contemplate.

What Mellows really signifies is not a turn to socialist republicanism but the first of a number of attempts to preserve intransigent revolutionary nationalism by tapping into perceived social discontent. Thus, in a late communication he takes up the issue of unemployment: 'The unemployment question is acute. Starvation is facing thousands of people. . . . The Free State government's attitude towards striking postal workers makes clear what its attitude towards workers generally would be. The situation created by all these must be utilised for the Republic. The position must be defined: Free State-Capitalism and Industrialism-Empire; Republic-Workers-Labour.'[41] All the ambiguity of social republicanism is in those lines: the Free State is identified with a mode of production – capitalism – but the Republic has no stated foundation except in solidarity with the vaguely defined cause of Labour. It was symptomatic that Mellows should have referred in his *Notes* to Wolfe Tone and the 'men of no property'. The Dublin Protestant who with the assistance of Belfast Presbyterian radicals would found the Society of United Irishmen in 1791 and play a crucial role in the events which culminated in the 1798 Rebellion was subsequently canonised as the 'Father of Republicanism'.[42] In 1796 Tone had written: 'Our freedom must be had at all hazards. If the men of property will not help us they must fall; we will free ourselves by the aid of that large and respectable class of the community – the men of no property.'[43] Rather than an 'embryonic socialist statement'[44] this is a bourgeois revolutionary's acknowledgement that in certain circumstances it may be necessary to make an instrumental and risky appeal to the 'lower orders'. As Richard Dunphy has recently noted of the limits of republican egalitarianism when it used the rhetoric of Tone, 'What was under attack was the notion of aristocracy, not the existence of socio-economic inequalities. The old, Anglo-Irish ruling class, together with the large farmers, the ranchers, distinguished by blood, by titles would make way for those who had worked their way to the top. Hard work, forbearance, meritocracy – these were the cornerstones of the egalitarian faith of the republicans. Such a man, having worked his way to success, would not be a bourgeois but a patriot. . . .'[45] This ambiguous populist egalitarianism would prove to be a potent resource for those who, in the next few decades, would indeed rework republicanism in a constitutional and 'radical' direction under the leadership of Eamon De Valera and the new political formation, Fianna Fáil.

The pan-class alliance of the War of Independence did not split along clear lines of class, but its ending released the defeated side from some of the restraints that had prevented Sinn Féin from taking up economic and social issues. Of course, there were still many in the anti-Treaty Sinn Féin and IRA who maintained a position of rigid and abstract opposition. The Irish Republic proclaimed in 1916 by a 'Provisional Government' had based its claim to the allegiance 'of every Irishman and Irishwoman' on a 'right' established by past insurrections: a real turn towards the solipsistic and self-referential, and away from those within the physical force tradition who still accepted the provision of the 1873 Irish

Republican Brotherhood constitution forbidding its 'Supreme Council' from initiating a war with England until they had the support of the mass of the people.[46] By the end of the Civil War there was much evidence of what Townshend describes as 'a Robespierrist vision of the public good. . . . A sense of democratic values existed, but it was modified by the belief that Sinn Féin understood what ought to be the will of the people if they were sufficiently nationally aware.'[47] Thus Mary MacSwiney, one of the most prominent of Sinn Féin diehards in the inter-war period, gave a typical response to the popular majority for the Treaty: 'The people of a nation may not voluntarily surrender their independence, they may not vote it away in the ballot box even under duress and if some, even a majority be found, who through force or cupidity, would vote for such a surrender, the vote is invalid legally and morally and a minority is justified in upholding the independence of their country.'[48]

Increasingly, however, the lack of popular credibility of such purism began to force a degree of rethinking in Sinn Féin and the IRA. This was aided by the increasingly clear conservatism of the governing party, now called Cumann na nGaedheal, which helped to 'socialize' the Civil War fracture. The first post-Mellows attempt to associate the republicans more clearly with social radicalism came in a number of articles written by Constance Markievicz for the Scottish socialist paper *Forward* and republished as a pamphlet, *What Irish Republicans Stand For*. As a close friend of Connolly's and a member of the Irish Citizens' Army who had received a death sentence (commuted because of her sex) for her role in the 1916 Rising, Markievicz was the Sinn Féin leader most able to put a red gloss on republicanism.

The basic theme represents a Gaelicized version of Connolly. Thus Britain had spent 800 years trying to replace the 'Gaelic State' with the 'Feudal Capitalist State'. The Free State was a further attempt to force 'the English social and economic system' on the Irish people. However, there was resistance, as the people 'cling instinctively and with a passionate loyalty to the ideals of a better civilization, the tradition of which is part of their subconscious, spiritual and mental state.' Connolly's admiration for 'his Celtic forefathers, who foreshadowed in the democratic organization of the Irish clans, the more perfect organization of the free society of the future', was quoted and linked to the claim that popular support for republicanism existed because 'the ideals embodied in that Republic touched all that was most vital and most Gaelic in the imagination and race memory of the people.' The Treaty was depicted as a counter-revolution 'for the purpose of breaking up the development of the Co-operative Commonwealth in Ireland'.[49] This was rewriting history with a dazzling mixture of red and green inks, and Markievicz was obviously strained to provide her readers with examples of revolutionary republicanism in action. Some were pure fabrications: the Democratic Programme was said to have been drawn up by De Valera and, perhaps even more incredibly, to 'emphasize and develop the ideals of the Gaelic state', predictably unspecified. Other instances may not have impressed many Scottish socialists: describing her stint as Minister for Labour, she spoke of how 'the people both employers and workers, believed in the justice of their own Republican government, and of our desire to act fairly, and to secure the best for the worker without ruining the employer.' There was an appeal to Irish shopkeepers, 'if they [did] not want their children to be reduced to the condition of starving wage slaves', to join the workers in reorganizing businesses on 'true cooperative lines'.[50]

This attempt to inflate republican social radicalism was one of the earliest indications of a move by a section of the anti-Treatyites from purity to politics and a more populist republicanism centring on economic protectionism – 'Why encourage the peaceful penetration of Ireland by English capitalism?' – and a distinctive Irish strategy of balanced economic development: 'we should guard against the conquest of Ireland by foreign capital, and the development of her villages along the lines that have created the "Black Country" and the this-world Hells to be found in Glasgow, Liverpool and all British industrial cities.'[51] Behind the whimsical mystifications there was a clear attempt to establish the popular credentials of the key republican political leader, Eamon De Valera, whose 'noble simplicity of life' was contrasted with the Free State government: 'the future aristocracy of Ireland . . . who are rolling around in limousines and acquiring fine residences'. Markievicz's articles represent the first substantial attempt by republicans to use class discontents and a populist Gaelic version of Connolly to criticize the new state. The mystificatory and manipulative version of this strategy embodied in these writings would soon be contested by a more substantial version from within the IRA itself.

2

Republicanism in Inter-war Ireland

The Civil War ended in April 1923 with a ceasefire signed by De Valera as President of the 'Government of the Republic of Ireland' and Frank Aiken as Chief of Staff of the IRA.[1] The declaration contained an ambiguous but significant clause: 'That the ultimate Court of Appeal for deciding disputed questions of national expediency and policy is the people of Ireland, the judgment being by majority vote of the adult citizenry, and the decision to be submitted to, and resistance by violence excluded, not because the decision is necessary, right or just or permanent, but because acceptance of this rule makes for peace, order and unity in national action and is the democratic alternative to arbitrament by force.'[2] For many of the defeated republicans, however, of whom over 12,000 were imprisoned at the time of the ceasefire,[3] democratic criteria would come into play only after the overthrow of the whole Treaty settlement – the 'people of Ireland' could not be truly represented through 'corrupt' institutions like the Free State and the Northern Ireland state. In the IRA were many who regarded physical force as crucial in bringing about change, and who saw 'politicians' as largely an unnecessary evil. The military front in the War of Independence had been opened independently of the Dáil and the government of the Republic, and during the war the military men showed increasing contempt for the politicians.[4] After the Treaty, the tendency to effective IRA autonomy developed to a high degree and although the IRA had taken an oath of loyalty to the Dáil during the War of Independence, the anti-Treaty IRA was largely independent of control by De Valera as president of the notional Republic.

However, military defeat gave the politicians an opportunity to reassert themselves. De Valera successfully urged participation in the general election of August 1923 and although the republicans did unexpectedly well, given the imprisonment of many candidates and election workers, the result inevitably stirred up the suspicions of some in the IRA that Sinn Féin was destined for incorporation in the Free State.[5] Certainly it became difficult to ignore the fact that while the Free State government lacked massive popularity and there was still substantial republican support, it was the support of a minority: a clear majority had voted for candidates who accepted the Treaty. The maintenance of a purist abstentionism held out little prospect of increasing Sinn Féin support against a state which could rely on popular memories and revulsion over the Civil War to isolate republicans so long as it seemed that they were simply preparing for a 'second round'.

By 1925, with more and more evidence that abstentionism was depleting popular support, De Valera and a substantial section of the Sinn Féin leadership had decided that the road to the 'Republic' lay in a long march through the institutions of the Free State and that this meant entering the Dáil. A pivotal role would be played by the Dublin-based Sinn Féin leader, Seán Lemass, soon to emerge as the economic strategist of the new party and the architect of its hegemony over the urban working class. Lemass was an abrasive critic of those in Sinn Féin whose idealist insistence on the 'de jure' republic of 1919 prevented them from acknowledging current realities: 'There are some who would have us sit by the roadside and debate abstruse points about "de jure" this and "de facto" that, but the reality we want is away in the distance and we cannot get there unless we move.'[6] The split in Sinn Féin came in March 1926 at a special Árd Fheis to consider De Valera's proposal that, once the oath of allegiance was removed, 'it becomes a question not of principle but of policy whether or not republican representatives enter the Dáil'. The proposal was narrowly rejected and De Valera and his lieutenants moved quickly to begin the process of organizing a new political formation – Fianna Fáil (Soldiers of Destiny) – which would rapidly consign the idealist intransigents of Sinn Féin to the margins of Irish political life. The relation of the new party with the IRA would be a complex and ambiguous one.

At the General Army Convention of the IRA in November 1925, Frank Aiken – the Chief of Staff and a De Valera supporter – admitted that some members of the 'government of the Republic' were discussing the possibility of entering the Dáil. He provoked substantial and angry support for a resolution from the Tirconail battalion in Donegal, calling on the IRA to sever its connection with the 'shadow' republican government composed of the Sinn Féin members of the second Dáil. The resolution was stridently anti-political: 'That in view of the fact that the Government has developed into a mere political party and has lost sight of the fact that all our energies should be devoted to the all-important work of making the Army efficient so that the renegades who, through a coup d'etat assumed governmental powers in this country, be dealt with at the earliest opportunity, the Army of the Republic sever its connection with the Dáil, and act under an independent Executive, such Executive be given the power to declare war when, in its opinion, a suitable opportunity arises to rid the Republic of its enemies and maintain it in accordance with the proclamation of 1916.'[7] This was proposed by Peadar O'Donnell, who would soon personify social republicanism and who would play a crucial role in republican political development in the inter-war period. O'Donnell saw himself as the link with the legacy of Mellows and set out self-consciously to politicize the IRA. Born in 1893 into a small farming family in Meenmore near Dungloe in Donegal, he trained as a teacher before the war. Radicalized in part by an uncle who returned from the United States where he had been a Wobbly, he was crucially influenced by a trip to Scotland, on which he had been sent by the people of Aranmore island off the Donegal coast, where he was teaching. He was to report on an agricultural strike that was affecting the seasonal earnings so crucial to the economy of the island, as to many other parts of the Donegal seaboard where tiny holdings of poor land could not provide for large families. Emigration to the United States was a structured necessity for such families – five of O'Donnell's eight brothers and sisters emigrated. For those who remained seasonal work as migrant harvesters in

Scotland was commonplace.[8] It was in Scotland that his radicalism was given a distinct socialist inflection: 'Glasgow was my doorway to the world of working-class struggle. There was no turning back for me.'[9]

O'Donnell left school-teaching in 1917 to become a full-time organizer for the Irish Transport and General Workers Union, now entering a period of rapid expansion, but his own priorities were soon apparent as he became involved in the IRA in 1919 and resigned from the union job in 1920 to devote himself full-time to IRA activities. By the time of the Treaty he was in command of the 2nd brigade of the IRA's Northern Division.[10] He opposed the Treaty, was captured in the battle for the Four Courts in June 1922, and imprisoned until his escape in March 1924.

Like Mellows, whom he got to know in Mountjoy Jail, O'Donnell became convinced that the anti-Treaty leadership would go down to defeat because of its lack of a radical social programme to win the masses to the 'Republic': 'The IRA, apart from himself, George Gilmore, Paddy Ruttledge, perhaps Seán Lemass, Seán Moylan and Tommy Mullins, were just as conservative as the First and Second Dáil governments.'[11] In a subsequent interview, he summed up the central inadequacy of the existing republican leadership: 'very dedicated men, almost religious men. . . . All they stood for was that they would not accept the Treaty, they had no alternative programme. They were the stuff that martyrs are made of, but not revolutionaries. . . . We had a pretty barren mind socially, many on the Republican side were against change. Had we won, I would agree that the end results might not have been much different from what one sees today.'[12] However, he saw his approach as more developed than that of Mellows, whom he saw not like some on the left as a socialist republican but rather 'a great Fenian (the Gaelic name for the insurrectionary nationalists of the IRB, associated particularly with their failed rising in 1867) who saw the poor as the freedom force of the nation as Tone did.'[13] For O'Donnell, social discontent was not something that an existing republican leadership could use for its own purposes; rather it demanded a transformation in republicanism, which would become a broad popular alliance capable of 'completing' the national revolution in a socially and economically radical way. As a leading member of the IRA after the Civil War – he was on the Army executive of 12 elected by the Army Convention and on the 7-man Army Council – he was in a strong position to attempt to socialize republicanism. He was helped by his own significant literary talents – he wrote four novels between 1925 and 1930 and would produce major works of auto-biography and contemporary historical analysis. For four years from 1926 to 1930 as editor of *An Phoblacht*, the IRA's weekly newspaper, he would use his position to help usher in a period of energetic if amorphous and contradictory republican leftism in an attempt to maintain a continuing and vital role for the IRA. This was all the more necessary given the increasing appeal of the Fianna Fáil party to many IRA members who were disillusioned with the post-1923 impasse of Sinn Féin. Fianna Fáil organizers who toured the country to build the new organization could often rely on local IRA commanders to bring their membership into the new party – numerous IRA companies were transformed into Fianna Fáil *cumainn* (branches). The skilful ambiguities through which the Fianna Fáil leadership expressed the party's own relationship to the physical force tradition allowed many such republicans to join Fianna Fáil without breaking their link with the IRA. It would be this ambiguous symbiosis that initially encouraged the social republican project and ultimately absorbed it.

Land Annuities and Left Republicanism 1926–32

There is now a considerable literature on both Irish socialism and republicanism in the twentieth century, yet little has been written about the agitation which attempted very clearly to link republican objectives to a major social and political issue: the movement against the payment of land annuities to England, which was launched in 1926 by Peadar O'Donnell in his native Donegal. A major reason for this neglect is ironically the very success of the movement which imposed itself on De Valera and the national leadership of Fianna Fáil. The Fianna Fáil victory in 1932 and its subsequent domination of Irish politics has tended to obscure the important role that left republicanism played in creating what Seán O'Faoláin referred to as 'a distinct social flavour about De Valera-ism'.[14] A related and important issue is the significance of the agitation for the understanding of the nature of social republicanism.

The early 1930s was to see one of the two major attempts since the Treaty to move the republican movement in a socialist direction – the Republican Congress of 1934. The reasons for the quick collapse of this initiative will be only partly understood if their origins in O'Donnell's project of the 1920s are not grasped. For in his writings of the period, and particularly in *An Phoblacht*, O'Donnell articulated perhaps the only serious attempt since partition to create a project of social and political transformation based on a Gaelicized version of Connolly's writings. This project of pushing republicanism to the left would exercise a continuing influence in subsequent decades. Despite its own failure it would become the unsurpassable limit of republican radicalism until the 1970s. However, its intrinsic subordination to a fundamentally nationalist political project meant that it would be incapable of undermining Fianna Fáil's populist appeal.

The land annuities were those due to be paid by Irish farmers under the 1891 and 1909 Land Acts and amounted to £3m a year.[15] Under the Government of Ireland Act 1920 the new governments in Belfast and Dublin were to have retained the annuities but this provision was held to have been superseded by the Treaty. The annuities were dealt with under the Anglo-Irish Financial Agreement of 1923, the terms of which were never published. The Irish government was to collect the annuities from the tenants and pay them into the British government's Purchase Annuities Fund. The Irish government's undertaking to pay the annuities was confirmed under the Ultimate Financial Settlement agreed with the British in March 1926. The political sensitivity of the issue was indicated by the fact that the Free State government did not publish details of the settlement until eight months after it had been signed.

Although the Labour Party had raised the annuities issue in the Dáil, the mainstream of anti-Treatyite Sinn Féin and later Fianna Fáil were notably slow to take up the issue. As O'Donnell explains in his own history of the agitation, he became aware of it when small farmers from his native Donegal Gaeltacht told him about the threats of legal action they had received from the Irish Land Commission for non-payment. Non-payment in parts of Donegal went back to 1918 when peasants supported by the local IRA Commander had decided to pay neither rent nor annuities. By the time Free State courts were established some peasants had accumulated up to eight years of arrears.[16] Similar situations existed in other small-farming areas in the west and south-west. For O'Donnell the harsh economic conditions that made it impossible for the small farmers to pay arrears, even if they had wanted to, was the most potent material symbol of the failure of the Sinn Féin revolution of 1919–21. As the manifesto of Saor Éire, which he had a hand in drawing up, was to put it in 1931, the first Dáil in 1919 'set its face against all tendency towards direct action by the masses to recapture their inheritance. . . . The small farmers and landless men demanded restoration of the ranches [sic] they demanded the relief of rent and in these vital issues the government betrayed them.'[17]

After the Treaty split there was on the anti-Treaty side a slightly more sympathetic audience for the views of agrarian radicals. In May 1922 the IRA Army Council produced an agrarian policy and P. J. Ruttledge, 'Director of Civil Administration', issued an order to local commandants to seize certain lands and properties and hold them in trust for the Irish people. These included all lands in the possession of the Congested Districts Board, all properties of absentee land-lords and those who spent the greater part of their time abroad, and all but 100–200 acres and mansion houses of landlords residing permanently in Ireland. Divisional land courts were to be established.[18] But that the leadership of the anti-Treaty side was predominantly unsympathetic to a clear identification with agrarian radicalism would soon become clear. Thus in his Notes, Liam Mellows reminded Austin Stack that the IRA already had a land programme which should now be actualized as part of the struggle 'if the great body of workers are to be kept on the side of Independence'.[19] But as O'Donnell was to say later of De Valera, 'he was numb rather than hostile to the working class struggle. He was as scared as

Griffith [the founder of Sinn Féin in 1905] of the gospel of Fintan Lalor.'[20]

For O'Donnell, the anti-Treaty leadership had failed to learn the crucial lesson of the War of Independence. This he stated clearly in a polemic with the purist Mary MacSwiney in the pages of *An Phoblacht*. His attitude to her organization, Sinn Féin, was the same as it was to the pre-Treaty Sinn Féin: 'It is a compromise with the conquest. To attempt to define Sinn Féin as the undoing of the conquest and restoration of the common ownership of· land, among other things, thus coming bang up against the order that has arisen out of the conquest – unthinkable. It would break up the "national" movement.'[21]

It was Connolly who had developed the notion that the substance of the socialist task in Ireland was the country's 'reconquest' from the capitalist structures which English colonization had imposed. This was an ambiguous notion. It could mean simply that, just as the imposition of foreign rule on Ireland had profound economic and social dimensions as well as political ones, the breaking of that foreign rule would necessarily involve equally radical economic and social transformations. However this facet of the notion was sometimes linked to a more romantic Gaelic revivalism. As a recent commentator on Connolly has noted, his major work *Labour in Irish History* must be placed firmly within the broad current of the Gaelic literary and cultural revival developing from the 1880s. Connolly was particularly influenced by Alice Stopford Green's *The Making of Ireland and its Undoing*, which focused on the destruction of Gaelic culture following the Conquest of the sixteenth and seventeenth centuries. This was presented as a rupture which rendered subsequent developments abnormal. The liberation of Ireland required a reconnection with the older traditions.[22]

Such a viewpoint inevitably tended to privilege those sections of the Irish population seen to be nearest to Gaelic traditions, and in the conditions of the 1920s it inevitably meant a focus on the peasantry of the western periphery. Of course, it was in these areas that the greatest concentration of small farmers was wresting a living from the poorest soils in Ireland. Agitation against annuities would inevitably have tended to focus on those areas where their burden was hardest to bear. But, for O'Donnell, there was more to the issue than material conditions in these areas. The annuities issue enabled him, he believed, to give the crucial material and class dimension to the republican struggle against the 'Imperialist' Free State regime: 'to talk of nationhood as something outside the people on which they are to rivet their eyes and struggle towards is wrong . . . organization will only come from the struggles of the hard-pressed to drive hunger out of their lives. I am convinced that the hard-pressed peasantry and the famishing workless are the point of assembly.'[23] The small farmers of the western periphery were crucial to his project for reasons that went beyond any strategic calculations of their conditions or class interests. O'Donnell in fact gave them a privileged role in the anti-imperialist struggle. As he plainly stated in his introduction to Brian O'Neill's *The War for the Land in Ireland*: 'In my opinion the relationship between the social rights of the toilers and the fight for national independence has been more persistently maintained by the small farmer population, even than by the industrial workers in the south.'[24] This valuation of the peasantry owed more to Gaelic revivalism than to socialist ideology. As Terence Brown has pointed out, the 1920s saw the confirmation of the west and of the Gaeltacht as the main locus of Irish nationalist cultural aspiration. The acutely depressed conditions in rural Ireland in this period, manifested in high levels of unemployment and emigration, weighed particularly heavily on the Gaeltacht areas, and for a central tendency in nationalism this became a critical issue. Brown quotes Douglas Hyde, the Irish Protestant who was co-founder of the Gaelic League, commenting on a recently published report of the Gaeltacht Commission in 1926: 'Remember that the best of our people were driven by Cromwell to hell or Connacht. Many of our race are living on the seaboard. They are men and women of the toughest fibre. They have been for generations fighting with the sea, fighting with the weather, fighting with the mountains. They are indeed the survival of the fittest. Give them but half a chance and they are the seeds of a great race . . . it will save the historical Irish nation for it will preserve for all time the fountain source from which future generations can draw for ever.'[25] O'Donnell made clear his fealty to an ultra-Gaelic version of Connolly's 'reconquest' when he specified that his objective was 'not merely to set up a Republic but to restore the old Gaelic civilization on the ruins of the capitalist state foisted on us by Imperialism.'[26] Clearly this meant that the preservation of the Gaeltacht areas was crucial, for their peasantries were the least corrupted bearers of Gaelic and anti-capitalist values. When decrees for non-payment of annuities were issued against peasants in the Tirconail Gaeltacht in Donegal, where the agitation had begun, O'Donnell responded in a typically revivalist way: 'Are the remnants of Gaelic stock to be sought out among the rocks and stripped naked under a cruel winter? Are these homes stamped unmistakably with the personality of these Gaelic folk – and they are as yet a vital, unbroken set of people – to be razed because tribute to England is not being paid?'[27]

However, thus Gaelicized, the annuities were an issue that had significant potential for Fianna Fáil. In April 1927 the desperate state of some small farmers was tragically revealed in the Gaeltacht area in west Cork with the death of a farmer, his wife and two of their five children from starvation. (O'Donnell took the name of the village where the deaths occurred, Adrigoole, as the title of a novel published in 1929.) *The Nation*, a weekly newspaper supporting Fianna Fáil, took up the issue in a way broadly similar to the approach of *An Phoblacht*: 'The policy of our efficient Minister of Agriculture is having unexpected success. He informed the country recently that as far as he was concerned, help would be given only to those farmers who can help themselves. . . . The Berehaven man, with his uneconomic holding could not help himself, and went to the devil. . . . If he had been one of the rich farmers he could have helped himself out of public funds. But unhappily for him and his kind he belonged to the Celtic fringe, he is a remnant of the old Irish that were driven by the invaders to the bogs and mountains. . . . Last year, 30,000 people, mainly from the Celtic fringe, left Ireland in order to escape the fate that awaits the landholder along the coast. Yet the grass is growing on the empty plains of Meath.'[28] There was a hint of the traditional agrarian radical demand for the break up of the grazing ranches. But *The Nation*'s main advice to its readers was, if they wanted to 'save the Gael', to vote Fianna Fáil in the forthcoming election. At this time Fianna Fáil had no concrete agrarian policy; although there was some sympathy for O'Donnell's campaign,[29] the position of the national leadership and of De Valera in particular was much more cautious.

It was the potentially divisive nature of the campaign which obviously worried De Valera. Soon after the extraordinary Sinn Féin Árd Fheis in 1926 and the subsequent decision to set up the new party, De Valera wrote to Joseph McGarrity, the leading figure in the Irish-American republican support group, Clan na Gael, explaining the decision: 'You will perhaps wonder why I did not wait any longer. It is vital that the Free State be shaken at the next general election, for if an opportunity be given it to consolidate itself further as an institution – if the present Free State members are replaced by Farmers and Labourers and other class interests, the national interest as a whole will be submerged in the clashing of rival economic groups.'[30] This clear avowal of the need to preserve Ireland from the dangers of class politics helps to explain much of the tortuous legalism which characterized De Valera's position on the annuities. In July 1927 he dealt with the issue in an interview with the *Manchester Guardian*: 'Our farmers ought certainly to pay something for the privilege of using the land. But perhaps what they pay should not be annuities calculated to compensate the landlord for his legal claim to rent, but rather a land tax which could be graduated more justly and scaled down in accordance with the farmers' ability to pay. Still I do not assert that those who advanced the money which the British Treasury used to buy out the landlords should not be repaid. But the question, by whom their money should be repaid, has still to be settled. I am not for a repudiation of debt. A future Republican government could not ignore all the acts of its predecessor, but the financial settlement which Cosgrave has made with England is absurd and will be reopened.'[31]

At the 1927 Fianna Fáil Árd Fheis a resolution proposed by a priest from South Mayo was passed calling on the Land Commission 'in urgent cases where writs have been issued and seizure or sale is imminent' not to take legal action where a farmer was able to pay the current annuity and was prepared to pay arrears by instalment.[32] There was considerable distance between this and O'Donnell's campaign in Donegal where the peasants had been organized to withhold annuities and resist seizures and sales. The decision of the conference to set up a special policy committee on the issue showed a determination that the party should benefit from it. But the report clearly demonstrated that the issue would be presented as a national grievance against England with the minimum possible social content. The basic argument was to be the legal one: that the continued payment of annuities was contrary to the Government of Ireland Act and the Treaty. In power, Fianna Fáil would reopen the question with Britain and uphold the right of the Free State to retain the annuities. The funds so retained would be used 'to help tenant farmers and to facilitate the purchase and distribution of land under the 1923 Act with special reference to the Gaeltachts and the Congested Districts'.[33] Legalistic appeals to British legislation had little attraction for either agrarian radicals or republican purists. Discussing the annuities issue at Sinn Féin's Árd Fheis, the party president J. J. O'Kelly 'referred to the means by which the lands of Ireland were confiscated by alien adventurers . . . his advice to Irish farmers was not to pay another penny in way of land annuities.'[34]

However, as O'Donnell admits, by the end of 1927 there was a great danger of the agitation collapsing in its original areas of support: 'I was desperately in need of some help to widen the area of struggle and to bring new voices onto the land annuities platform.'[35] In a significant article, he implicitly recognized the limits of a strategy too closely tied to the peasant periphery. He spoke of 'a quivering uneasiness in the collective mind of the working masses . . . a tiredness, a distrust, a cynicism', and of the feeling that the peasantry were 'a hard, mean, clutching, self-centred, self-seeking lot who really want to pay out nothing.'[36] It was symptomatic of the large element of idealism that remained in even so 'materialist' a republican as O'Donnell that suspicion of the peasantry is explained by factors like 'tiredness' and 'cynicism'. Urban working-class lack of interest in the annuities issue reflected the failure of even radical republicans to link it to a broader strategy of economic and social change. O'Donnell saw in the annuities issue a symbol of the continuing imperialist burden which the Free state government was prepared to impose upon a large section of the Irish people. This approach assumed that in the struggle against this burden an effective radical alliance could be built between 'peasants' and workers. As we shall see, the social republicans' grasp of the political possibilities in urban Ireland was a tenuous one. But even their rural strategy failed to appreciate the complexity of rural class structure. It was this failure which ensured Fianna Fáil's easy 'capture' of the issue.

The situation of peripheral isolation encouraged a move towards Fianna Fáil and this was facilitated by an approach from Colonel Maurice Moore, a member of the Free State Senate who had been waging a campaign against the legality of the continued payment of annuities to England. Moore had produced a pamphlet, *British Plunder and Irish Blunder* which he wished O'Donnell to serialize. Until then *An Phoblacht* had taken little notice of his speeches for, as O'Donnell admitted, '. . . it would not occur to me to link up with a Free State Senator who could invoke no better argument than British acts of Parliament.'[37] However, Moore was now a member of Fianna Fáil and on its executive was able to put his case strongly to De Valera. Association with Moore made it easier to go about the task of getting Fianna Fáil TDs on to annuities platforms: De Valera had banned them from appearing on platforms with O'Donnell. In February 1928 a national anti-annuities campaign was launched at a meeting presided over by Moore in the Rotunda, Dublin. O'Donnell shared the platform with three Fianna Fáil TDs: Gerry Boland, Dr Jim Ryan and Patrick Ruttledge, one of the foremost agrarian radicals in Fianna Fáil, whose frequent speeches on the poverty and unemployment in Mayo were well received in *An Phoblacht*. In his speech, O'Donnell raised the 'Call off the Bailiffs' and 'No Rent' slogans which continued to embarrass De Valera, and Ruttledge made the point that while 'the platform held people who did not agree on some points . . . on this matter of ending the payment of an illegal and immoral tax to England, they could agree and work in harmony, maybe opening the way to big things in the future.'[38]

A national 'Anti-Tribute League' was created, with a leadership dominated by western radicals who personified the very close links – both ideological and familial – that still remained between the IRA and Fianna Fáil. Its chairman was Frank Barrett, chairman of Clare County Council. An ex-member of the Army Council whose brother was still in the IRA, he was now a leading member of Fianna Fáil.[39] The vice-chairman was Eamonn Corbett, an IRA comrade of Mellows, who was now chairman of Galway County Council.[40] The campaign attempted to get county councils in areas where annuities agitations existed to pass resolutions against the payment of the annuities to England and also demanding the suspension of legal action for arrears. By the end of the year such resolutions had been passed by Clare, Galway, Kerry and Leitrim county councils and the campaign was getting good publicity and support from the *Mayo News* and other western tribunes of agrarian radicalism.[41] But the radicalism articulated by the *Mayo News* represented only one strand and, for all its importance, a minority strand in Fianna Fáil. As De Valera's semi-official biographers have noted, one of the major problems facing the new party was the fear amongst sections of the public of its supposed radicalism. In drafting an election address in 1927, De Valera protested that 'the sinister design of aiming at bringing about a sudden revolutionary upheaval, with which our opponents choose to credit us, is altogether foreign to our purpose and pro-gramme.'[42]

The linking of the annuities issue directly to the conditions and needs of the small farmers, the anti-big farmer ethos of the campaign and its aura and rhetoric of direct action to resist the bailiffs were not the forms in which De Valera wanted the issue to be articulated. The increasing involvement of the Fianna Fáil leadership in the annuities question was associated with a sustained attempt to drain it of any specific class dimension. Thus *The Nation* began to publish articles by lawyers proving the illegality of the payments to England. If they made any appeal to history then it was done in such a way as to include the majority of the agricultural population. In a typical article by a lawyer, the regional and class dimensions of O'Donnell's revivalism is obliterated in a simple identification of 'historic struggles' and 'the farmer': 'As a matter of political economy, the need to help the agricultural industry requires no emphasis. But the farmer has surely other claims that go nearer to the hearts of his countrymen. He, above all, is the Gael of age long tradition. Far away in the dawn of history, he it was who tilled the land, built up its traditions and fought the battles for the liberty of our country.'[43] The secretary's report to the 1929 Fianna Fáil Árd Fheis could report on the party's 'vigorous pursuit of the campaign for the retention of the land annuities. No question, in recent times, has aroused such widespread interest among the people, as is evidenced by attendance at public meetings and the demand for literature on the subject.'[44] However, in February of that year, the National Executive had already adopted a resolution committing the future Fianna Fáil government to using the retained annuities for the abolition of rates on agricultural land. The conservatism of this proposal was clear to many western radicals. As the *Connaught Telegraph* noted: 'What affiliation have the congests of the west with the Farmers' Union which is composed of the men monopolizing the grazing ranches of the country? How will derating affect the thousands of congests in Mayo with the 14/- worth of land as compared with the grazing farmers having hundreds of acres of which he tills not a sod?'[45] Such an approach was clearly radically different from O'Donnell's, although he accepted that after the repudiation of the payments to England the peasants would continue to make some payment. However, all arrears were to be cancelled, something which De Valera had set his face against, the payment was to be not in excess of half the present annuity, and the money was to be used for agricultural credit and for the financing of cooperative enterprises.[46] But as the world depression hit Ireland in 1929 O'Donnell began to predict confidently that a tide of radicalism would force Fianna Fáil to the left if it wanted to survive.

Fianna Fáil strove, with some difficulty, to adapt and mould the themes of the annuities campaign to other pre-existing themes of its discourse on the land question. The object was to create an agrarian stance radical enough to consolidate its support amongst the small farmers of the west but not liable to alienate the more solid members of the farming community.

Thus while the republicans under O'Donnell's influence might agitate against payment of the annuities, De Valera's approach was to emphasize that annuities would continue to be paid but then retained in Dublin. To make this more palatable, he promised that while some of the money would be used for derating, it would also be used to speed the process of land purchase and redistribution particularly in the Gaeltachts and Congested Districts.[47]

From 1929 to the election of 1932, *An Phoblacht* and O'Donnell formed a bloc with the agrarian radicals in Fianna Fáil in an intense assault on the 'imperialist' Free state regime and its main internal class support – the 'ranchers'. The basic assumptions of the agrarian radicals were clear enough. Out of 378,000 Irish agricultural holdings, some 255,000 or 67.5% were valued at under £15 per year. These were the small men of rural Ireland: the total valuation of all these holdings did not reach £2m, whereas the total valuation of all the holdings together exceeded £9.5m. It took 315,000 of the smaller holdings, or 92% of the whole, to reach a valuation of half of the Free State, while the remaining half was accounted for by 33,000 holdings (sometimes non-residential and ranching) or a little over 8%.[48] For the radicals the political implication was obvious: the lands valued at £5½m should be divided and peopled by agriculturalists on holdings from twenty to fifty pounds in valuation. Thus the *Mayo News* declared: 'the spoken and written statements of Eamon de Valera our great chief, openly and candidly convey to the ranchers that this state of things which keeps our people in poverty must end, as a consequence they are putting forth every effort to defeat him. Those men who lock up God's storehouse have the acres, but they have not the votes.'[49] The *Mayo News* was typically blasé about the major obstacles to such radicalism: 'Roughly we have agriculturalists living on land valued at two million pounds. They are our only originating source of wealth, and all other classes in the community are directly or indirectly deriving their income from them. They are a small number of men occupying land of the valuation of £5,500,000 whose sole occupation is, as the late Michael Davitt put it, watching cows' tails growing. They confine the land to growing blades of grass. They are practically worthless as an originating source of wealth to the community. The loss to the community per acre of such land is the difference between the life sustaining capacity of an acre of tilled land and an acre of grass.'[50]

A typical rural radical dismissal of any productive role for urban social classes, and displaying the moralistic 'tillage' mentality which blithely dismissed meat, the mainstay of Ireland's exports, as 'practically worthless', this passage ignores important political realities. It was one thing to target the top 8% as 'enemies of the people', but quite another to target the top 32.5% in this category. Yet implicitly this article identified Fianna Fáil with 67.5% of Irish farmers and against the 32.5% at the top. However much some western radicals might like such an approach, the Fianna Fáil leadership attempted to avoid it; their adoption of agricultural derating was a sign of their willingness to compromise with larger farmers.

Nevertheless, the weight of the western small farmer and landless labourer component in the party's support base, together with the undoubted influence of the annuities agitation in giving a national political focus to intensifying agrarian unrest from 1929 on, forced even De Valera to sound a radical note. Thus at a meeting in Irishtown, County Mayo, where the Land League had been launched in 1879, he presented Fianna Fáil in terms of a utopian rural radicalism: '. . . the Ireland his party stood for was the Ireland of Fintan Lalor – an Ireland which still was their own from sod to sky . . . with the country's resources fully developed, employment and the means of existence for a population of 20 million could easily be supplied.'[51] In the 1932 election campaign he seemed to be willing to contemplate a much more radical attack on the large farmers: 'What about the rich lands? Have they been divided? In Meath the richest land in Ireland, 5% of farmers own 41% of the land. These are the farmers who own 200 acres each; 631 persons own 234,575 acres: 631 own practically a quarter of a million acres of the best land in Ireland. . . . In Tipperary 485 persons own 200,000 acres and in Kildare 6% of farmers own over 172,000. . . .'[52] In office Fianna Fáil would disappoint many of its rural supporters. Nevertheless its first years of power were to see a considerable increase in the pace of land redistribution. The Land Act of 1933 was crucial here: under it, the Land Commission was empowered to expropriate, with compensation, any property that seemed suitable and distribute it among small farmers and the landless. This was coupled with the withholding of the land annuities which precipitated English tariff reprisals on Irish exports and brought the dislocation of the crucial cattle export trade. A brief upsurge of Irish fascism in the form of the Blueshirt movement was the intense and fevered reaction of the large farmers who saw the Fianna Fáil victory as a form of agrarian 'Bolshevism'.

The radical element in Fianna Fáil's appeal in 1932 was heavily influenced by the pressure of social republicanism. The annuities campaign had developed in a way that appeared to vindicate O'Donnell's line inside the IRA. He put this forward very clearly in an exchange with Mary MacSwiney who opposed the introduction of class issues into republican discourse: 'My method of influencing an organization is to raise issues behind it and force it either to adjust itself so as to ride the tidal wave or get swamped. . . . If we wake up the country Fianna Fáil would either have to rearrange itself to stand for the people's demand or it would be swept as wreckage around the steps of the Viceregal Lodge.'[53] Implicit in this was the idea that although Fianna Fáil had forsaken the pure ground of the Republic, it was still a party which could be forced in a progressive and anti-imperialist direction. For O'Donnell, the conversion of the IRA to social republicanism was a prerequisite to a reconstitution of anti-Treatyism through the transformation of Fianna Fáil or, if that proved impossible, a new united front of 'anti-imperialist' forces. Ironically he was to have more success in pushing Fianna Fail in a radical, autarkic nationalist direction than transforming the IRA.

Saor Éire and the 'Lurch to the Left'

'By the end of the 1920s the world economic crisis had made itself felt so sharply in Ireland as an agricultural crisis that middle and even bigger farmers found the current annuity an embarrassment, and suddenly our movement became self-propelled.'[54]

One of O'Donnell's motives in instigating the IRA's break
with Sinn Féin and the Second Dáil in 1925 had been to get the
IRA involved in social agitations. However, he admits he was
to be relatively unsuccessful. Although a member of both the
Executive Council and the Army Council and editor of *An
Phoblacht* he had been unable to involve the IRA as a body in
the annuities agitation.[55] His use of *An Phoblacht* to publicize
the annuities issue was a source of conflict in republican ranks:
'Quite good-intentioned fellows are sizzling with anger
against me for using *An Phoblacht* to push my own set of
activities in republican groups in the country. The working
class note will split the compactness of the 'real republic' I am
threatened . . . It is my firm conviction that it is by making the
working class ideals active and dominant within the Republican movement that good can come to the revolutionary
movement in the country.'[56]

In January 1929 a proposal by O'Donnell and a small group
of left IRA men to found a radical political organization
tentatively called Saor Éire was rejected by the Army Convention. Instead volunteers were permitted to join a new
political organization, Comhairle na Poblachta, which was
designed as a united front of non-Fianna Fáil republicans.[57]
The first statement of the new organization on Irish unity
reflected the attitudes of IRA chief of staff, Moss Twomey, 'a
dedicated right-wing Fenian, scrupulous in his religious
observance'[58] rather than those on the left: '[Irish unity] has
become an absolute necessity if Ireland is to remain a Christain
entity in a world rapidly becoming pagan . . . to get the clean,
Gaelic, Christian mind of Ireland in revolt against the
beastliness of English Imperial paganism should be the task of
every right minded citizen of Ireland.'[59]

But as the 1929 slump cut off emigration outlets in the USA
(between 1926 and 1930 over 90,000 had emigrated there[60]),
there was a major decline in the remittances which had helped
many small farmers eke out their living. The deteriorating
economic and social conditions gave a new immediacy and
attractiveness to O'Donnell's ideas. He was later to claim that
it was the inadequate response of the IRA leadership which
prevented a revolutionary resolution of the crisis and benefited
Fianna Fáil: 'there was no political face to this mass unrest . . .

it was a great lurch to the left on definite terms . . . As it became clear that the government had in mind to subject the IRA to a mounting system of police thuggery, the possibility of another armed clash forced itself into Republican discussions and with it came talk of the need for a Republican policy. We were back to Mellows. At any time the IRA chose, it could have put itself at the head of the whole Republican movement, pushing past Fianna Fáil, De Valera and all, to reach the 1919 position at one stride, by releasing its members into the land annuities agitation.'[61] However, the essential ambiguities of social republicanism are apparent in the fact that a few pages later in his account of this period, O'Donnell gives a very different evaluation of the possibilities. What he now appears to have desired was active IRA involvement in the annuities movement as a means of returning a Fianna Fáil government of a particular type, one forced by popular pressure to adopt agrarian and other economic policies considerably to the left of what they were committed to: 'Facing a general election we believed we could add enough push to De Valera's campaign to overrun the government party. . . . De Valera and those round him wore no halos for us . . . These men would be incapable of the comprehensive, state-sponsored schemes, which alone could reach out to the small farm countryside, expand industry . . . National leadership was not the challenge facing us. . . . Our task was to give coherence to the Fenian radicalism that characterized the crisis. The way to do that would be to put forward a short list of candidates to serve as a rallying point for second tier leadership to impose this militancy on the Fianna Fáil Executive.'[62]

This essential lack of clarity as to what was possible in 1931–32 reflects the fundamental strategic void at the heart of physical force republicanism, whatever its ideological complexion. Its alternative to Fianna Fáil populism was either the ideal 'Republic' to be brought about by another attempt at the forcible overthrow of the Free State or an equally abstract social republicanism. Although the latter was prepared to dirty its hands with material grievances, it would seek to direct them to an objective which, for all its Marxist coloration, was effectively as detached from the possibilities of the situation as the 'Republic' of purist dreams.

The apparent radicalization of the IRA leadership in the two years after the rejection of the Saor Éire proposal represented a desperate attempt to staunch what Bowyer Bell has described as the 'wholesale desertion' of its members to Fianna Fáil as it moved towards power.[63] A movement which was estimated to have 20–25,000 members in 1926 had declined to a hard core of about 5,000 at the beginning of 1929, although even then its paper *An Phoblacht* sold 8,000 copies while the Fianna Fáil weekly, the *Nation*, sold 6,000.[64] John McHugh has suggested that in the late twenties there were three main elements in the IRA – the left led by people like O'Donnell and George Gilmore, which was a definite minority but with disproportionate influence through its effective control of *An Phoblacht*; a strong bloc of apolitical militarists, well represented by the chief of staff, Twomey; and another relatively small group who adhered to Catholic social doctrines.[65] The largest group which, like the bulk of the ordinary volunteers was drawn from small farmers, landless labourers and urban workers, was not unsympathetic to the left. Its own conditions and experiences were reflected in diffuse social-radical variation on traditional republicanism. The further attraction of social republicanism was that it offered volunteers a deeper rationale for refusing incorporation in constitutional politics through the blandishments of Fianna Fáil.

But while the language of publications and meetings would be increasingly affected by borrowings from the Comintern, and a few republicans like O'Donnell would have close and friendly relations with the tiny coterie of Irish Communists, the substance of the relationship was largely instrumental. Here was a declining movement in desperate need of the issues and language to justify its continued existence. One of the police reports which the Cumann na nGaedheal government was using in an effort to alert the Catholic hierarchy to an approaching 'red' threat that included the IRA, gave an astringent estimate of the actual relationship between the IRA and social radicalism: 'There can be little doubt that there are in the IRA men who dislike Communism and similarly in Communist circles men who regard the IRA as merely sentimental, old-fashioned patriots, but a union has evidently been arranged on the basis that both parties will do their best to destroy the present order of things. The value of this from the IRA point of view is obvious, every unemployed man, every small farmer who has to pay a Land Commission annuity, every struggling small trader, every discontented worker, will now be told that the IRA is his ally. . . . The depression in agriculture and the repercussions here of the world-wide industrial slump will thus be turned into motive power for the IRA. It was fairly clear that the IRA could not continue to live on its original base. The number of people who are prepared to imperil their lives and fortunes for the difference between the existing state on the one hand and a Republic such as the USA or France on the other hand is negligible. That a civil war – even a short one – was fought even partly on such a basis was due to purely temporary and personal causes which have already lost much of their force. The men who wished to keep the IRA alive had therefore to look around for support, springing from some other motives than the traditions of Irish independence and they found support in the widespread movement against the system of private property and private enterprise. . . .'[66]

Undoubtedly the predominant tendency in the IRA looked to the annuities movement and to the intensification of problems of unemployment and agricultural depression, as the material from which a 'second round' could be engineered. The intense problems of the small farmer in the West, exacerbated by depression and the effective closure of emigration outlets, produced optimum conditions for a recrudescence of a form of republican intransigence which can be identified primarily as a form of traditional rural resistance to an 'oppressor' state. It was in many ways a land war disguised as a national struggle.

O'Donnell, who attended a congress of the Comintern's European Peasant Committee (Krestintern), was eager to give his annuities agitation an 'internationalist' flavour, and in March 1930 the Anti-Tribute League was transformed into the Irish Working Farmers Congress, which met in Galway. The rhetoric of the meeting did much to convince the police and the government of the reality of a 'red' menace: 'This Congress accepts the platform and programme of the European Peasant Congress . . . by fighting on this platform, in alliance with town workers for the common interest of all

toilers against capitalist exploitation, against land annuities
. . . the working farmers are at the same time fighting for the
complete independence of our country.'[67]

In fact, the alliance with urban workers was as speculative a
construction as the link between the farmers' struggles against
annuities and the fight for 'complete independence'. The
substantial reality was a widespread spirit of lawlessness in
many rural areas. At the centre of this was the incapacity of
tens of thousands of farmers to pay annuities, the growth of
arrears and the resultant action by the Land Commission to
recover them, which could take the form of seizure of animals
and even of the land itself. O'Donnell had always seen in the
occasions of conflict between bailiffs and farmers the opportunity to demonstrate the 'imperialist' nature of the Free State
and the possibility of a new republican offensive which unlike
the usual IRA military activities of the period – arms raids,
shooting of policemen, intimidation of jurors – would not
leave the masses cold or hostile. By 1931, as the police
complained of a 'growing feeling against payment of debts
and against private property',[68] and the government adopted
an increasingly repressive demeanour, the IRA's secret paper
commented on 'an amazing resurgence of feeling throughout
the country during the present year. . . . Several companies
and battalions have doubled and trebled their strength.'[69] This
'Fenian Radicalism', as O'Donnell termed it, drew its strength
predominantly from the areas with a history of participation in
the annuities agitation. According to the police the areas most
disturbed by illegal drilling and other forms of 'irregularism'
were Tipperary, Kerry, Leitrim and Donegal.[70] These were
also often areas with strong traditions of agrarian agitation and
anti-Treatyism. There was in many parts of the western
periphery a potent mixture of present economic grievance and
an abiding ideological tradition which the Department of
Justice characterized thus: '. . . for generations there has been
in Ireland the tradition of opposition to the state – a readiness
in word and action, to question the authority of its institutions.'[71]

For the mainstream of the IRA leadership and much of its
membership, the Saor Éire radicalization was opportunistic. It
held out the prospect of using material grievances to launch a

new campaign. For them, O'Donnell's re-coding of republicanism in the language of class struggle held out the possibility
of enlisting new masses for traditional objectives. The
ambiguities of social republicanism were apparent in
O'Donnell's address to a massive republican gathering at
Bodenstown in June 1931: 'What is the state machine? To
understand the machine it is necessary to see that the British
ruling class pushed in here, not just to place soldiers in Dublin
Cork, and Belfast but to enrich themselves by the order of life
they would establish here. . . . Every struggle that arises,
every strike in the cities, every fight on the land must be
interpreted in this light so that the mass of the people may be
led into revolt against the machinery of the state . . . not
merely against the police.'[72] One sense of this replicates
Connolly's identification of the conquest with imposed
capitalism and real freedom with socialism. This was probably
O'Donnell's intended meaning. However, articulated at the
grave of Wolfe Tone to a gathering of republicans, most of
whose knowledge of Connolly's writings would have been
minimal,[73] its actual significance was different. It was an
invitation to republicans to reinterpret concrete economic and
social grievances and struggles as part of the national struggle.
While this may have had the temporary advantage of raising
IRA morale by apparently opening up new opportunities, it
also had the effect of interpreting the 'class struggle' in Ireland
in terms of fundamentally nationalist objectives. For most of
the republican masses – the small farmers and workers – the
most appropriate mixture of social objectives and nationalism
would be that provided by Fianna Fáil. In 1930 and 1931, for
many of those in the IRA, the growth of social tension, the
increasingly repressive response of the government and the
radical noises of even the Fianna Fáil leadership presaged a
massive attack on the whole Treaty settlement, in which the
IRA would be able once again to become a popular force. In
one sense, therefore, a move to the left also appealed, as
holding out the possibility of intensified state repression and,
in response, a non-parliamentary break with the institutions
of the Free State. For a brief period, this appeared a possible
outcome. But the IRA, too narrowly entrenched in the
traditional redoubts of rural resistance, underestimated the

urban and rural appeal of Fianna Fáil's mild social reformism and pacific, gradualist dismantling of the Treaty settlement.

The IRA's General Army Convention meeting in Glendalough in April 1931 had adopted the Saor Éire programme. Its goal was now apparently 'to achieve an independent revolutionary leadership of the working class and working farmers towards the overthrow in Ireland of British Imperialism and its ally, Irish Capitalism.'[74] The initial public manifestation of the new programme was its first congress in Dublin attended by over 150 delegates in September. *An Phoblacht* predictably hailed it: 'Saor Éire gives a lead which, if acted upon, will achieve the Reconquest.'[75] Claiming continuity with the 1916 Proclamation, the manifesto attacked the first Dáil for opposing 'the direct action of the masses' and denounced Fianna Fáil, '. . . the party of the Irish middle class. . . . [By] retaining much of the phraseology of their more robust days, Fianna Fáil ties up to their party a strong backing among the National population. They promise a higher tariff wall, so they get the small manufacturer and delude a section of workers in Irish industry; they promise to prevent the shipment of land annuities to England and make that, with derating, a gesture towards farmers. But the crisis is exposing them. They fail to campaign for the maintenance of the unemployed; they fail to support workers against wage cuts; they are unable to support the campaign against forced sales; they oppose the slogan "No Rent", they refuse to support the demand for the overthrow of the land monopoly without compensation and to the consternation of their own youth they condemn rising IRA activity.'[76] This denunciation implicitly recognizes the real ideological and material appeal of Fianna Fáil policies to both workers and small farmers, but then blithely denies it, either classifying it as illusory or simply raising more 'leftist' demands for which there was in fact no substantial constituency. The shallowness of this attempt to overtake Fianna Fáil by windy appeals to 'organized committees of action amongst industrial and agricultural workers' was apparent even at the time, as were some of the more ludicrous aspects of the attacks on De Valera's party. Sean Hayes, who presided at the conference and was a veteran of the annuities campaign, was a Fianna Fáil county councillor and would soon be a TD for the party.[77] The links of personality, ideology and outlook between many in the IRA and Fianna Fáil made the Saor Éire denunciations distinctly unimpressive. Even more demoralizing for the minority of serious leftists in the IRA was the shallowness of the new commitments. O'Donnell was later to criticize Saor Éire as 'evasive action', the adoption of a social programme as an alternative to active involvement in popular struggles.[78] And a more forthright dismissal of the whole venture came from Frank Edwards, a member of the IRA in Waterford city and later an International Brigadier: '. . . it was a most undemocratic way to send out invitations [to the Saor Éire Congress], just the Commandant and the Adjutant. It was IRA through and through. They got a county council member from Clare [Hayes] as chairman. . . . He startled everybody by commencing with a religious invocation. Then to cap it all Fionan Breathnach stood up later and said we should adjourn the meeting as some wished to attend the All Ireland in Croke Park that afternoon. It showed you how seriously they were taking their socialism.'[79] A convinced socialist who was selling 600 copies of An Phoblacht a week at the time, Edwards emphasizes that for all their proclaimed leftism, the IRA effectively functioned not as the scourge but rather as the left wing of Fianna Fáil. Of An Phoblacht's readers he concludes disconsolately: 'I suppose it was the people who voted for Fianna Fáil afterwards who bought them. We, Republicans had nothing to offer them politically.'[80]

The Republican Congress Minus Workers and Protestants

The Catholic bishops received their copies of the Department of Justice memorandum on 'subversive teachings and activities', and duly responded in a joint pastoral on 18 October 1931. Saor Éire was condemned as a 'frankly communistic organization' trying to 'impose upon the Catholic people of Ireland the same materialistic regime, with its fanatical hatred of God, as now dominates Russia and threatens to dominate Spain.'[81] The government introduced new Public Safety

legislation under which twelve organizations including Saor
Éire, the IRA and the Revolutionary Workers' Groups
(precursors of the Communist Party of Ireland) were banned,
military tribunals were introduced and hundreds were
arrested. Sean Cronin claims that the church-state offensive
took the IRA by surprise: 'they had moved out of the shelter of
"national rights" into the exposed ground of "social rights"
and were bombarded by everyone.'[82] Certainly the Catholic
Church's offensive demonstrated the clear ideological con-
straints on the agrarian radicalism of which people like
O'Donnell had such high hopes. The *Mayo News*, which, as a
militant supporter of small farmer agitation, had published
one of O'Donnell's pamphlets,[83] made its position on Saor
Éire very clear. Reprinting the manifesto in full, it then
attacked it at length, particularly for its claim to continuity
with 1916: 'Patrick Pearse and his co-signatories of 1916
placed "the cause of the Irish Republic under the protection of
the Most High God". The engineers of the new Workers'
Republic at their first conference sent fraternal greetings to the
Russian Soviets whose proclaimed policy is anti-God, who
excel in obscene caricatures of the Blessed Virgin. The
proclamation on which Saor Éire takes its stand, was drafted
not by Patrick Pearse, but by Mr Stalin in Moscow. The
whole programme is foreign as well as anti-Christian, it is
against every tradition and principle of Irish nationality. . . .
[If] the mask of Republicanism under which it is mas-
querading were torn off this face, it would show itself in all its
anti-National and anti-Christian ugliness.'[84] The response of
the bulk of republicans was to discard the Saor Éire programme and forcibly assert their fidelity to nation and
Catholicism. The remnants of Sinn Féin were produced to
vouch for the soundness of those who had unfortunately
produced a 'misguided' social programme. Mary Mac-
Swiney, while opposing Saor Éire ('It is a bad national policy
to divide the people on a class basis') claimed that of those who
produced the policy "most . . . are practising Catholics and
not one single one of my acquaintance would stand for an
anti-Christian state. . . .'[85] A stalwart of the IRA and the
annuities movement like Eamonn Corbett would publicly
proclaim: 'many of us are indifferent or hostile to com-

munistic ideas and propaganda but feel very strongly on the national question.'[86] When the periodical *Irish Rosary* claimed that on a trip to Moscow in 1929 O'Donnell had been trained in 'anti-religious propaganda' he sued (unsuccessfully) for libel, denying the charge and adding: 'on the contrary I am a Catholic.'[87] Republicans were long used to withstanding attacks from the Church – they had been excommunicated during the Civil War. But such anathemas had concerned their role as an 'armed conspiracy' and had not questioned their Catholicism. The new assault provoked a headlong retreat from a public leftism which had never been securely grounded anyway. The organization now joined the broad opposition front including Fianna Fáil, Sinn Féin and the Labour Party, which denounced the increased repression and the government's conservative incapacity to deal with the economic crisis, but from a safely Catholic position.

Sinn Féin's Árd Fheis dissociated the 'republican move-ment' from 'anti-Christian propaganda' and proposed a social order based on 'Christian principles'. For people like MacSwiney and the leading IRA man and later supporter of the left Republican Congress, Michael Price, this meant the principles set out in papal encyclicals. Price quoted Aquinas, Pius V and Leo XIII to back up his ideas for social reform.[88] James Connolly had set the pattern for this dressing up of radicalism in theological garb in his *Labour, Nationality and Religion*. Understandable in some ways in a country where Catholicism had such deep popular roots, this approach created problems with which, by definition, it could not cope in dealings with Ireland's substantial Protestant population. But the pressure to conform was irresistible, as one organiz-ation after another proclaimed its fidelity to social reform according to Catholic social principles. As a leader of the Labour Party put it: 'they already had the framework of an equitable social system especially suited to the people in the Encyclicals of Pope Leo XIII and his illustrious successor, the present Holy Father.'[89]

For De Valera and Fianna Fáil it would prove relatively easy to ignore the government's allegations that they were party to an upsurge of 'Bolshevist' agitation and to benefit from the discomfiture of social republicanism. De Valera was in some ways more robust in his response to the government assault

than the leadership of the IRA. Quick to point to the paltry
number of communists in the Free State, he went on to
establish that any 'extremism' was caused by the country's
manifest and major economic and social problems. These
demanded a solution, but 'a solution having no reference
whatever to any other country, a solution that comes out of
our own circumstances, that springs from our own traditional
attitude towards life, a solution that is Irish and Catholic.'[90]
De Valera's own tendency to substitute a spiritual republican
asceticism for economic policy (he informed the *Manchester
Guardian* that he wanted to free Ireland 'from the domination
of her grosser appetites and induce a mood of spiritual
exaltation for a return to Spartan standards'[91]) was quite
compatible with electoral promises to provide employment
for all who wanted it[92] and to solve the problems of the
congested districts and the Gaeltachts.

In less than a decade his hopes for an Ireland of twenty
million would appear empty – a product, as Ó Tuathaigh puts
it, of his conventional nationalist belief in the creative powers
of political sovereignty.[93] However, in 1931 and 1932 such
beliefs inspired the hopes of many small farmers and unemployed workers, while the IRA could only vacillate
between its desire to re-establish its national credentials and a
residual tendency to criticize the new Fianna Fáil government
from the left. The Church's assault notwithstanding, the
rising political tensions produced by the government's drive
against 'anti-state' organizations and the frequent clashes
between republicans and the newly-formed Army Comrades
Association (a precursor of the fascist Blueshirts) led to a
generalized upsurge of republican sentiment and activity. This
benefitted both Fianna Fáil and the IRA whose membership
increased, passing 8,000 by 1934.[94] In the 1932 and 1933
elections, the IRA told its volunteers to campaign for Fianna
Fáil, adding the proviso that such support did not imply
acceptance of the limits of De Valera's objectives.

When it came to specifying the difference between Fianna
Fáil and IRA objectives, the political hollowness of militant
republicanism became evident. The mainstream evinced an
uneasy and ambiguous attitude, lending some credibility to
the government's gradual dismantling of the Treaty, but

rejecting De Valera's requests for the disbanding of the IRA and a 'fusion of forces' against the 'anti-national reactionary forces'.[95] A vestigial radicalism was also maintained: thus an IRA statement of 1933 urging members to vote for Fianna Fáil also registered dismay at the government's 'attempt to stabilize and build up an economic system, which for all that it relieves unemployment at the moment, will perpetuate the evils of social injustice. . . .'[96] However, the IRA Convention in March 1933 adopted a new policy statement, 'The Constitution and Governmental Programme of the Republic of Ireland', which formalized the retreat from Saor Éire. It promised social reforms, restrictions on wealth and welfare for the poor, but also stressed the individual right to private property and provided for the safeguarding of private enterprise. There was nothing here that De Valera could not agree with, and at least one thing that must have seemed a boon: the Convention also issued an order prohibiting volunteers from writing or speaking on economic, social and political questions.[97]

For Moss Twomey, Sean MacBride and the majority of the IRA leadership, there would have been little dispute with the claim (from a Fianna Fáil negotiation document) that 'they (Fianna Fáil and the IRA) have at bottom the same national and social outlook.'[98] The recreation of republican unity through fusion was desired by both; at issue were the terms of the fusion. In De Valera's view, Fianna Fáil, which he insisted on characterizing as a broad national movement, 'the resurrection of the Irish nation'[99], should absorb the IRA. The latter appeared to envisage a much more equal partnership, in a united front to reestablish the Republic. Meantime, they would maintain their separate existence and right to take military action. De Valera had offered fusion on the basis of the republican ceasefire proposals of 1923, which among other things claimed that 'the sovereignty of the Irish Nation and the integrity of its territory is inalienable'.[100] In five meetings with Sean MacBride in the first eighteen months of Fianna Fáil rule, he maintained that, apart from the 'outstanding difficulty' of partition, the spirit of these proposals could be implemented by his government.[101]

As the government withheld the annuities and entered the

Economic War with England and was assailed by a strident big-farmer onslaught in the form of the Blueshirts, its republican credentials were validated not only by the republican electorate but also by increasing numbers of IRA volunteers who were absorbed into the army and a new volunteer force. O'Donnell later commented on this period: 'I realized when Fianna Fáil came to power in 1932 that the IRA had no meaning as an armed force. They could offer so many concessions to the Republican viewpoint that it was bound to blur the issues that still divided us. But it would reinforce more than ever my early belief that a government was permitted in Dublin only so long as it remained a bailiff for the conquest.'[102] The development of the Blueshirts in 1933 was to provide O'Donnell and his supporters in the IRA with another issue which they hoped would allow a clear political demarcation between 'real' and 'fake' republicanism to be drawn: the struggle against Irish fascism would displace the anti-annuities movement as the main mobilizing issue for social republicanism. The Blueshirt movement originated in the anti-republican Army Comrades Association founded in 1931 from veterans of the Free State army. After the Fianna Fáil victory in 1932, the ACA opened its membership to the general public. In March 1933, De Valera called a snap election which increased his parliamentary majority, and in the same month he sacked General Eoin O'Duffy, Cumann na n Gaedhael's appointee as Chief of Police. O'Duffy made himself the focus of the ACA, which he re-christened the National Guard, and gave it a distinct fascist style when he instituted the fascist salute and the wearing of a blue shirt as a uniform. At its height, it claimed a membership of 100,000, and for a year from the autumn of 1933 it seemed a formidable force. However the challenge would be easily defused; the movement's collapse reflected the leadership's failure to create a broad-based coalition of opposition. They were too dependent on one social group, the big farmers and their sons, particularly the large cattle farmers in Limerick, Cork, Waterford and Kilkenny, who were suffering from the disruption of the cattle trade by the Economic War.

However, for O'Donnell and his supporters, Irish fascism represented the issue that would allow the IRA to take the initiative against De Valera's increasingly successful incor-poration of its constituency. Throughout 1934, there were continuous clashes between republicans and Blueshirts and the police and army. The Blueshirts had adopted the tactics of the anti-annuity movement, organizing non-payment of rates and land annuities, and resisting attempts to seize animals. Republican attacks on Blueshirt meetings allowed the govern-ment to adopt a statesmanlike stance, more or less even-handedly dispensing 'justice'. In 1934, the military tribunal established to deal with such disturbances convicted 349 Blueshirts and 102 IRA men. Naturally, the IRA bitterly denounced any action against them as a betrayal, but there is no sign that it decreased the government's popular appeal. For the left in the IRA, De Valera could never defeat the Blueshirts because he left the economic and social basis of the movement – the large farmer class – untouched. An apocalyptic vision of the fascist threat merged with traditional obsessions: 'The British preparations for war are being reflected here in the hectic drive of the Imperialists for power. Britain at war can only be safe when Ireland is gripped in the steel jacket of the Imperialist-Fascist dictatorship.'[104] Precisely because there was so little evidence of the Blueshirts' capacity to mount a real challenge to the state (after all, 'constitutional' republican-ism of the Fianna Fáil variety could easily label Irish fascism as an essentially anti-national minority, given its Free State origins), social republicans were driven to portray it mythic-ally, as part of a British assault on the Irish nation. Fianna Fáil would now be portrayed as a government unable to satisfy the demands of its small farmer and worker supporters and, more critically, unable to prevent a political counter-revolution from the 'imperialist' elements in the country. Social republic-anism would be proved correct in its estimate of Fianna Fáil's reformism. But such prescience as it could claim was small compensation for the continuing subordination of its social radicalism to a nationalist political project. So much became apparent in the short-lived Republican Congress.

At the 1934 IRA Army Convention, Michael Price, who had moved considerably from his position of opposition to Saor Éire, proposed that the IRA should adopt as its objective a

Republic as visualized by Connolly. The leadership, no doubt mindful of the recent intense assault from the Church on Saor Éire, opposed the Workers' Republic as a goal, and when his resolution was defeated Price withdrew. Then, O'Donnell and George Gilmore proposed a resolution that the IRA should mobilize a 'united front' campaign for a Republican Congress, a rallying of republican opinion which 'would wrest the leadership of the National Struggle from Irish Capitalism'.[105] A majority of the delegates supported the resolution, but the vote of the leadership ensured its defeat and O'Donnell and his supporters left the IRA.

The Congress supporters established a newspaper and local groups in preparation for a national conference to launch the united front. The almost immediate collapse of the project when the conference met in Rathmines in September 1934 demonstrated the strict limitations of even the most radical forms of social republicanism. The immediate cause of the split was a division between those who wished for a commitment to the slogan of a Workers' Republic and those, led by O'Donnell and Gilmore, who wished the Congress to mobilize around the struggle for the Republic, which Fianna Fáil was incapable of leading to a successful conclusion.[106] The O'Donnell position, which had a Pyrrhic victory, was consistent with the dominant tendency of social republicanism since the annuities campaign. It aimed at a united front of IRA members, rank-and-file Fianna Fáilers, Labour Party members, and workers and small farmers, who would be appealed to on an amalgam of national and social issues. But within this combination, the nationalist inflection was quite systematic.

The first issue of the Congress's paper had defined the main task as the struggle against the Blueshirts: 'above all else, an organ of mass struggle against fascism: that must be the slogan of every committee working towards the Republican Congress.'[107] But fascism was portrayed as a stalking horse for the traditional enemy: 'once in power, British backing beyond anything given those that played England's game in 1922 would be given. For, Britain seeks to have Ireland in chains before adventuring into the war for which she is feverishly preparing.'[108] Like the annuities campaign, anti-fascism was to provide material for a popular upsurge to 'complete' the national revolution. Fianna Fáil's alleged inability to deal with the Blueshirts was traced to its unwillingness to challenge the 'conquest' in rural Ireland by expropriating the ranchers without compensation and redistributing their land to the small farmers and the landless. In a pamphlet written at the beginning of the Economic War, O'Donnell had argued that the anti-rancher policy was the central task in completing the national revolution: 'the thinning down of the rural life and the organized dependence on Britain was the economic organizing of our national enslavement. It is the national issue that is in the forefront in breaking down that dependence and increasing rural employment. This rancher-based cattle trade versus tillage fight is now primarily a fight on the national issue.'[109] Large-farmer and rancher support for fascism appeared greatly to strengthen the social republican case against Fianna Fáil policies. In fact, there was not a lot of evidence that small farmers were as yet dissatisfied with the pace of the government's agrarian reforms, and, more significantly, even the Congress's paper had to record serious rural unease with the radical tone of social republicanism. A supporter from Tipperary reported: 'very few people in the country districts know anything about James Connolly. There is a prejudice against his policy.'[110] More specifically, another supporter complained that the slogan 'Seize the ranches' was not well received and served to generate much confusion: 'The words "confiscation" and "communism" and all sorts of other isms are thrown at those who use it and unfortunately some small farmers believe that the adoption of such a policy will lead to the seizure of their little farm.'[111] If the fascist threat to the government and its agrarian reforms had been as substantial as the Congress supporters claimed, there would perhaps have been some hope for its strategy of arousing the countryside. The Congress analysis of Fianna Fáil's supposed weakness in the face of the Blueshirts directly followed Marx's diatribe against the failure of European bourgeoisies to carry through the revolutions of 1848: 'Fianna Fáil cannot fight Fascism. Irish Capitalism is caught between two threats – the threat of Imperialist dictatorship on the one hand and the fear of the roused working class and small farmer population on the other. This is the secret of Fianna Fáil's hesitation.'[112] In fact, the 1934 local government elections in Mayo, in which O'Duffy had been predicting a major victory, represented a substantial defeat for his movement – as the *Mayo News* commented: 'The county council and municipal elections in the Irish Free State have pricked and deflated the Blueshirt balloon.'[113] The mainstream IRA, which had consistently refused to accept the Congress analysis of the fascist threat, noted that the election 'proved conclusively that the Imperialist-Fascist organization commands the support of only a minority of the people.'[114] No doubt the IRA leadership was pleased to see the main mobilizing efforts of the Congress so quickly deflected. The Rathmines split would reveal the other strategic weaknesses of social republicanism.

The initial statement of the Congress group had declared that the way to make 'the Republic a main issue dominating the whole political field' was to identify it with the workers and small farmers: a Republic of a united Ireland will never be achieved except through a struggle which uproots Capitalism on its way.'[115] But there was no evidence that the discontents of parts of rural Ireland had any affinities with the struggles of urban workers, and even less on which to base the Congress's hopes in urban Ireland. Here the social republicans were fatally handicapped by a broader republican incapacity to relate seriously either to the existing labour movement or to the Protestant workers of Ulster.

Michael Price, addressing the Woodworkers Union for the Congress organizing committee, explained that the Irish Labour Party was not being invited to participate. Part of his attack on the Labour Party was that 'they are certainly not leading any struggle for the overthrow of capitalism' – which was certainly true if unsurprising – but the core of his complaint was that it had 'betrayed the Connolly teaching and tradition in 1922 . . . the Irish Labour Party is shifty on the Republican issue.'[116] Price and the other social republicans were true to Mellows here in choosing Labour's relation to republican objectives as the fundamental test of its progressive claims. In a communication to Frank Gallagher (later a key member of Fianna Fáil), Mellows defined the left-republican position on the leadership of the Labour Party: 'By their acceptance of the Treaty and all that it connotes . . . they have betrayed not only the Irish Republic but the Labour movement in Ireland and the cause of the workers and peasants throughout the world.'[117] Throughout the period of social-republican dominance, *An Phoblacht* was characterized by a lack of serious coverage of the labour movement, especially as compared to the intense concern with the annuities campaign. What it did have to say tended towards denunciations of the 'anti-national' role of the leadership. Particular venom was reserved for the man who had led the Labour group in the Dáil, Thomas Johnston. An Englishman, Johnston brought out the more xenophobic impulses in his republican critics. O'Donnell seems to have been typical of those whose judgement of the labour movement was permanently distorted by the passions of the Civil War. (A biographer relates an incident which reveals the depth of republican resentment at Labour's 'betrayal': when O'Donnell was in jail during the Civil War, his wife went to Johnston's office and 'warned him to his face that if anything happened to Peadar, he himself would not be alive that night.'[118]) As the annuities campaign developed, the lack of interest in it in urban Ireland and particularly in the labour movement seems to have alienated O'Donnell even more. The labour movement was charged with forsaking the legacy of Connolly, and although this was sometimes argued in the ultra-left language of the Third Period Comintern, the core charge against Labour was a nationalist one. In a typical blast in an article on Connolly, O'Donnell appeared to dismiss not only the leadership but the rank and file of the Labour Party as well: 'I have not the slightest doubt but that outside the Republican movement . . . there are no right elements. That section of the working class element that follow Johnston will supply the thugs and police to be hired by the Imperialists in the event of any treasonable goings on such as 1916.'[119] At the heart of social-republican alienation from the Labour Party and those workers who supported it was the belief, encouraged by O'Donnell in particular, that the small farmers were the 'oppressed' group most receptive to a nationalist inflection of their grievances. O'Donnell put this clearly in his introduction to Brian O'Neill's 'Marxist' *The War for the Land in Ireland*: 'in my opinion the relationship between the social rights of the toilers and the fight for national independence has been more persistently maintained by the small farmer population, even than by the industrial workers in the south.'[120] The only concrete proposals that social republicanism offered the working class were a mixture of Third Period leftism – to forsake the existing 'reformist' trade unions and set up rival rank-and-file committees – and the nationalistic demand that all unions in the Free State should have their headquarters there.[121] This attack on the role of the British-based 'amalgamated unions' ('English Unions for English interests') was a traditional nationalist one: Arthur Griffith had bitterly attacked James Larkin as an emissary of 'English trade unionism' before the war. It would be taken up and encouraged by Fianna Fáil and, together with Catholic anti-communism, was to provoke a long and debilitating split in the trade union movement in 1944.[122]

If social republicanism's lack of rapport with the working class in the Free State was ultimately a product of its subordination of class to nationalism, the intense interest which the Congress displayed in developments in the Protestant working class in the North might appear surprising. The republican position on the Ulster Protestants varied between a hostile view of them as the bigoted descendants of alien Planters and a more sympathetic, if ultimately patronizing, view of them as a section of the Irish people who, for a variety of reasons, had been separated from their place in the nation by British machinations. *An Phoblacht* expressed both views. A hostile editorial in 1928 outlined a flippant, but common, nationalist 'solution' for the Ulster Protestants: 'There are in our North Eastern counties a large number of people who pride themselves on both their Scottish ancestry and their loyalty to the English crown. Why not swap these worthies for our exiles in Scotland, who will give an undivided allegiance to Ireland.'[123] Here there was much common ground with Fianna Fáil. When De Valera was arrested in Northern Ireland, *An Phoblacht* gave prominent coverage of a large protest meeting in Dublin addressed by Fianna Fáil TDs. The sentiments expressed towards the Ulster Unionists were uniformly hostile and bellicose: 'buy no

Belfast goods . . . until they were willing to become part of the Irish nation.' They were referred to as 'the Orangemen and Freemasons of Belfast', and Sean McEntee, soon to be a cabinet minister, declared that he and his comrades 'would not rest until the Republican flag was floating not alone on Cave Hill but on Stormont.'[124] For the social republicans, the very notion of the 'reconquest', while it could at times be expressed in suitably 'left' anti-capitalist terms, was hard put to incorporate Protestant workers. It was usually presented as an 'uprising' of Gaelic Ireland and of the urban and rural poor to seize back their rightful inheritance, and many who used the notion clearly had difficulty in applying it to Ulster, where the 'Planter' element included a working-class majority. Some simply erased the Protestant working class from their view of Ulster. Thus Eithne Coyle, president of the republican women's organization Cumann na mBán and a signatory to the original Republican Congress manifesto, obviously saw the 'reconquest' in atavistic terms: 'we must show these tyrants in the North that the land of Ulster belongs to the real people of Ireland and not to the planter stock of Henry VIII.'[125]

The dominant strain in social republicanism and in the Congress was what Clare O'Halloran has dubbed the stereotype of the hard-headed and practical Unionist who respected plain speaking and would respect republicans who stuck to their principles.[126] While certainly less obnoxious than the planter/bigot stereotype, it was for all that based on a failure to engage with the substance of the Unionist movement and state. If the mass of Protestant workers were hostile to the legacy of Wolfe Tone, this was to be explained by their failure to distinguish the secular and non-sectarian nature of republicanism from the sectarianism which had corrupted nationalist politics in Northern Ireland. Thus An Phoblacht speculated that 'if you could succeed in discrediting organized political sectarianism on the Catholic side the Orange Order would not long survive.' It attacked the leading northern nationalist, the MP for West Belfast, Joe Devlin, his role in the Catholic organization the Ancient Order of Hibernians, and the main Catholic daily, the Irish News: 'for nationalism that paper substitutes Catholicism; for Imperialism it substitutes Protestantism, fanning the flames of sectarianism and keeping the Catholic and Protestant exploited in disunity.'[127] Such recognition of the role of sectarianism in nationalist politics represented one of the more honest and attractive features of social republicanism, but it still functioned to sustain a political strategy which ultimately failed to come to terms with the fact that, for many republicans, nationality and Catholicism were integrally linked and that 'secular' republicanism was very much a minority creed.

The onset of the Great Depression and the sharp increases in unemployment in the heartlands of the Protestant working class formed the basis for a new optimism about the possibilities of winning Protestant workers to 'anti-imperialist politics'. In an address to 'the men and women of the Orange Order' on the 12th of July 1932, the Army Council of the IRA informed the Protestant workers that, because of the world depression, Britain was no longer able to support the economy of Northern Ireland and that their future was therefore bound up with the rest of the Irish people: 'the industrial capacity, and training of you, industrial workers of North-East Ulster ensure for you a leading influence and place in the economy and life of a Free Irish Nation.'[128] How the export-oriented shipbuilding, engineering and textile industries of Belfast would be integrated into an autarkic social republic was not explained. The superficialities of the address would be sustained by the outbreak of serious working-class discontent during the Belfast Outdoor Relief Strike and accompanying riots in October. As Protestant and Catholic workers campaigned and rioted together, social republicans proclaimed the beginning of an historic shift in Protestant allegiances. George Gilmore, a republican from a northern Protestant background, described the ODR strike as 'the most important event in that city for centuries'. Here there is a clear repetition of Connolly's tendency to see in every serious strike involving Protestants the beginning of a break with Unionist ideology. For republicans of the left and right, Unionism was a reactionary ideology whose mass base had to be explained by assuming a Protestant working class blinded to its own interests. Conversely, any sign of even a limited economic and social awareness was read as the beginning of the end of Unionism.[129]

The Republican Congress would make much of the need to involve the newly awakened Protestant working class in 'anti-imperialist activities'. Its paper claimed that 'the advance of the vanguard of the Protestant workers into active struggle for the Workers' Republic is no longer a matter for day-dreaming. It has taken place.'[130] The supporters of Congress made much of their ability to bring a contingent of Protestant workers from the Shankill Road to the 1934 Wolfe Tone Commemoration march at Bodenstown and of their success in establishing local sections of the Congress in Belfast. It was certainly an achievement to get even 'two lorry loads'[131] of Protestant workers to a traditional Republican occasion but then, as before and since, the actions of small groups and individuals were assigned a wholly spurious representative significance. These few Protestants were then used to shore up an approach to the mass of Protestant workers which, if they were aware of it, evoked only hostility.

O'Donnell could claim in Dublin that a 'great awakening' was taking place amongst Protestant workers. But economic discontent and even dissatisfaction with the Unionist regime hardly justified his claim that 'workers of non-nationalist stock are realizing that their place is in a united front with their comrades in the south.'[132] The dominant strain in the coverage of the North in the *Republican Congress* was to emphasize that economic class consciousness was not enough, that Protestant workers had to move beyond the politics of the Northern Ireland Labour Party. 'The main weakness of anti-imperialist activities in Belfast working-class organizations has been a shying away from the national struggle for freedom.'[133] In an address to trade unionists in the Independent Labour Party hall in Belfast, O'Donnell attacked the NILP for 'dodging the Republican issue . . . the working-class movement in the North East has weakened the whole national struggle by its failure to see that its own freedom is inseparably bound up with the unity and freedom of an Irish Workers' Republic.'[134] In the face of developments like the sectarian riots in 1935, this incapacity to gauge the depth of Protestant working-class antagonism to 'the national struggle' could only sustain its optimism by more frantic attacks on the 'pro-imperialist' leaders of the northern labour movement and the reactionary and sectarian role of the IRA leadership in Belfast.

Prior to the ODR riots, *An Phoblacht* had criticized northern republicans for being little more than a Catholic defence force and making no attempt to establish contacts with Protestants. Belfast republicans were said to be 'on the whole possessed of a bigotry that is dangerous to the cause they have at heart.'[135] The failure of the Belfast IRA to get involved in the ODR strike as an organization was also attacked by O'Donnell, who claimed that they had been encouraged to make contacts with the Protestant working class; 'but always the reply was a thousand and one good reasons why it could not be done. Even on the eve of the ODR workers uprising the local OC pooh-poohed the idea that such a development was likely.'[136] It was true that outside a small number of socialist-inclined volunteers and a small number of Protestant IRA men, the Belfast organization was not fertile ground for social republicanism. Its concerns were predominantly military and geared towards its role of communal defence. As O'Donnell bluntly put it: 'we haven't a battalion of IRA men in Belfast; we just have a battalion of armed Catholics'.[137] However, to claim, as the Congress did, that 'the erection of the border was made possible by the separation of the Republican movement from the working class movement'[138] was greatly to exaggerate the role of these negative features of Belfast republicanism.

The failure to achieve the Republic was explained away on the republican left by various failures of leadership – the 1919 failure to support the demands of the small farmers and landless men, or the Belfast IRA's lack of proselytising activity amongst the Protestant workers. That the problem lay in the objective was never raised as a possibility. Social republicanism emerged as a strategy evolved to overthrow the Treaty settlement. Its use of the language of class and its attempt to link republican objectives to social and economic issues did have some real effects. Most crucially, it ensured that Fianna Fáil sounded the note of agrarian radicalism in 1932. But although it could play a role in pushing Fianna Fáil to the 'left', it could achieve little more. Attacks on De Valera in power only alienated its rural constituency, which feared 'socialism'. Left republicans had the weakest of roots in the southern working class and only illusions about Protestant workers. The Congress would split and disappear, divided between a majority led by O'Donnell, who still held to the strategy of mobilizing the masses by demonstrating that only an economically and socially radical strategy could achieve traditional republican objectives, and a minority led by Michael Price and two of Connolly's children, who argued that only a specifically socialist objective could ensure the support of the Protestant workers of Ulster.

The majority position completely failed to take account of the fundamental change that Fianna Fáil's victory had brought about. Before that, it was possible to argue for a radical republican movement to force Fianna Fáil to the left or even to displace the party altogether. With the resources of state power, De Valera had proved able to siphon off large elements of the republicans' constituency. It was much more difficult to mobilize an 'anti-imperialist' united front when the government could not be so easily portrayed as a reactionary pro-British rump. The minority position failed to attract because of the manifest difficulties facing any exponent of a 'Workers' Republic' in a state where the headquarters of the tiny Communist Party had recently been burned down by a clerically-inspired mob. Nevertheless, its supporters made some highly pertinent criticisms of the arguments of O'Donnell and Gilmore. These had emphasized that the only principled approach to adopt in Northern Ireland was to put the republican position straight to Protestant workers: 'it is harder to go among Protestant workers and insist that they must team up with the Republican masses against British Imperialism than to go under the banner of a Workers' Republic.'[139] In response, it was argued not simply that such propaganda would get nowhere in Belfast, but even more significantly, that the continued affiliation to republican objectives would tie the movement to some of the most integrative and reactionary political currents in the south. In an astonishingly prescient attack on the proponents of a republican united front strategy, Michael Price recalled a recent bellicose statement by Sean T. O'Kelly, a Fianna Fáil cabinet minister, threatening to impose the Republic on the north by force of arms and an offer by O'Duffy, the Blueshirt leader, to sink his differences with De Valera in a common campaign against Ulster. 'The united front movement might lead them to become involved in an attempt to make positive the jurisdiction of an all-Ireland Republic.'[140] In fact it would be the IRA, not the Congress that would soon be involved in such a campaign. The social republicans had greatly exaggerated the radical potentialities of the rural and urban masses, and were unable to combat the absorptive capacity of Fianna Fáil's populist nationalism to which they had contributed. On the issue of Protestant Ulster, social republicanism had failed utterly to escape the iron cage of nationalist assumptions, and while they might look with dismay at the subsequent IRA attempt to 'complete the national revolution' forcibly, O'Donnell and his supporters would continue to judge all issues by their relationship to an objective they happily shared with the most conservative and militaristic elements of the IRA.

3

In De Valera's Shadow

For almost thirty years after the collapse of the Republican Congress, physical force separatism was the overwhelmingly dominant form of republican activity. The debacle of Congress was used to reinforce traditionalist nostrums concerning the futility of 'politicisation' while in reality the leadership of the IRA was content to accept De Valera's objectives as legitimate, reserving a continued role for the IRA by simply emphasizing the need for an intransigent point of pressure to ensure that the risks of Fianna Fáil vacillation were minimized.

But as De Valera pressed ahead with creating a state that would satisfy the republican aspirations of broad swathes of the population, the IRA pretensions to the status of an alternative leadership became increasingly ludicrous. Membership of the IRA, which had soared in 1931–32, fell to 7,358 in 1935 and 3,844 a year later. In the same period the membership in Dublin almost disappeared, falling from 490 in 1934 to 93 in 1936.[1] The collapse in Dublin membership reflected the specific effects of an increasingly hard government line against the last vestiges of IRA 'radicalism' – its intervention in a transport strike in Dublin in March 1935, when volunteers sniped at army lorries used to replace trams, and shot policemen.[2] As the situation in Spain moved towards civil war, a wave of anti-communist feeling developed in Catholic Ireland, with Dublin most liable to its irruptions. At the 1936 Easter Commemoration march, contingents from the Communist Party and the remnants of the Republican Congress were stoned by the crowd.[3] A substantial number of left IRA men were among the 400 or so Irish who fought for the Republic in Spain.[4]

The IRA leadership was increasingly dominated by those who saw the key to the 'Republic' in a military campaign in either Northern Ireland or Britain or both. Fianna Fáil would be forced to complete the national revolution, not, as the Congress had predicted, through the activation of a grass roots radical coalition but by armed action which would rekindle popular nationalist sentiment and force a confront-ation with Britain. In part, of course, the IRA had little choice. Its very existence required at least the prospect of action. By 1936 it was clear that military activity in the south would invite a quick and predictable response from De Valera. After a number of IRA armed attacks on opponents, culminating in the murders of a retired Vice-Admiral in Cork in March 1936 and a policeman in April, the government proscribed the IRA and arrested many of its leaders, including the Chief of Staff, Moss Twomey.[5] For one of Twomey's successors, Sean Russell, an archetypal anti-political republican, there was no feasible way of shaking Fianna Fáil and the Treaty settlement except through exemplary violence *outside* the Free State, which he mistakenly assumed De Valera would have more difficulty in repressing.

In 1937 Sean MacBride, Chief of Staff and the main political intelligence left in the leadership after the Congress schism, accepted De Valera's new constitution with its 'de jure' claim to jurisdiction over the 32 counties as fulfilling most of the republicans' objectives. Any remaining national goals could be achieved peacefully, and thus, he declared, the IRA had no further role.[6] In marked contrast was the bitter denunciation uttered by the *Irish Democrat*, a paper produced by the remnants of the Republican Congress: 'De Valera has sancti-fied the property system arising from the Elizabethan, Cromwellian and Williamite Conquest with religious phrases.' But still O'Donnell and another prominent social republican who had temporarily returned from the Spanish war, Frank Ryan, counterposed to Fianna Fáil conservatism an abstract appeal for an all-Ireland conference of 'Separatists and Labour bodies' to restore the unity destroyed by the Treaty. This coalescence of nation and class appeal had as its premiss a real popular commitment to a progressive 32-county republic: 'we accuse the Fianna Fáil government of this: in a time of trial for the Nation, they ask less of the people than the people are eager and able to achieve.'[7] That there was considerable and growing dissatisfaction with the limits of the post-1932 reforms, particularly in the countryside, would very soon become clear. But this dissatisfaction, while it might hold out possibilities of changing political alignments *within* the southern state, could not shake the broad popular sympathy for De Valera's movement towards a truncated but nevertheless effective form of sovereignty.

Popular aspirations for a full 32-county republic and a more egalitarian economic and social order may well have existed, although it was undoubtedly an exaggeration to claim that 'the 1916 Proclamation was always read to promise a triumph of the poor over the small group of rich men who trafficked in their misery.'[8] But such aspirations could not easily be made the basis for an alternative national strategy to that of Fianna Fáil. This was not simply because as essentially Irish Catholic aspirations, they had no appeal to the obdurate Protestants of Ulster. More fundamentally, they shared with Fianna Fáil the assumption that the attainment of full political sovereignty made the economic and social regeneration of Ireland a simple matter of governmental will. This ingrained nationalist commonplace linked De Valera and many of his most bitter critics. By the end of the thirties the limits of Fianna Fáil policies for economic and social regeneration were becoming clear: 'The great leap forward did not materialize. Emigration and rural depopulation were not halted. The link with sterling was maintained. The free flow of capital and labour between Ireland and Britain was not interfered with. Full-blooded protectionism was being strongly diluted by the late thirties. Between the Coal-Cattle Pact of 1936 and the Anglo-Irish agreement of 1938 Ireland's trade pattern was returning to 'normal'; that is to say the economy of the Irish state was being reintegrated into the larger trading economy of the neighbouring state'.[9]

But just as the IRA militarists were trapped in a prisonhouse of assumptions centring on the notion that the two states had evolved from 'betrayal' – from the twists and turns of human desires and weaknesses rather than any factors of a more structural nature – the remnants of social republicanism were trapped in the assumption that the manifest inequalities and oppressions of Irish life could be cured through a more radical, nationalist, political coalition, using the state to institute the social republic they claimed was implicit in 1916.

A striking characteristic of both the IRA and social republic-anism throughout this period is that, whether 'left' or 'right', its focus was on completing the revolution by action, military or agitational, that would impose itself on the state governed by Fianna Fáil. In the dispute over whether a military campaign should be aimed at Britain or Northern Ireland the proposal for a northern focus came from the veteran IRA leader Tom Barry from Cork. He proposed an attack across the border to seize a northern town, hold it as long as possible and withdraw, having, it was hoped, roused the population and forced the issue of partition upon a reluctant De Valera.[10] The rejection of this plan, which led to Barry's withdrawal from the IRA, had nothing at all to do with arguments against it from the IRA in Northern Ireland. As Bowyer Bell has noted of the IRA leadership from the 1920s to the 1940s: 'despite the size and enthusiasms of the IRA in the Six Counties, the north had played only a minimal part in the leadership of the IRA. Rarely had a northerner served on GHQ much less the Army Council, and rarely had the Dublin leadership given consideration to the problems of the north.'[11] Just as, for a brief period, an exaggerated view of the effects of the Great Depression on the Protestant working class had led the social republicans to accord the north a privileged place in their strategy for 'reconquest' of Ireland as a whole, so now a military campaign in Northern Ireland was proposed on the basis of little interest in, or knowledge of conditions in the north, for what was essentially a southern purpose. The defeat of Barry's proposal may have reflected some residual distrust of the more sectarian and 'defenderist' aspects of the northern and particularly Belfast IRA. However, given the barrenness of the strategy that was decided upon, this appears doubtful. Rather, the debate over the objectives of the military campaign illustrates that the leadership regarded itself as still potentially a major force in Irish political life. It had failed utterly to understand De Valera's effective closure of anti-Treaty aspirations.

Throughout the 1940s and 1950s, the attempt to relate republicanism to the actualities of Irish life went on outside the IRA. Absorbing the remaining members of the 'government' of the second Dáil in 1938,[12] the IRA under Sean Russell's leadership 'declared war' on England and launched a campaign of sabotage and terror which confirmed its increasing marginalization in Ireland where, buttressed by the massive popularity of his policy of neutrality, De Valera could take stringent measures to repress the IRA with little fear of popular repercussions. Military courts, internment and a small number of executions and deaths from hunger strikes, together with the predictable internal bickerings and charges of 'betrayal' born out of patent failure, had effectively destroyed much of the organization by 1945. In February 1939 Russell had established contact with the German Intelligence organization, Abwehr II, who were to send agents to Ireland to encourage IRA activity in the north aimed at disrupting the British war effort. In May 1940 he arrived in Berlin where he met prominent Nazis including Joachim von Ribbentrop, the Foreign Minister, and received training in sabotage. He was being transported back to Ireland by submarine when he took ill and died. Russell's intrigues with Germany, which came to nothing, were not uniformly popular in the south, where some IRA men looked askance on contacts with the Nazis.[13] In the north, the dominant response was to welcome anything that might lead to British defeat. Those few Belfast IRA men who had been touched by the thirties radicalism could only look on in amused contempt as their comrades in jail jubilantly plotted the eastward march of the German army into the Soviet Union.[14]

Towards a Border War

Defeat and marginalization would teach no lessons. Neither would the increasing evidence of rural and urban discontent with the De Valera dispensation. Dissatisfaction with the limited nature of Fianna Fáil agrarian reforms and its failure to deal seriously with the continuing problems of underemployment and emigration in the West was expressed in the temporary success of a western peasants party, Clann na Talmhan (Children of the Land) founded in 1938. It won 11% of the vote and 14 seats in the Dáil election of 1943. The limits of the industrial policies of tariff protection and job creation were also clear by the 1940s, and in the 1943 election the Irish Labour Party substantially increased its vote – from 10% to 15% – almost doubling its Dáil representation from 9 to 17.[15] Although this advance would be soon checked by a major split in both the Labour Party and the Irish TUC – fuelled by nationalism, antagonism to British-based unions and anti-communism[16] – there was clear evidence that the material for a radical attack on Fianna Fáil existed.

When it came, it was led by the ex-IRA leader Sean MacBride, who founded a new party, Clann na Poblachta (The Family of the Republic) in 1946. Rumpf has summed up its fundamental dynamics as expressing 'the dissatisfaction of the more constructive members of the younger generation of Republicans, both with the growing conservatism and machine politics of Fianna Fáil and with the arid brutality which had characterized the IRA. . . .'[17] Its specific policies on the economy – repatriation of Irish capital invested abroad, breaking of the monetary link with sterling, substantial government investment to stimulate a depressed economy – resembled a revamped radical Fianna Fáil platform of the 1920s. Its achievement of 13% of the vote and 10 seats in the Dáil in 1948 was a central factor in displacing Fianna Fáil from office for the first time since 1932. However its acceptance of places in a coalition government which included the anti-republican Fine Gael only alienated many of its supporters. More fundamentally it demonstrated the problems for any political party in the southern state which combined its appeal to social radicalism with an inchoate hope that, just as it was possible for a Dublin government to take a more active role in dealing with unemployment, poverty and disease, so it was open to it by a simple act of will also to 'solve' the national question.

The result of MacBride's brief irruption into mainstream politics was a self-interested scramble for nationalist credentials between the Coalition parties and Fianna Fáil, manifested in the declaration of a Republic in 1948 and the launching of an all-party Anti-Partition Campaign. This campaign, with its origins in the dynamics of inter-party competition in the south, highlighted the 'affront' of partition in an intense propaganda onslaught in Ireland and internationally but failed miserably, though predictably, to alter the situation. However, its effect on the IRA was substantial.

The initial success of Clann na Poblachta encouraged the remnants of the IRA (in 1948 the 'General Headquarters Staff' estimated that the organization had 200 activists and some hundreds of sympathizers[18]) to equip themselves with a political arm by re-establishing the link with Sinn Féin – by taking it over. This politicization had two notable characteristics. The first and more important was to be the clear subordination of the political organization to the IRA Army Council. The second was the staggering backwardness of its economic and social programme.

The 'National Unity and Independence Programme' of Sinn Féin referred to a 'reign of social justice based on Christian principles'[19]. These were the corporatist vocational principles which had so enamoured the Blueshirts and the Catholic hierarchy in the 1930s and which Fianna Fáil, to its credit, eventually rejected.[20] In the late 1940s, they had been narrowed down to the matter of intense Church opposition to any attempt to 'import' the 'socialistic' welfare state from the United Kingdom. It was the attempt by the radical Minister of Health, Noel Browne of the Clann, to provide free health care for pregnant women and nursing mothers, which would destroy the Coalition and MacBride's new party.[21] In this crucial conflict between a government minister and the Catholic hierarchy, the republican movement's position was an implicitly miserable one. While the Unionist government in the north used the 'Mother and Child' affair to intensify its depiction of the Republic as priest-ridden and backward, Sinn Féin, now the mouthpiece for an organization which had decided in 1948 to prepare for a military campaign against the 'occupied Six Counties',[22] declared itself for vocational principles and against the welfare state.[23] The new monthly paper of Sinn Féin, the *United Irishman*, swore its fidelity to the republican saint Wolfe Tone and his objective of destroying English rule by 'unity of Protestant, Catholic and Dissenter'.

But at the same time it persisted in the characteristic Catholic, nationalist fixation with the supposed power of Southern Free Masonry,[24] and was content to reject blithely such manifestations of the 'British link' as the welfare state, which was massively popular with the Protestant working class.

Of course, most IRA members were little interested in social philosophy, Marxist, Catholic or otherwise. Most would have been practising Catholics with no time for politics, particularly if they were tainted by 'communism' (a capacious term in post-war Ireland). Like their Chief of Staff Tony Magan, they were dedicated to a republican ideal narrowed down to reunification by physical force. There were exceptions to this general rule, and some of these 'exceptions' would play a key role in the 1960s. Thus, in a book which recalls one of the darkest and most arid periods for the IRA – the English bombing campaign – Brendan Behan claims to have declared to his captors that he had come over 'to fight for the Irish Workers and Small Farmers Republic'.[25] He typically differentiated his own variety of republicanism from those of '. . . your wrap-the-green-flag-round-me junior Civil Servants that came into the IRA from the Gaelic League, and were ready to die for their country any day of the week, purity in their hearts, truth on their lips, for the glory of God and the honour of Ireland.'[26] A working-class background in Dublin's north side was shared with a friend, Cathal Goulding, who had joined Fianna Éireann – the junior wing of the IRA – in 1937 at the age of eleven. His grandfather had been an Invincible –the group responsible for the murder of the two most senior British officials in Ireland in 1882 – and his father and uncle had both been in the IRA. His father was a painter who, like many anti-Treatyites, found it extremely difficult to get work in the aftermath of the Civil War because of hostility from many employers. He set himself up as a self-employed contractor and his son would combine work as a painter and active membership of the IRA. Both his parents had been sympathetic to social republicanism, and Austin Stack's pamphlet *The Constructive Work of Dáil Eireann*, outlining the 'responsible' attitude taken by the First Dáil to divisive land and labour issues, was used as a primer on the dangers of reactionary degeneration within the republican movement.[27]

But class consciousness was not to act for Goulding as a solvent of republican intransigence and militarism until the collapse of the IRA's next military campaign. In Dublin at least, it was possible for traditions of working-class militancy to influence some members of the IRA, even in its most militarist and reactionary period. In Goulding's north Dublin James Larkin, the charismatic leader of the 1913 Lockout, had been elected to the Dáil in 1928 with over 8,000 votes as a candidate of the Irish Workers' League which he had founded as the Irish Section of the Third International.[28] Yet such class consciousness tended to be sublimated into a militaristic intransigence and self-justifying belief that the fundamental mistake of people like O'Donnell and Gilmore was to take action that put them outside the 'army', and that ultimately the task was to win the IRA to radical politics. This formidable task was made no easier by the fact that these faint echoes of the Congress debates were soon drowned out by strident anti-partitionism. In the late thirties and forties, the IRA was composed predominantly of people whose focus was still on the Civil War and the subsequent divisions and redivisions of anti-Treatyism. For all its often barren bitterness it still, especially in its urban form, had a capacity to express a deep, intransigent opposition to the Irish state. From 1949 onwards, as the anti-partition campaign dominated public life in the south, a new generation of IRA members emerged whose focus was largely an extreme variant of official propaganda. The new members who flocked into Sinn Féin and thence to the IRA had received their formative political education, not from the stock republican litanies of the evils of 'Free Statism' but from the leaflets and pamphlets on the evils of partition produced by the southern state. For Tomás MacGiolla, later president of Sinn Féin, political education began with a massive all-party rally held in O'Connell Street in 1949 to condemn the passage of the Ireland Act at Westminster as an 'iniquitous' solidification of partition. The 'national question' became identified with the ending of the British-supported 'Orange State' thanks to the thorough and well-produced pamphlets detailing Unionist discrimination and gerrymandering which the all-party assault had produced.[29] Then came the collapse of the Coalition government and the return in 1951 of a lacklustre Fianna Fáil administration whose energies were totally absorbed in an unimaginative response to the Republic's burgeoning economic crisis. For many like MacGiolla, enthused and mobilized in 1949–50 and observing the lack of results from the campaign of the constitutional parties, membership of Sinn Féin was a natural progression, as was support for the armed assault on Northern Ireland to which the IRA had been committed since 1948.

Republicans could not have been unaware of the massive crisis of the Republic's domestic economy in the mid-fifties, as unemployment rocketed and emigration levels reached and surpassed their worst pre-independence levels. However, these developments were treated not as evidence of the bankruptcy of De Valera's ideals of economic autarky but rather as signs that 'Free-Statism' could only corrupt and violate what were essentially sound principles of national development. Thus while the crisis impelled Fianna Fáil to jettison the economics of Sinn Féin and to reintegrate the Republic into the world economy, it confirmed the republican movement in its full-blooded protectionism. MacGiolla and other republicans watched trains arrive in Dublin's Westland Row station from the west of Ireland, packed to capacity with those who were going straight on to the mailboats at Dun Laoghaire and emigration. They gave out leaflets at rallies of the unemployed in O'Connell Street.[30] The message was the consoling one that until the 'British occupation' of the Six Counties was ended the economic depression would not be ended – a prediction that would prove more damaging to the IRA in the Irish Republic than the predictable failure of their armed campaign in Northern Ireland, which was launched at the end of 1956.

Idealism and Sectarianism in the 1956 Campaign

Within less than a year, the 1956–62 campaign had clearly failed, and for reasons that were predicted before it commenced. The delay in launching the campaign, which had caused much dissatisfaction in the ranks and led to a couple of anticipatory splinter attacks in Northern Ireland, reflected a debate inside the IRA leadership over the viability of a guerrilla campaign in the midst of a hostile majority population. As an alternative to a guerrilla campaign, some leaders suggested a longer-term strategy: first, sabotage of transport and communications to bring everyday life to a standstill, and second, preparation of the nationalist population for a civil disobedience campaign. The latter, it was calculated, would provoke repression from the police and the highly unpopular B Special constabulary (unpopular among Catholics, that is) and provide the space for the IRA to emerge as a 'people's' defence force.[31]

Instead it was decided to opt for Sean Cronin's 'Operation Harvest': a plan for a guerrilla campaign waged initially by 'flying columns' from the south who would sabotage communications, destroy police barracks and ultimately create 'liberated areas'. Cronin, a Kerry man and ex-member of the Free State army who had recently returned from the United States, was a forceful personality, and the acceptance of his strategy seems to have owed as much to the energy and conviction with which he argued it as to any more substantial factor. It was sadly deficient in any grasp of northern realities. Indeed, one of its attractions was precisely its effective suppression of the dynamics of northern sectarianism. For as long as the IRA's activities were focused on creating 'liberated areas' in some of the predominantly Catholic borderlands of Northern Ireland, the question of the repercussions of such activities on Catholic-Protestant relations, particularly in the sectarian cockpit of Belfast, could be ignored.

The IRA Army Council was also well aware that action in the north was necessary to undermine support that had emerged for heretical anti-abstentionist ideas amongst some republicans. The key figure was Liam Kelly, an IRA man from Pomeroy in County Tyrone. Influenced by the formation of Clann na Poblachta and particularly by Sean MacBride, Kelly persuaded a majority of Tyrone republicans to support the idea of a new political organization, Fianna Uladh (Soldiers of Ulster) and a new military organization, Saor Uladh (Free Ulster). Kelly agreed with MacBride that the 1937 Constitution should legitimize the southern state, particularly now that the Coalition had taken the Free State out of the Commonwealth and established a Republic in 1948. As a consequence he argued for an end to abstentionism in the south and a concentration of republican effort against the state of Northern Ireland. Expelled from the IRA in 1951 for planning an operation without authorization, he was elected to the Stormont parliament for Mid-Tyrone in 1953. His support base by then extended to Derry and Belfast, where some younger republicans – including a later leader of Official republicanism, Billy McMillen – were attracted by his mixture of political and military activism. Jailed for making 'seditious statements', Kelly was nominated by MacBride and elected to the Irish Senate in 1954. His release from prison in August 1954 was the occasion of a serious riot in Pomeroy, County Tyrone, when thousands of his supporters clashed with the RUC. In November 1955 Saor Uladh attacked the RUC station at Roslea, County Fermanagh, and in November 1956 Saor Uladh and another splinter group attacked six customs posts along the border.[32]

These developments made some sort of 'decisive' response from the IRA inevitable. The Army Council was no doubt encouraged by the 1955 Westminster election results. Two IRA arms raids on army barracks in Armagh and Omagh in 1954, the second of which led to the capture and imprisonment of eight IRA members, had done much to restore republican morale. In the election Sinn Féin contested all twelve constituencies, half of them with men in prison for the Omagh raid. The result was the largest anti-partition vote since the formation of the state – 152,310 votes – and two victories in Mid-Ulster and Fermanagh-South Tyrone.[33] Interestingly, the only constituency with a large Catholic population in which the Sinn Féin candidate did not perform well was West Belfast. Here Sinn Féin's neglect of economic and social issues ensured that it trailed behind an Irish Labour Party candidate – the Catholic proletariat would remain wedded to various versions of labourist and republican labour politics until the late 1960s.[34] Meanwhile Cronin's strategy would direct the IRA's attentions to the redoubts of intransigent rural republicanism in the border areas and north Antrim.

On the night of 12 December 1956 approximately 150 men

were involved in attacks on ten different targets in Northern Ireland as 'Operation Harvest' began. By its end six members of the RUC and eleven republicans were dead – relatively few people by the standards of the post-1969 campaign.[35] Its highpoint was the abortive attack on Brookeborough RUC station in Fermanagh in January 1957. Like all the 'flying columns' this one was composed of IRA men from the south with only the skimpiest knowledge of local conditions. Two of the group, Sean Garland from Dublin and Daithi O'Connaill from Cork, would play crucial and conflicting roles in post-1962 republican rethinking. The key figures in the attack would be the two IRA men who were killed during it – Sean South and Feargal O'Hanlon. The deaths of two young idealists – as they were widely perceived in Catholic Ireland – resulted in a powerful spasm of public emotion: 'When the bodies of South and O'Hanlon were carried across the border, their transmutation from young men into martyrs began. There began a week of all but national mourning. Crowds lined the route of South's funeral cortège to Dublin. . . . Town Councils and County Corporations passed votes of sympathy.'[36] In the general election which occurred soon after, Sinn Féin's 19 candidates got just over 5% of the vote and it had four TDs elected. These were unexpected victories but as Rumpf has noted the result was 'ultimately insignificant'.[37] Mass concern over the Coalition government's lack of response to a massive economic crisis was the decisive issue in giving De Valera a last impressive election victory. In 1956 he had made it clear to emissaries from the IRA who had asked for his cooperation or connivance in the planned campaign that he thought partition could not be ended by force.[38] As the campaign futilely sputtered on, producing only internment (eventually over 250 people were interned in Northern Ireland) and a massive mobilization of the police and 13,000 B Specials,[39] interest and sympathy evaporated. In July 1957 after the IRA had killed an RUC man in County Armagh internment was introduced in the Republic and nearly 200 were interned.[40] Catholic disillusionment was plain in the Westminster election in October 1959 when the Sinn Féin vote slumped by over a half.[41] In the Republic the Sinn Féin vote in the 1961 general election declined to 36,393 for 21 candidates – 3% – and only one was elected.[42]

The IRA's Army Council had addressed an appeal to the Protestants of Northern Ireland to support the independence movement, in the very midst of their military campaign.[43] The exotic futility of this gesture should not obscure the nagging doubts and suspicions which some southern republicans had about a too-direct mobilization of the forces of grievance and traditional animosity which existed in the Catholic population in the north. It is still unclear whether, as some claim, a decision was made not to include the Belfast IRA in the campaign, so as to avoid the possibility of sectarian conflict,[44] or whether Belfast's non-involvement reflected fears that its personnel were too well known to the police.[45] What is clear is that the order from the IRA GHQ that all possible steps had to be taken to avoid shooting members of the part-time Protestant constabulary – the B Specials – was intensely unpopular with northern IRA men and their sympathizers.[46] Regarded by the government and the Protestant population as the 'eyes and ears' of the state, with a detailed knowledge of their Catholic neighbours, the Specials were the focus of much fear and animosity. Attacks on the Specials were opposed on the basis that their deep roots in local Protestant communities would ensure that such attacks would provoke bitter sectarian animosities. As the IRA campaign reeled under its own futilities and the introduction of internment north and south, some began to query the wisdom of excluding action that would at least restore flagging Catholic interest and support.

Ironically, it was Sean Cronin, whose original plan had effectively marginalized the appeal to Catholic communalism, who in 1959 appeared willing to contemplate the risky venture of a Belfast campaign. By then the leadership was bitterly divided over whether the campaign should be called off, with Cronin to the fore in pressing for its continuance. He hoped to ensure revival through a sharp change in focus from the border areas to Belfast. Sean Garland, a survivor of the campaign's most martyrogenic action – the attack on Brookeborough RUC station in which Sean South and Fergal O'Hanlon were killed – was chosen to mobilize the Belfast IRA. Disguised as a Glasgow university student but largely ignorant of the city and its republican sub-culture, he had just enough time to discover widespread demoralization before he was arrested and gaoled in the Crumlin Road prison, where his mission was received with sullen resentment by the many IRA prisoners who regarded the campaign as by then an obvious and definitive failure.[47]

For some in the Belfast IRA, the failure of 'Operation Harvest' stemmed directly from its fastidiousness. As the national leadership settled its divisions by intrigue – Cronin was displaced by an organized letter-writing campaign from Irish-America which used anti-communism and other disreputable charges against his radical American wife[48] – the remaining republicans in Crumlin Road speculated on what, if anything, their future might be. Attempts to politicize such discussion were received with hostility.[49] More typical would have been the jocular remark of a future leading Belfast Provisional, that a military campaign of the 1956 sort was 'no use' and that the only way forward was to 'shoot a lot of priests and ministers', thus ensuring a strong communal base for the IRA in the resultant sectarian polarization.[50] Such sentiments reflected a stubborn reality of the northern situation which the idealist rhetoric of 'Wolfe Tone' republicanism found hard to recognize, let alone deal with.

4

A Limited Reassessment:
The IRA after 1962

In June 1963, an incident occurred in Belfast which epitomized the contradictory impulses at the heart of republicanism as it sought to recover from the failure of the border campaign. A march was to be held to celebrate the 200th anniversary of Wolfe Tone's birth. It was part of a series of activities organized by the Wolfe Tone Society, which had emerged from discussions between Cathal Goulding. Sean Cronin and Dick Roche in Dublin and a small group of republicans, nationalists and labourites there and in Belfast.[1] In Belfast, the urge behind the Wolfe Tone Society – to create a broad coalition of 'progressive' and 'nationally-minded' forces – ran up against the brutal wall of communal assertiveness. The Belfast IRA had been asked to act as a colour party, but when the police forbade the carrying of an Irish Tricolour, the IRA commander in Belfast, Billy McKee, assented. This decision was bitterly contested by the bulk of Belfast IRA men and despite Goulding's attempt to mediate, McKee was forced to resign and was replaced by Billy McMillen. A march inspired by a strategy apparently aimed at building a new 'anti-imperialist' alliance to include at least a section of the Protestant community would in fact herald a period of intensifying conflict between the police and republicans on an issue which could reinvigorate communal solidarity amongst Catholics but left even progressive Protestants cold.[2]

Goulding was now Chief of Staff of the IRA, his reputation for leftism notwithstanding. Imprisonment in England during the first three years of the border campaign meant he was untainted by its failure and in any case, the general demoralization was such that no-one else wanted the job.[3] The Army Convention in 1962, at which his tenure commenced, marked the beginning of a process of assessment of the state of the IRA and a reassessment of the history of the republican movement. For Goulding, such a reassessment meant, in part, a return to the debates of the inter-war period, with the aim of reconstituting the IRA as a vanguard of social republicanism. It was in this context that his overtures to intellectuals outside the IRA were made. The nature of this external input has been the subject of bitter controversy but not much useful information or analysis. The split in the IRA and Sinn Féin in 1969–70 would see Goulding's opponents claim that he had allowed 'Marxists' to take effective strategic direction of the republican movement. These claims have been rather uncritically repeated in Bishop and Mallie's recent history of the Provisionals.[4] What was the significance of these external influences?

The two key individuals were Anthony Coughlan and Roy Johnston. Both had lived in England and been involved in the activities of the Connolly Association, which had emerged from the disintegrating Republican Congress. A London branch reconstituted itself as a Connolly Club and this was subsequently revived by an influx of Irish International Brigaders.[5] Its monthly paper the *Irish Democrat* had been edited since 1947 by Desmond Greaves, a member of the Communist Party of Great Britain and author of a major, if tendentious, biography of Connolly.[6] Under his leadership the Association concentrated on organizing among Irish emigrants for two aims: 'first their own defence, second the freedom of their country'.[7] It also sought to influence the British labour movement away from what was seen as its dangerous mixture of apathy and pro-Unionism on the Irish question. During the border campaign the Connolly Association concentrated on attacking the Unionist government for interning republicans and began to press the British government to use its power under the Government of Ireland Act to legislate for civil rights in Northern Ireland.[8] As early as 1955, the *Irish Democrat* had put forward the idea of a civil rights campaign as the way to shatter Ulster Unionism.[9] For a year in 1960–61, Coughlan acted as a full-time organizer for the Connolly Association, promoting 'anti-Unionist political activity in Britain',[10] including a march from London to

Birmingham to raise the issue of British acquiescence in Unionist rule.[11] A graduate of University College Cork who had been in London from 1958 doing post-graduate work, Coughlan returned to a lectureship in social administration in Trinity College Dublin in 1961. He was a fervent republican in the sense that he saw the central issue of Irish politics as the completion of the national revolution. However this could not be achieved by the physical force tradition but only by the creation of a broad national coalition in which the labour movement would play a central role. The objective of this movement was 'real' independence, not socialism. In Northern Ireland the objective would be to destabilize Unionism by reforms which would detach enough Protestants from the Unionist Party to create a 'progressive' coalition: 'Stormont could then be used against imperialism', to quote his friend and mentor Greaves.[12]

Coughlan was invited to join the Wolfe Tone Society in 1964 when it was decided to maintain it as a permanent 'think tank' of 'active people with roots in the language, trade union, cooperative, republican and other organizations. . . .'[13] The Society was to provide the intellectual resources for a unification of 'the bulk of the radical-minded elements in the existing Trade Union and Republican movement' in a new revolutionary political organization.[14] Goulding and Cronin had played a role in initiating the Wolfe Tone Society, but its subsequent development was not heavily influenced by the IRA. Rather the IRA was undergoing a parallel process of development in which some of the central ideas propagated by the Wolfe Tone Society were to play a crucial if controversial role.

Coughlan's ideas on the economic conjuncture and subsequently on the reform of Stormont had considerable influence on the IRA's reassessment. Although he made a direct contribution to the Army Council's discussions on future strategy he was determined to maintain a position of independence, and refused all requests to join the organization.[15] The person responsible for bringing such ideas directly into the IRA's internal education programme was Roy Johnston. From a middle-class Protestant background in Dublin, Johnston had a Science doctorate from Trinity. In England between 1960 and 1963 he had been active in both the Communist Party and the Connolly Association.[16] On returning to Dublin he joined the Wolfe Tone Society but unlike Coughlan became deeply involved in the IRA's reorientation. Goulding had met him in the Wolfe Tone Society and was impressed with his abilities. Goulding was unburdened by the common IRA disdain for civilians and, with a background which predisposed him to social republicanism, he was eager for Johnston to play an active role in internal discussion and education. It was possible for individuals to join Sinn Féin and not be a member of the IRA but the clear subordination of the 'political wing' to the army meant that 'real' membership of the republican movement dictated membership of the IRA. For this reason, Johnston joined the IRA, and it was this and in particular his role in the education of volunteers rather than his position as education officer for Sinn Féin that caused intense disquiet among more traditional members.[17]

Goulding appears to have had a largely instrumental attitude to people like Coughlan and Johnston and to his generally good relations with Irish communists, particularly those in Belfast. He would later observe of this period that 'most of our people were very naive about making political demands'.[18] The IRA needed to import some theoretical assistance for its rethinking process. However he also clearly believed that such ideas would be relatively easily harnessed to the principal purpose: 'we knew that if we were to retain the leadership of the movement, and maintain the movement itself as a revolutionary organization, we would need to have a policy for the next phase of the fight against British Imperialism in Ireland.'[19] The long severance between the IRA and social republicanism dictated that this tradition had to be reappropriated from largely external sources, but for Goulding this would create the conditions not for the demise of the IRA but for its reconstitution as armed guarantor of the social and political gains of a revolutionary popular movement. For all its dramatic effects in the 1960s, the new thinking was in central respects traditionalist.

Regressive Modernization

There was much that was critical and innovative in the approach of Coughlan and Johnston. In particular there was an emphasis on the republican movement's intellectual bankruptcy. In a key analysis, Coughlan emphasized the need for theory: 'it is time that Irish republicans began to take ideas and theory seriously.'[20] Republicanism had proven itself incapable of developing 'the substantial body of theoretical writing' of the major Irish revolutionaries of the past and applying it to contemporary circumstances. As a result it had no engagement with some of the most crucial questions of contemporary politics: 'We ask where has the republican movement put forward an authoritative criticism of the Second Programme of Economic Expansion of the Fianna Fáil party as it leads Ireland back towards economic union with Britain? (In 1964 the Fianna Fáil government published its Second Programme of Economic Expansion to continue the process of trade liberalization and attraction of foreign capital begun with the First Programme in 1959.) Or of the reasons for the failure of the Irish cultural and language movement to achieve more success in the past forty years than it has in fact done? Where is the ruthless analysis of the failure of either republicanism or labour to significantly influence government policy in the twenty-six Counties since the southern state was founded?'[21] But although there is no doubting the radical and progressive intent of this approach and its desire to demilitarize the republican movement – 'Superior ideas are more effective than armies in that the changes they bring about are more permanent'[22] – it was ultimately limited by its traditionalist ideological horizon. This was set out most clearly in the constitution of the Wolfe Tone Society, which as a description of 'Ireland Today' said little that a leader writer in the *Irish Press* (the pro-Fianna Fáil daily) would have disagreed with: 'The Irish people, north and south, are one nation sharing common history on a common territory. . . . No real conflict of interest exists between any section of the common people, either between different sections of the people of the north, or between north and south. Propaganda which depicts imaginary causes for division, which fosters artificial conflicts, or which exaggerates regional differences in character in order to justify the political division of the country, is false propaganda. . . . The Partition of Ireland is inimical to the interests of all Irish people; is the cause of all the exceptional political and economic problems from which Ireland has suffered for past 40 years and today is the main barrier to the solution of those problems. . . . Economically . . . Partition is responsible for Ireland's exceptional problems of unemployment and emigration. . . . The basis of Partition in the Six Counties is an artificially fostered sectarianism, an anti-Catholic prejudice and bigotry which has become identified with the State system . . . without which the system could not survive and without which there would be no reason for its existence. . . .'[23] The traditional nationalist assumptions of one nation, 'artificial' divisions implanted by Britain, the identification of the popular basis of Ulster Unionism with sectarianism, the identification of reform as a prerequisite for winning Protestants to the cause of national independence were thought to have a renewed and radical significance precisely because Fianna Fáil was in the process of openly and flagrantly betraying them for the first time.

In the debate that split the Republican Congress, O'Donnell had claimed that the slogan of a 'Workers' Republic' would allow De Valera to continue to hegemonize workers and small farmers by identifying Fianna Fáil with the 'Republic'. The real task was to demonstrate to the masses, not that Dev was not a socialist but that he was not a real republican. The difficulty in the 1930s was that the Economic War, the adoption of protectionism and other development policies by Fianna Fáil allowed it to maintain a claim of continuity with traditional republican objectives. Now, it was claimed, the conditions for a united front of republicans and trade-union and small-farmer organizations against Fianna Fáil were much more favourable. Crucial here was the break with the protectionist measures of the thirties, which the Fianna Fáil government of Seán Lemass had initiated at the end of the 1950s in response to the grave economic crisis.[24] The gradual phasing out of protectionism, the vigorous attempts to attract foreign capital, the preparation of Ireland for EEC membership simply signified the final capitulation of Fianna Fáil:

'. . . whereas De Valera's efforts at economic independence were half-hearted . . . at least some effort was made during the 1930s and 1940s to weaken some of the links with Britain. But Lemass has given up the effort entirely. And between De Valera's compromise and Lemass's capitulation there is difference enough to justify Britain in turn changing its tactics.'[25] Now that the leadership of Fianna Fáil had acquiesced in 'their present ignominious role of local managers for imperialism', Britain had been encouraged to change its strategy towards Ireland as a whole. Partition was no longer the best possible way of keeping the country in a weak and dependent position; Lemass's capitulation had encouraged Britain to seek a more radical constitutional change, of which the Anglo-Irish Free Trade Agreement in January 1966 was seen to be a portent: 'Britain now hopes to snare Lemass back into the United Kingdom. The Free Trade Agreement will do the trick. . . .'[26] The basis for speculating about such a drastic possibility was not argued out at any length. A Sinn Féin document prepared by Johnston's Education Department pointed to Britain's economic problems as a symptom of 'deep crisis': 'the imperialist power . . . [is] finding it increasingly difficult to maintain the huge profits it has been drawing from the neo-colonial exploitation of its former empire . . .'[27] In such a situation, 'Britain will be increasingly anxious to weld Ireland more tightly to her side as a secure neo-colony. . . .'[28] Fianna Fáil's economic 'capitulation' was seen as the basis for a total reversal of classical republican objectives and it was now denounced as a 'Unionist' party. The opportunities had never been greater for a broad anti-imperialist alliance in the Republic to challenge the hegemony of 'anti-national ideas and theories' which had as their hallmark 'the abandonment of the aims of the 1916 men and the republicans of the past as "impractical" and impossible of attainment in the world of today.'[29] This alliance would reflect the interest of the mass of the people – '. . . the workers and small farmers and those sections of small business and the intellectuals who are adversely affected by the domination of British and foreign captital in Ireland.'[30]

At the centre of what Sinn Féin would label its 'economic resistance' campaign was the notion that a 'truly' republican government could use its sovereignty to establish 'real' economic independence. The proposals were largely a résumé of past critiques of the timidity of De Valera's policies in the thirties, in particular his failure to control the movement of Irish capital abroad and to repatriate Irish capital invested abroad by banks, insurance companies and individual Irish investors.[31] A certain novelty was achieved by the attachment of the idea that in a world of decolonization and old and new 'anti-imperialist' powers Ireland could count on what the republicans referred to, in coy deference to the strength of anti-communism, as 'mighty friends'.[32]

While such ideas certainly provided republicans with a broader set of strategic options than had been current in the forties and fifties, their ultimate capacity to assist in the modernization of the movement was limited. This was not, as some of their opponents would claim, because they were 'foreign' or 'Marxist'. It was the case that the two small Irish communist parties had adopted programmes in 1962 which contained many similar themes – particularly on the need for 'anti-imperialist' alliances against the Fianna Fáil 'sell-out'.[33] But both the communists' programmes and the core ideas of republican rethinking were deeply dependent on the pre-given categories of nationalist thought – particularly that unfulfillable quest for 'real' independence, which assumes political will can compensate for the realities of a small island with (relatively) tiny resources. The most striking characteristic of the thinking of the period is its capacity to deny the significance of certain massive realities which a 'Marxism' less influenced by nationalism would have paused to reflect on.

Centrally, the republican analysis failed even to begin to comprehend the appeal of the new economic policies to the working class. In terms that echoed O'Donnell's disdain for the labour movement the trade unions were castigated for their narrow concern with wages and conditions: 'only a militant trade union movement with a national consciousness . . . can work towards the expansion of employment opportunities and control over the export of Irish capital.'[34] The absence from the recent Irish Trade Union Congress of any resolution expressing opposition to the Anglo-Irish Free Trade Agreement was noted, as was the general failure to

oppose the 'economic capitulation' of the Fianna Fáil government.[35] What was completely absent was any recognition that
the policies of economic liberalization, while they threatened
indigenous industry, built up behind tariff walls since the
thirties, held out the promise of new employment by foreign
capital. For devotees of economic nationalism, such employment was a sign of dependence and did not enter their
calculations as anything else but an indication of national
decadence. This blinded them to the popularity of the new
policies with large sections of the working class who saw them
as the only way out of the morass of the fifties. The concern
with the 'anti-national' aspects of the new policies also blinded
the republican movement to the increasing role that the state
itself would play under the new Economic Programmes in
generating employment through an expanded public sector.[36]
Thus the post-1962 'turn to politics' was accomplished under
the direction of types of thinking that would prove to be out of
touch with key realities of political and economic life in the
Republic. On the other hand, the new emphasis on challenging 'British Imperialism' through the development of a
broad coalition mobilized on a range of political, economic
and cultural issues, did have radical and, for many, unsettling
implications for the role of the IRA.

Towards an Army of the People

An editorial in the Wolfe Tone Society's newsletter, *Tuairisc*,
in the year of the fiftieth anniversary of 1916, challenged 'the
illusion still current in some pockets of the Republican
movement that a simple-minded armed struggle against the
British occupation is alone sufficient to generate sufficient
popular support to complete the national revolution.'[37] These
'pockets' of illusion were in fact far from residual elements in
the IRA. Goulding was keenly aware that any rethinking must
maintain a role for the IRA as a military organization. He
subsequently described the situation: 'we had on our hands
trained physical force revolutionaries who were, to some
extent, still armed. They would decide for themselves what
would happen next, if we didn't decide for them.'[38] As the

conception of anti-imperialist activity was broadened, there was a clear necessity to devise a role for the IRA which was subordinated to this broader strategy while not stampeding those in the organization who saw it first and foremost as an army. An IRA document produced in the early 1970s gave one version of how this process had transformed 'an army of militarists, rigid and inflexible, and geared only for a military campaign against British forces in Ireland', into a 'revolutionary army, an army of the people, capable of developing and exploiting a revolutionary situation for the benefit of the people'. It was no longer an elitist force divorced from popular struggles, but existed to 'assist the people in what is THEIR liberation struggle'.[39] As will become apparent, this was a rather romanticized description of the role of the Official IRA in defending Catholic ghettoes in Northern Ireland and 'retaliating' against the British Army. It was a 'people's army' with no actual relation to the bulk of the population in the two Irish states other than that of assertion. But this role was not in fact one that the rethinking of the 1960s had wished to prepare for. Until 1969 the role of the IRA was increasingly defined as that of ultimate 'guarantor' of the gains of popular struggles.

The first major result of the rethinking was a nine-point programmatic statement put to a special Army Convention in 1964. The points included involvement in economic and social agitations, the creation of a national liberation front of republicans, trade-union and small-farmer organizations and other radical groups, and, most controversial, the end of abstention from Irish and British parliaments.[40] All except the last, which the Army Council had recommended be rejected, were accepted. Such new commitments sat uneasily in relation to the IRA's traditional military role. However, implicit in a number of important republican documents of the period is an attempt to maintain the IRA's primacy while transforming its most fundamental functions. Thus in the Sinn Féin document 'Lessons of History' a key element for the success of the 'national revolution' was said to be 'an organized body of men, prepared to resort to arms if necessary and therefore subject to discipline. . . .'[41] Yet this was only one of four factors identified as crucial; the others were 'the existence of a body of theoretical thought; the extent to which the interest and political and social outlook of the "men of no property" predominate in the national independence movement; a political crisis for imperialism'.[42] The resort to arms was clearly envisaged as the ultimate defence of a popular movement's gains in an 'anti-imperialist struggle', and even then was not declared inevitable. The primary role of the IRA was clearly political: 'rousing the consciousness and understanding of the common people'. [43] An IRA document captured by the police in the Irish Republic in May 1966 gives a clear idea of the problems this policy was encountering and the radical implications that were by then being faced up to. Little progress had been made in developing Sinn Féin as a relatively independent political organization and most educational work was being carried on inside the IRA.[44] Recruits to the movement joined for traditional reasons and the methods of training them did little to discourage 'militarist' thinking. There was a need to change the emphasis away from arms and battle tactics to 'Social and Economic objectives': 'It is felt that a recruit graduating from recruits class finds that there is a lot of unromantic and possibly boring work to be done before he gets a chance to use his military training. This accounts for the high turnover in membership at present. . . .'[45] Recruits needed to be clear that military activity was to be geared to backing up and consolidating 'revolutionary action initiated legally'.[46]

The document, which the IRA denied had ever been adopted as policy,[47] indicated the general direction of the new thinking. Most disturbing for some would have been its proposed 'Organizational Principles'. Thus it was argued that the 'basic movement will be a political national and social revolutionary organization with an open membership and legal existence'.[48] At a time when the republican movement was struggling to recover from the collapse of the military campaign and hold together a depleted membership, some of the proposals were grandiose. For example the new political organization was envisaged as leading a 'vast and diversified movement under the Republican umbrella', including trade unions, cooperatives, tenants associations, youth groups.[49] At their heart was the aspiration to use such an expansionary perspective as a means of justifying a radical transformation in the role of the IRA. The vanguard role of the IRA in the republican movement, although linked to its continuing military function, was now defined differently: it was the wider movement's 'back bone', composed of the 'best and most conscious members . . . the most advanced elements'.[50] Its leadership principle was thus being transformed from the military idealism of traditional Fenianism into a semi-Leninist one.

If the movement was to be radically politicized in this way, there were also clear implications for the existing hegemony of the IRA. As the document noted, 'the current position that the [Sinn Féin] Árd Fheis is a rubber stamp for the Convention is an imposition on the many sound people in SF'.[51] In the interim the Army Convention would continue as the effective policy-making body, but this role would be attenuated 'as the basic policy decisions are seen to be made correctly and openly by the National Conference'. Ultimately it was envisaged that the role of the Army Convention would be downgraded to that of a 'specialist conference of certain people in the Movement for examining technical problems connected with the military aspect of the revolution'.[52]

Such ideas were seen by many members of the IRA as subverting the very existence of the physical force tradition. Certainly they raised an old conflict between champions of self-referential military action to arouse the masses and those who stressed the need for popular mobilization as a pre-liminary to the use of force. Nonetheless, even the most militant proponents of the second position, like Goulding, were in no doubt that the trickle of people who were joining the IRA in the 1963–67 period had joined predominantly in the hope of another campaign. Consequently, although Goulding could, in moments of exasperation, startle his volunteers with unguarded declarations of the effective redundancy of the IRA,[53] it was believed that the road to politicization entailed a compensatory range of military activities. The blowing up of Nelson's Pillar in Dublin in 1966 has encouraged the idea that these activities were essentially frivolous diversions for the bored volunteer. In fact the strong resistance to the new direction ensured that more serious activities had to be contemplated. In 1964, a plan for an arms raid on a Territorial Army barracks in Newry was only aborted at the last moment when a local guide did not turn up.[54] The document seized by the police in 1966 included a military plan for another northern campaign, which would eschew 'classical guerrilla type operations' of the 1956·type and instead 'learn from the Cypriots and engage in terror tactics only.'[55] The seizure did not put a stop to the planning of activity in this area. In 1966 a special military council was established by the Army Council with the task of planning a new northern campaign and a member of the Army Council went to England to set up a network of support for such a campaign.[56]

Such developments reflected Goulding's approach to introducing change in the republican movement, which was to seek to maintain maximum unity, bringing as many traditionalists along as possible. His implicit point of reference was O'Donnell and the Republican Congress. By moving outside the IRA and refusing the task of struggling for change from within, the Congressites had condemned themselves to nullity. For Goulding the only way forward was within the 'Official Army'.[57] This necessitated the maintenance of a commitment to 'armed struggle', the more strongly because the main thrust of the new policies and, in particular, the use of 'outsiders' like Coughlan and Johnston in discussions of strategy and in internal education, had brought fierce resistance.[58] Yet the contradictions were painfully clear. In an interview with the main Belfast evening paper, Goulding claimed that the IRA had no immediate military plan and repudiated past unilateral militarism: 'we want to have the bulk of the people with us'. Most crucially, he explained that he wanted 'to try and get through to the Protestant working class'.[59] For Goulding, any real prospect of a new campaign was unthinkable before there had been radical political and ideological developments in the Republic and Northern Ireland. But as long as the new thinking was confined to paper and declarations, the IRA had nothing to offer its members as an attractive alternative to the inevitable hankering for 'real' action. In this context the creation of a structure for planning a new campaign in the north was only a slightly more sophisticated variant of the activities which the local leaderships of the

IRA embarked on as a means of maintaining or recuperating morale.

In Belfast, the local commander, Billy McMillen, was aware of the criticisms of a number of veteran republicans who had left the movement since 1963. Initially hostile to the new direction himself, and eager to convince the rank-and-file members that the increased involvement in politics would not make them redundant, he ensured that not only was the training of new recruits solely a military matter, but that scope was provided for its exercise.[60] McMillen was able to build up the membership of the Belfast IRA from a tiny 24 in 1962 to around 120 by 1969, thus allowing the creation of three 'battalions' centred on the 'Third Battalion' based in the Lower Falls area, where McMillen and his 'adjutant' Jim Sullivan had formidable popular reputations.[61] He would later claim that the 'selective' use of force was crucial in allowing the IRA to maintain itself and expand during the period.[62] Certainly the young Catholics who did join the IRA at this time were uninfluenced by the post-1962 rethinking. After the Divis Street riots during the 1964 Westminster election (these were provoked by the RUC's removal of a Tricolour from the window of a shop being used as a Sinn Féin election headquarters for McMillen, the West Belfast candidate) a couple of dozen recruits were made.[63] For McMillen the 'patriotic fervour' generated by the riots and motivating these young IRA men was an unalloyed blessing for the republican movement in the city. For those who joined, 'politics' and the republican movement were often opposing universes,[64] and clandestinity, gun lectures, and instructions for destroying telephone kiosks and pillar boxes the centre of revolutionary activity. As the pace of IRA political involvement in the Republic accelerated in 1967, McMillen and the Belfast leadership insisted that they be allowed a 'happy blend of political agitation and military activity'.[65] Well after the IRA's Army Council had decided to promote a civil rights campaign in Northern Ireland as the best possible way of undermining the Unionist Party's hegemony and getting through to the Protestant working class, the Belfast IRA launched a series of large fire-bomb attacks on Territorial Army bases in Belfast and Lisburn.[66] Goulding saw the Belfast IRA in terms which recall the dismissive attitude of earlier IRA radicals to the 'reactionaries' in the Belfast movement. The resistance of the Belfast leadership to the new thinking was explained by the fact that the movement there was dominated by 'Catholic bigots'. Goulding often found it more congenial to get his information about conditions in the north from Communists with whom he was friendly. Echoing the Republican Congress's criticism of the Belfast IRA's lack of connection with the Protestant working class, he attached a perhaps exaggerated significance to the Protestant working-class credentials of some members of the Communist Party in Belfast. His lack of rapport with the leadership of the Belfast IRA was symbolized in some of his trips to Belfast when he would meet the local Communists and return to Dublin without contacting the IRA leadership.[67] This recoil from republican Belfast was an unconscious recognition of the terrible obstacles which the sectarian realities of Ulster posed for even a modernized republican project.

The fundamental dynamic envisaged in the rethinking had been one of a build-up of agitational coalitions to rescue the IRA from the self-imposed isolation of a physical force campaign in Northern Ireland. Much of this new dynamism was expected to develop in the Republic, and this would pull the organization away from a militarized fixation on the northern state. Yet almost exactly three years after the Army Council decided on the support of a gradualist campaign of civil rights reforms in the north, the northern situation would deal a major blow to the whole Goulding strategy. No adequate understanding of the division of the republican movement and the subsequent decades of violence is possible without an appreciation of the assumptions and limitations of the IRA's northern strategy.

Civil Rights and Abstentionism

In August 1966 a meeting of members of the Wolfe Tone Society was held in Northern Ireland in the Maghera home of Kevin Agnew, a prominent republican notable. Goulding was present but it was a young graduate from Cork, Eoghan

Harris, who had been recruited into the Wolfe Tone Society by Goulding, who read a paper agreed by the IRA Army Council on a civil rights strategy for Northern Ireland.[68] The replacement of the geriatric Unionist Prime Minister, Lord Brookeborough, by Terence O'Neill in 1963 and the latter's adoption of certain modernizing themes had encouraged some hopes of reform of the sclerotic Protestant regime. Then came the 1964 election victory of Harold Wilson, who had publicly proclaimed his desire to force change on the Unionist regime. The work of Dr Conn McCluskey and his wife in Dungannon – since the early 1960s they had publicized discrimination against Catholics in jobs and housing, and founded their Campaign for Social Justice in 1964 – clearly demonstrated the existence of a reformist agenda. But the failure of either O'Neill or Wilson to deal with these injustices created conditions of growing Catholic frustration which republicans could hope to mobilize. At the same time the fact that O'Neill's largely cosmetic modernizations had provoked intense intra-party disputes, and that he was already being attacked by the emerging Protestant populist Ian Paisley for 'betrayal' of Loyalist interests, demonstrated the difficulties awaiting any strategy that depicted a reformist agenda on civil rights as a means of forging popular alliances between even sections of the Catholic and Protestant working class.

The paper Harris read was in fact closely based on a long article, written by Coughlan, which was published that month in *Tuairisc*. Through his activities in the Connolly Association and the influence of Desmond Greaves, Coughlan had come in contact with a perspective which regarded civil rights issues as the Achilles heel of Unionism.[69] The issue had assumed an even more crucial significance, it was argued, because of a transformation in British strategy towards Ireland: 'The far-seeing leaders of British imperialism saw that the bright young men of Fianna Fáil might prove a better bet for preserving British influence in Ireland than the bigoted fanatics of the North.'[70] As part of the British master-plan to 'snare Lemass into the United Kingdom', the Northern Ireland prime minister, Terence O'Neill, had been ordered to play down discrimination and provide a cosmetic modernization of his regime.[71] The opportunity thus existed to use this thawing of political life to press for a much more thoroughgoing set of reforms: 'the Unionists should be squeezed by popular demands from the disenfranchised, the gerrymandered, the discriminated against, the oppressed Catholic and nationalist minority within the North itself, demands for reforms, for civil rights, for genuine democracy and opportunities for free political expression.'[72]

The 'most progressive' outcome would be the releasing of the energies of 'the people', which was then specified as the Catholics and the Protestant working class. The analysis was characterized by its fundamental optimism about the likely response of Protestant workers to the development of a civil rights agitation: 'If things change too much the orange worker may see that he can get by alright without dominating his Catholic neighbour.' The emergence of Paisleyism was recognized, as was the possibility that he would overthrow O'Neill, but this was dismissed as unlikely. The reasons provided demonstrate the distance that separated even the most progressive and intelligent republican analysis from a serious grasp of Unionism: 'If Paisley and his followers are opposed by both the British government and the main Unionist leadership, who have switched their policy, how can he possibly win? Britain has changed its tactics relating to Ireland as a whole, consequent on the Dublin Government's capitulation. The Orange Card is no longer as useful as it was. At present the Orange rank and file in the North don't know what has happened. They are in a state of deep doubt and confusion and Paisley is the only one who has come forward as a guide. But the old certainties of anti-Catholicism and bigotry peddled by Paisley no longer suit imperialism as well as they did in the past. The Orangemen are being sold down the river and they do not know it. For years the basic fundamental of their faith has been their trust in Britain. Whatever they did, Britain would stand by them and back them up. But if this rock of faith is removed, if Britain betrays them – what then?'[73]

The long-term prospect was seen as one where republicans could break through to the Orange masses and explain imperialism's real motivation, thus liberating them at last from their illusions and allowing them to join the national struggle. This undoubtedly serious commitment to winning Protestants through a process of political reform, and the stated opposition to Catholic sectarianism and any resort to violence, could not compensate for the unreconstructed assumptions that survived from the traditional nationalist project. Centrally, the internal dynamics of the Unionist movement were overlooked in favour of a largely externalist explanation. Orangeism was seen as a phenomenon that existed for the convenience of the British state. When the latter changed its strategy, the basis for Orangeism was effectively removed. From James Connolly through to recent Árd Fheis speeches by leading Provisionals, and including the main theses of constitutional nationalism as set out in the 1984 Forum Report and constantly repeated by John Hume, there is an unbroken thread of analysis to which the modernizing republicans in the 1960s maintained fealty. It is that Unionism's substance is the British 'guarantee'; if British support is removed, Ulster Protestants will wake up to their real interests.

In the two years between the Maghera meeting and the first civil rights march from Dungannon to Coalisland in August 1968, the Wolfe Tone Society, northern republicans and some communist trade unionists assumed the motivating role in the creation of the Northern Ireland Civil Rights Association (in January 1967).[74] In this period, the main concern of the IRA leadership remained the development of the movement in the Republic, where, by 1967; there was clear evidence of a crisis. Although the special IRA convention in 1965 had accepted the bulk of the leadership's recommendations for change, there had been considerable resistance to their implementation. As a result, there was a feeling of disarray and demoralization in the movement. A meeting of the IRA's local leadership in August 1967 assessed the state of the movement in terms of membership, finance, arms and political development. It was a depressing stocktaking: 'they suddenly realized that they had no movement at all. They only thought they had a movement . . . the circulation of the *United Irishman*, for example, which in 1957–59 had been in the hundred thousand bracket had fallen to fourteen thousand.'[75] The way out of this state of affairs lay in a more intense propagation of the new policies.

Thus the 1967 Sinn Féin Árd Fheis, in line with a previous decision by the August IRA gathering, amended the party's constitution to define its aim as the establishment of a Socialist Republic.[76] That year would also see the organization establish a number of citizens' advice bureaux and, most important, the Dublin Housing Action Committee, which quickly mobilized a considerable popular constituency by a campaign which focused on the contrast between the housing crisis and the unprecedented level of office building in the city.[77]

A crucial factor in republican calculations was the emergence of the Irish Labour Party as a significant political force in urban areas, particularly in Dublin. In the sixties, the Labour Party made significant gains in seats and membership in Dublin, and in the process shifted away from the staid conservatism which had characterized it in the forties and fifties.[78] The improving economic conditions in the Republic, associated with the liberalizing policies of Lemass, resulted in a decline in emigration and an upsurge of industrial militancy.[79] The disintegration of De Valera's Ireland released Labour from its traditionally timid public poses; for the first time since the thirties, Labour politicians could publicly identify their objectives as socialist. The progress of the Labour Party in Dublin was a main consideration in Fianna Fáil's unsuccessful attempt to get popular endorsement for a constitutional amendment to abolish proportional representation in 1968.[80] However, although the dominant tendency in the IRA and Sinn Féin leadership favoured a broad national liberation front, including trade unionists and Labour Party members, there was no shift in the traditional republican disdain for the leadership of the Labour Party. As a result, the growth of support for the Labour Party was deeply disturbing to the architects of the new policies.

The position was set out clearly in a major article, 'The Dilemma of Sinn Féin', in the *United Irishman* for November 1968: 'The organization [SF] has grown and developed in the last few years. Yet its impact is still marginal. The radical position which it had been carving out for itself will not be easily established in the face of the growth of Labour, backed by the trade union movement. This is in fact the core of Sinn Féin's present dilemma. It is not Fianna Fáil or Fine Gael which need worry Sinn Féin, but the fact that Labour has a readymade broad base in the trade union movement. It is the lack of a corresponding base that is Sinn Féin's major problem. Two radical movements are not feasible on a small island. The relation of Sinn Féin to the trade union movement and also to the Labour Party is the hitherto unresolved problem for Sinn Féin. Campaigns such as that on housing are only of a limited value if the political advantages are going to be picked up by Labour.'

In 1967–68 Sinn Féin and the IRA would emphasize their involvement in an 'economic resistance campaign'. Some of these activities, like the IRA's destruction of buses used to ferry scabs in an industrial dispute involving an American company in Limerick, its blowing up of a foreign-owned oyster boat and its attacks on farms owned by foreigners, served to demonstrate that for republicans the function of all economic and social agitation was to reassert the 'national dimension' which the trade union movement and the Labour Party neglected.[81] In an article provoked by the recent influx of a number of university-based intellectuals, most prominently Conor Cruise O'Brien, into the Labour Party, Roy Johnston warned those who saw in this the prospect of Labour's radicalization. People like O'Brien would not accomplish the essential task facing Labour, which was to 'clarify its ideas and policies on all aspects of the national and social questions, involving its whole membership in the study . . . of the socialist ideas of James Connolly.'[82] For Johnston, the Labour leadership was exposed in its true colours by the telegram of congratulation it had sent to Harold Wilson after his 1966 victory, so demonstrating its disregard for the British party's 'manifest imperialist record'. The influence of people like O'Brien would in fact make the Irish party more like the British, and the best that could be expected from that was a '1945 type victory, giving a government that can be controlled by the large property owners behind a facade of socialist words'. That Johnston could dismiss the substantial achievements of the Attlee administration, particularly in welfare policy, indicated not so much ultra-leftism as a typical republican disdain for economic and social reforms that left the 'imperialist' link unquestioned. Nevertheless, precisely because the Labour Party was expanding and even winning support from young radicals in the universities, the question of Sinn Féin's self-imposed political marginalization by its abstentionist policy took on a new and controversial significance.

By the time the 1968 Sinn Féin Árd Fheis took place, the police attacks on the second civil rights march in Derry on 5 October had propelled the northern question into the centre of politics in Britain and Ireland. In both marches northern republicans had played a central role as stewards and participants – in the confrontation with the police in Derry they had ensured that the front line of dignitaries and MPs was pushed into the police line. The emergence of a mass civil rights movement seemed to offer rich opportunities, which Goulding and his supporters in the leadership were eager to take. In his presidential address, Tomás MacGiolla described October 1968 as 'historic', linking the civil rights explosion with the defeat of Fianna Fáil in the referendum on proportional representation – a blow from which he incautiously predicted Fianna Fáil would never recover. The implication was clear; in both states the traditional parties of government were in disarray, and in Northern Ireland the Nationalist Party too had been discredited by the civil rights mobilization. A political space had opened up and republicanism had a unique opportunity to move into it.[83] Nevertheless, the leadership was unsure of its ground, however optimistically MacGiolla described the political possibilities. The adoption of the commitment to a socialist republic, even as sanitized by the qualification 'in accordance with the Democratic Programme of the First Dail',[84] had caused some disquiet amongst older and more traditional republicans. MacGiolla was at pains to quell their fears: 'socialism has nothing to do with either Atheism or Totalitarianism, as is evident from even a superficial reading of Connolly. Neither is it a philosophy which must be imported. It is part of the Republican tradition since the founding of the United Irishmen.'[85]

In a speech earlier in the year, Sean Garland had referred to 'mealy-mouthed sentimentalists' who wished to 'preserve the movement as traditionally constituted', and warned that the movement must be prepared for any 'structural or organizational changes' necessary to obtain its objectives.[86] However, at the 1968 Árd Fheis, he proposed an amendment to the resolution calling for a constitutional change to allow elected representatives to take their seats in the Republic's parliament. Garland's amendment called for the creation of a commission 'representing both branches of the movement' to examine how 'the new political situation in the south' could be turned to the advantage of republicanism.[87] The purpose of the commission was to avoid a bitter debate and the possibility of a split. By postponing a decision on the abstention issue for another year, it was hoped that resistance could be marginalized. There was some disquiet that some of the anti-abstentionists, particularly the energetic and articulate Seamus Costello from Bray, an Army Council member and prominent Sinn Féin activist, were unnecessarily abrasive and had needlessly alienated some of the traditionalists, who, it was thought, might ultimately have been won over or neutralized.[88] Costello's passionate contribution in support of the amendment served only to convince traditionalists that it was a manoeuvre to ensure their defeat, a feeling that the report of the commission did little to undermine.

The wording of the amendment and the report (when it was published in March 1969) made clear the degree to which the dominant section of the leadership saw the main axis of progress as a southern one. The report, *Ireland Today and Some Questions on the Way Forward*, maintained that while the 'Six Counties are the key to English control, the 26 Counties are the area in which the greatest anti-imperialist unity is possible and where there is most experience of the economic laws of neo-colonialism in operation . . .'[89] There was a section on the class structure of the north, which contained an evaluation of the progress of the civil rights movement. Here the deductive optimism of Coughlan's 1966 analysis was maintained, despite the evidence of increasing sectarian polarization, particularly after the Peoples' Democracy's 'long march' from Belfast to Derry in January 1969. The growth of support for Paisley was recognized but dismissed; 'this is not the English strategy: they want integration of the whole of Ireland with the UK, under the control of a puppet regime constructed from the O'Neill brand of Unionism and the

Lemass/Lynch brand of neo-Unionism.'[90] The classical fixation of republicanism with 'England' as the source of all Irish ills had the effect of blinding the republican leadership to the rapidly deteriorating situation in Northern Ireland. The document envisaged the achievement of the objectives of the civil rights movement and the development of a situation where the way was open 'for the linking of the economic demands to the national question'. The disintegration of Unionism would enable sections of the Protestant working class to be won from the Northern Ireland Labour Party and ultimately towards 'the framework of an all-Ireland movement towards the achievement of a 32-country democratic republic'.[91] The victories of a number of civil rights candidates in the Stormont election in February 1969 were hailed as demonstrating that 'the Six County people' were prepared to support a radical alternative to unionism on a non-sectarian basis. The defeat of the candidates of the old Nationalist Party demonstrated the innovative and disruptive effects of the civil rights marches. However, the document simply ignored those features of the electoral returns which showed the major crisis that was developing within the Unionist state and party. O'Neill, whose victory over Paisley had been defined as most likely, was increasingly beleaguered and would soon resign. The Northern Ireland Labour Party would see its electoral base disappear, but not to the advantage of a new progressive republicanism. As 1969 progressed, the analysis of civil rights and Northern Ireland which had underpinned the new political line of Goulding's leadership would diverge ever more markedly from the realities of the northern crisis.

Ireland Today depicted the gradual development of a 'broad anti-Unionist and anti-Imperialist alliance' in the north, which would eventually link up with a similar alliance in the Republic. The fundamental difference was that while in Northern Ireland the process of civil rights reforms had to be accomplished before 'anti-imperialist' issues could be raised, such issues were seen to be at the heart of current politics in the Republic. The central question in the document was that of the leadership of the anti-imperialist alliance, the 'national liberation front', in the Republic. Here it was asserted that the republican movement represented 'the great mainstream of the national and social revolutionary tradition', while the Labour Party's tradition was condemned as one of 'national and social compromise'.[92] Yet it was also clear that the commission was aware of the realities of a situation where republicanism had no comparable influence to that of the Labour Party in the urban, particularly Dublin, working class. In what was probably the most open and extraordinary admission of weakness, the document pointed out that the membership of the republican movement in Dublin was not much greater than that of the Irish Workers Party (as the CP in the Republic was then known), and that Dublin sales of its *Irish Socialist* were comparable to those of the *United Irishman*.[93] The new politicized and agitational style of republicanism was helping develop a radical ambience in the Dublin universities (which were influenced also by the international student and worker militancy of 1968) but so far this had benefitted the Labour Party: 'there is a steady stream of young radicals into the 26-county Labour Party. These would come to us if we were more credible.' As long as the republican movement could only use its resources as a radical and agitational group to the left of the Labour Party, it risked forcing the 'opportunist' Labour leadership into a fake radicalism which would reap the benefits of republican efforts.[94] Only a decision allowing Sinn Féin to get candidates elected and participating in the Dáil would allow the party to challenge the Labour Party for the leadership of the urban working class.

Some of the ways in which the idea of a national liberation front was presented in the document provided its opponents with easy and lurid targets – particularly the positive attitude adopted towards work with the communists. Given Johnston's and Coughlan's association with Greaves and the Connolly Association, charges of a 'red' infiltration were predictable. Anti-communism was not the only reason for the subsequent split. Much of the opposition to the document arose from the fear that behind the rather speculative proposals for popular alliances north and south lay another internally radical agenda centred on the future role of the IRA. *Ireland Today* contained a number of proposals for organizational change, of which the central one was for 'the integration of the existing Movement into a unified whole. . . .'[95] Although it made some gesture to traditionalists by stating that 'the historic link with the Republican government, at present vested in the Army Council, must be preserved', the core proposal was for a 'single-unified leadership'. This integration of the 'military' and 'political' leaderships seemed to imply the effective marginalization of the IRA. Of course there was a very large degree of overlap between the leadership of Sinn Féin and that of the IRA – given the history of the effective subordination of the one to the other, this was unsurprising. Yet the document clearly envisaged that the main business of the new unified leadership would be political – the attempt to develop the national liberation front. Thus, in a section dealing with the various 'specialist functions' to be represented at the meetings of the Árd Chomhairle (executive committee) of the unified organization, 'action groups concerned with the physical defence of the people' came last, after 'commemorations, youth work, trade unionists' groups, farmers groups and the *United Irishman*.'[96] Such a rebaptism and downgrading of IRA activity was bitterly resisted by those who saw in the developing northern crisis a very different road to the rebirth of republicanism.

Abstentionism was not a point of principle for all those who were to challenge Goulding's leadership at the end of 1969. Kevin Mallon, who later became a leading Provisional, had been one of a group of six prominent Tyrone republicans who resigned from the movement at the beginning of 1969 in protest at the failure to get rid of abstentionism.[97] Many northern republicans were willing to consider any tactic that maintained pressure on the Unionist regime and brought a crisis nearer. However, that crisis was seen to hold the possibility of a new and successful military campaign, and as 1969 progressed, the gradualism of the original civil rights strategy, essential to its objective of winning Protestant support, was confronted with communal upsurges that undermined its basic premisses.

The main premiss was the vulgar Marxist assumption that as the Republic was breaking with protectionism, the British interest in partition had gone, and, with it, the fundamental force supporting Loyalism. Once it became clear to the Protestant working class that it was being betrayed by the state on which it had lavished its deluded loyalty, a real political realignment was possible. Since Britain no longer had an interest in partition, any move towards the abolition of the Stormont parliament and the imposition of direct rule from London had to be resisted, as meaning unmediated control of the north by imperialism. As the crisis of the Northern Ireland state deepened, the response was to intensify demands for Britain to use its powers under the Government of Ireland act to enforce reforms of the Stormont regime. In fact, because the republican tradition had always underestimated the relative autonomy of Unionism as a political force, it was now incapable of recognizing that the institutional manifestation of that autonomy – the Stormont regime – was disintegrating under internal and external pressure for change, and that this disintegration was fraught with massive possibilities of communal violence. By externalizing the sources of the intractable sectarianism of Northern Ireland, the dominant republican analysis, particularly as put forward by Coughlan, appeared increasingly lacking in credibility in the northern Catholic ghettoes.

The *United Irishman* warned of 'dangerous illusions' among some supporters of the civil rights movement. The core illusion was to see the main enemy as the 'Orange Order and the local Unionist junta'. These could not remain for long if 'English' support was withdrawn. The main enemy was 'English Imperialist rule which has used religious sectarianism to delude generations of Protestant workers that in some way Irish democracy is the enemy'.[98] The way to end such domination was by forcing the imperialist power to legislate for democratic reforms in Northern Ireland; a reformed Stormont was the only way of releasing Protestant workers from their illusions. There was, of course, a fundamentally attractive impulse here – to move politics forward through peaceful political and ideological struggle aiming at Protestant–Catholic unity. In an Easter 1969 address in Belfast, Sean Garland had declared that if the civil rights movement was to succeed it would have to recreate the unity of purpose between Protestant and Catholic workers seen in the 1907 Dock Strike and the 1932 Outdoor Relief agitation. However, he then went on to define the role of republicans in the civil rights movement as to press on with the primary task 'of ending British domination of our country'.[99] As in the thirties, left republicans were convinced that a successful national-liberation struggle had to win substantial Protestant working-class support. They once again tended to see in their more traditional comrades, particularly in Belfast, one of the major obstacles to this objective. But these undoubtedly positive impulses could not compensate for their basic tendency to treat popular Unionism as a superficial imposition on what would otherwise be an integral part of the Irish People.

The republicans' problems in relation to the Protestant majority in the north would be sharply intensified by the unresolved question of what exactly the role of the IRA should be. And as the possibility of severe communal conflict increased in 1969, the exact nature of the IRA's capacity became a major issue not simply for the republican movement but for sections of the ruling party in the south.

Fianna Fáil and the IRA

In a speech to a conference of Republican Clubs (due to a government ban on Sinn Féin in the mid 1960s this was the name of the political wing of the movement in Northern Ireland) held in Carrickmore, County Tyrone, in July 1972, Tomás MacGiolla provided a very comprehensive account of how what was now the Official republican movement understood the major political and military developments since 1969. He emphasized the 'revolutionary' significance of the civil rights mobilization: 'There was no way by which the Stormont or British government – could defeat the people's demands or break their unity and determination . . . the Dublin government had lost all influence and control of the situation since the eclipse of the Nationalist Party in the spring of 1969. Control of events and the leadership of the peoples' struggles was in the hands of the Republican movement, although many other forces were also at work.'[100] The 'forces of imperialism' had then intervened to change the character and course of the struggle, initially through the encouragement of sectarian confrontations. The intense communal violence which began in Belfast on 13 August 'was no spontaneous communal riot or uprising by the Protestant people against their Catholic neighbours. It was organized by the forces of the state following a political decision at the highest level.' While the Stormont regime and its British controllers were held responsible for the August violence, it was the Fianna Fáil regime that was made to bear prime responsibility for reactionary developments on the Catholic side: 'The Republican movement and the Civil Rights movement had set their faces against sectarianism and the AOH and Nationalist Party were dead. So a new Catholic sectarian force was needed . . . As early as February the Dublin government had begun their part of the imperialist plan by making their first contacts with Republicans and Civil Rights workers in the north. Following the August pogroms they intensified their work on much more fertile ground. By concentrating on those republicans and ex-Republicans who saw their role as Catholic defence groups and by playing on their latent sectarianism and militarist desires, they created a split amongst republicans in Belfast and offered money and guns to those who would reject the leadership of the Republican movement.'[101]

The claim that Fianna Fáil was attempting to split the republican movement had appeared in the *United Irishman* as early as November 1969, in a story claiming to be based on two months of investigations. After the split, it became a staple of Official attacks on the Provisionals that they were the creatures of Fianna Fáil. MacGiolla's Carrickmore speech is simply a polished and comprehensive example of this; Rosita Sweetman's widely publicized *On our Knees: Ireland 1972,* which was written from a clearly pro-Offical perspective, also emphasized the supposed role of Fianna Fáil. In their recent substantial history of the Provisionals, Bishop and Mallie dismiss the Official account: 'the theory of a government-inspired conspiracy to remove the dangerous leftists of the new IRA and replace them with the manageable stooges of the old tradition is characteristically fanciful and vain.'[102] While some of the Official analysis deserved the charge of being fanciful, the role of a *faction* of Fianna Fáil cannot be so easily dismissed.

The central weakness in Official analysis of the factors leading to the split was its incapacity to acknowledge the significance of the communal polarization in Northern Ireland in 1969. As the Scarman Tribunal subsequently commented: 'while the Catholic minority was developing confidence in its power, a feeling of insecurity was affecting the Protestants. They became the more determined to hold their traditional summer parades, particularly those in Londonderry and Belfast. In these circumstances sectarian conflict was to be expected. . . .'[103] The IRA, particularly in Belfast, was inevitably affected by the polarization. In April, during serious riots in Derry, the police discipline disintegrated, and one Catholic, Samuel Devenny, was seriously injured by the RUC and later died.[104] This served to intensify popular Catholic hostility to the police, already significant after major riots in Derry in January 1969. In response to the April disturbances, the Belfast IRA attacked several post offices in the city with the aim of diverting police resources from Derry.[105] Such actions were inevitably used by the Unionist government in its claims that behind the civil rights mobilization was a more sinister subversive purpose.[106] In fact the Belfast IRA was pitifully inadequately prepared for any such role, with a membership of not much more than a hundred and a grand total of twenty-four weapons.[107] After anti-police riots in Ardoyne, a largely Catholic district in North Belfast, the IRA came under strong communal pressure for 'defensive' action. Such pressure was initially resisted by McMillen.[108] However, as sectarian confrontation intensified in July, particularly in the Ardoyne and at the Unity Flats complex at the bottom of the Shankhill Road, such abstinence came under increasing pressure from within republican circles.

At the minimum, Belfast republican traditions – and popular memories of the IRA's role in communal defence during the violence at the formation of the state and in the sectarian riots of 1935 – demanded that the IRA take on a similar role for the Catholic communities in which it was based. In July IRA members were called together and told that they would have to defend Catholics in the Unity Flats area.[109] At this time, Ardoyne and Unity Flats were part of the IRA's First Battalion area, but the realities of numbers and arms mocked the nomenclature. This battalion was supposed to cover North Belfast – Ardoyne, the New Lodge Road and Oldpark area – as well as two other small Catholic ghettoes, the Markets and the Short Strand. It had fewer than forty members and scarcely any weapons.[110]

McMillen, himself a late and reluctant convert to the new policies,[111] was well aware of the criticisms that many older republicans in Belfast were making of the move away from traditional concerns. Some of the critics were people like Joe Cahill, who had left the organization soon after the new emphases became apparent.[112] Others had remained but continued to voice their opposition. Jimmy Steele was the preeminent republican veteran in Belfast, with status derived from his leading role in the IRA and the more than twenty years in prison that had resulted from this. He took the opportunity of the reinterment of Barnes and MacCormack – two IRA men executed in England during the 1940s campaign – to launch a bitter and comprehensive attack on the direction the movement had taken since 1962. The speech, given at Mullingar in July 1969, enraged many of the national leadership present and Steele was 'suspended' from the movement. This had a catalytic effect in Belfast, where it encouraged many of those who opposed the new policies to intensify their opposition.[113]

Support for the national leadership was concentrated in the Lower Falls area, where McMillen and Sullivan reigned supreme in the republican sub-culture. It was here as well that most of the meagre resources of men and weapons were concentrated. In large swathes of Catholic west and north Belfast, the dominant republican notables were hostile to Goulding's leadership. In Andersontown the Drumm family and Leo Martin exercised influence; in Clonard the Hannaways and Francis Card (down to the split Goulding and his supporters had considered Card an ally;[114]) in Ballymurphy Joe Cahill and Gerry Adams's family.[115] Some of these figures had remained active, many had dropped out, but their recognized role and status in their fiercely localistic communities gave them a major resource when the prolonged and serious violence erupted in August 1969.

The IRA leadership in Belfast was increasingly ground

down between two conflicting impulses – to aid and assist in the development and intensification of the civil rights demands, or to become the armed defenders of Belfast Catholics. The first impulse, which arose from the belief that a sectarian state was no longer in the interests of 'Imperialism', was now compromised by the rise to dominance of forces which the analysis had proclaimed historically redundant. This would lead to a simple inversion of the original position. Now it would be argued that because of the threat of a united people, 'Imperialism' had turned to the revival of sectarian animosities in order to defend its interests. In a few months the *United Irishman* would shift from emphasis on the irrationality of Paisleyism for the British state's strategy of a modernized Ireland reintegrated in the UK, to the claim that 'Civil War is Britain's aim'.[116]

The large scale communal violence of August 1969 was the most disturbing evidence to date of the limits of the IRA's civil rights strategy. It had been recognized that a Protestant backlash was possible, but this had been downplayed. When it occurred, the unresolved issue of what would be the IRA's military role inevitably came to the fore. That a reform of the Northern Ireland state, especially if partly impelled by a largely Catholic mobilization, would generate severe tension and possibly violence, was hardly unpredictable. The IRA's lack of preparedness reflected not simply the weakness of its strategic analysis but also a recoil from the implications of what communal violence would mean for its objective of reaching the Protestant working class. Many regarded such fastidiousness as the sign of ultimate degeneracy. For as the northern crisis erupted, it briefly, if powerfully, encouraged a widespread feeling that the 'unfinished business' of 1918–23 was on the agenda again. The Officials exaggerated the role of Fianna Fáil, but they did not imagine it.

The communal violence in Belfast on 14–15 August was the first major outbreak since 1935 and the most intense since the violence that attended the formation of the Northern Ireland state in 1921 and 1922. It clearly surprised the leaders of the civil rights movement as well as the IRA. The chairman of NICRA, Frank Gogarty, told the Scarman Tribunal: '. . . we all on the Executive underestimated the strength of militant

Unionism at this time, and had we foreseen the holocaust which did occur in mid-August we most certainly would not have entered on such an enterprise as we did. . . .'.[117] He was referring to the decision made by the executive of NICRA on 13 August to organize demonstrations throughout Northern Ireland to relieve pressure on the Catholic population of the Bogside in Derry, who were in the second day of bitter rioting against the police, following the traditional Apprentice Boys' Parade on 12 August.[118] The executive had intended to exclude Belfast from their plans precisely because of fears of sectarian confrontation, but as Scarman noted: 'we have no doubt that some activists, so far from accepting the decision, did cooperate with some in Londonderry to call for demonstrations in Belfast.'[119]

The IRA in Belfast had no qualms about initiating action to relieve the Bogside. The first public manifestation of this was a march to Springfield Road RUC station to hand in a petition against police brutality in Derry. This was organized by the IRA: the man who handed in the petition (referred to by Scarman as 'Malachy' Doran[120]) was a young volunteer, Anthony Doran, and he was accompanied at the head of a large crowd, which sang the Soldiers Song and carried an Irish Tricolour, by Joe McCann, another recent recruit, who was soon to acquire near-legendary status as an Official IRA leader. Before organizing the march, the volunteers had prepared a sizeable number of petrol bombs for the subsequent anti-RUC riot.[121] This one incident crystallizes the dilemma of the national IRA leadership. Their representatives on the Executive of NICRA supported the decision not to involve Belfast, but the Belfast leadership was in the forefront of activities which, at the very least, helped to exacerbate an atmosphere of fevered communal fears and animosities.

Gerry Adams has spoken of two separate, if overlapping agendas, being followed by republicans at the time: 'one group was intent on exposing the irreformable nature of the 6 county state: the other was following a gradualist approach to reform the state.'[122] This is a useful but overneat description of a situation where dividing lines were not so clear-cut and the 'two agendas' were often in confusing interaction in the same people. The policy of *Ireland Today* had, after all, envisaged that civil rights would create the conditions for the subsequent raising of the issue of national rights. In conditions of intensifying crisis for the Stormont regime, many supporters of the civil rights strategy would see no real contradiction in activities that more directly confronted the state. A small group like the IRA in Belfast, whose leadership was only very recently converted to the need for 'politics' and whose rank and file had had as yet virtually no political education,[123] was faced with an accelerating political crisis which by its nature encouraged a traditional response.

Just before the eruption of violence in Belfast the prime minister of the Republic, Jack Lynch, had made a television broadcast in response to the rioting in Derry. He claimed the Stormont government was no longer in control of the situation, described the violence as the result of decades of Unionist rule, demanded the introduction of a UN peace-keeping force and requested the British government to enter into negotiations on the constitutional position of Northern Ireland.[124] With its portentous, if ambiguous, declaration that 'the Irish government can no longer stand by and see innocent people injured and perhaps worse', the broadcast contributed powerfully to the mixture of fear and expectation that gripped the Catholics of Belfast in the subsequent weeks.

The death toll in the two days and nights of intense rioting in Belfast was seven: five Catholics and two Protestants. Four of the Catholics were killed by police gunfire[125] and, as Scarman commented, 'The absence of any sustained heavy shooting by civilians . . . was a feature of the disturbances.'[126] In a subsequent comment on earlier pressure which the IRA had come under to use weapons in the defence of Catholic areas, Billy McMillen explained: 'this we were reluctant to do as we realized that the meagre armaments at our disposal were hopelessly inadequate to meet the requirements of the situation and that the use of firearms by us would only serve to justify the use of greater force against the people by the forces of the Establishment and increase the danger of sectarian pogroms.'[127] Here, a very realistic estimate of the possibly disastrous effects of IRA armed action coexists uneasily with the notion that such a disaster might be less likely if the IRA had more arms than it then possessed. The evidence given to the Scarman Tribunal fully supports McMillen's qualms about the use of weapons. On the night of 14–15 August the use of IRA guns in the Lower Falls, in a situation of inter-communal rioting, simply served to incense the Protestant crowds and encouraged the RUC to introduce armoured cars with heavy machine guns.[128] Given the intensity of communal feelings by 13 August, serious disturbance in Belfast was likely. However, the frenzied, systematic burning of Catholic houses in the Lower Falls, Clonard and Ardoyne was not inevitable. The IRA's use of guns contributed powerfully to the remorseless intensity of the Protestant onslaught in these areas.

It was therefore merciful that the IRA's resources were so pitiful. In the Lower Falls – the heart of IRA resistance and strength – there were thirteen weapons in all, including a submachine gun and a couple of rifles. [129] It was these that were used in what Scarman referred to as the only 'sustained heavy shooting by civilians',[130] when IRA members occupied a primary school building for an attack on a Protestant mob. In the Ardoyne there were no IRA arms at all – four weapons had been sent in some time previously but due to the disorganization of the local republicans they had subsequently been withdrawn.[131] The Short Strand, a small Catholic ghetto in East Belfast, had no weapons either and after 14–15 August the IRA leadership was able to despatch only seven volunteers and two defective pistols for the defence of this area.[132] However, there was little evidence of McMillen's initial qualms about the use of weapons in the passionate and semi-euphoric atmosphere that existed in the working-class heartlands of Catholic Belfast in the aftermath of the August violence. Barricades had gone up, citizens' defence committees were created, and the intense sense of communal solidarity would admit no nuances in the depiction of the two days and nights of violence as a pogrom launched jointly by the police and Protestant mobs on an ill-defended population. Catholics had so obviously borne the brunt of the violence in lives and property, and distrust of the government and the police was so intense that many people became locked into a sense of communal righteousness that allowed only one disastrous conclusion: August 1969 was a product of the defencelessness of Belfast's Catholics.

This profound communal feeling was to have irresistible effects on the IRA, in part at least because of the way it was taken up and refracted back on Belfast by an important current in the Fianna Fáil government. The development of the civil rights movement, the crisis in the Northern Ireland state to which it massively contributed, and the onset of serious violence brought the 'national question' back into the centre of the southern government's concerns. As *the* republican party, with the first of its constitutional aims being 'to secure the Unity and Independence of Ireland as a Republic', Fianna Fáil faced a potentially explosive problem when serious disorder developed in Derry and Belfast. For a while it appeared that the whole 1921 settlement, which it had execrated for decades, was disintegrating. This inevitably raised the question of what Fianna Fáil strategy should be in such an eventuality.

Seán Lemass (Taoiseach 1959–1966) had reconstituted Fianna Fáil's approach to Northern Ireland by emphasizing the need to create the economic and social conditions in the Republic which would make unity a more attractive notion for northern Protestants. Under Lemass and his successor, Jack Lynch, the focus of concern in Northern Ireland was the need for internal reform as a prerequisite for the essential transformation of attitudes which would allow a majority of Protestants to reconsider their British affiliations. Both maintained their formal fidelity to the notion that partition was wrong: 'a deep throbbing weal across the land, heart and soul of Ireland' was how Lynch described it at the 1970 Fianna Fáil Árd Fheis. There was, however, no question of encouraging the notion that partition could be eliminated by some simple policy option like British withdrawal or that there was any way around attempting to persuade Unionists to alter their attitudes to unity.[133]

The northern crisis was a major check to this process of modernization. It stimulated a strong upsurge of traditionalism, and not simply in those parts of the Republic like the border areas and the west where fundamentalist attitudes where strongest. There was a wave of sympathy for the victims of what was commonly perceived as a state-sponsored pogrom, and demands for strong government action to defend northern Catholics. After the August violence, representatives of the various citizens' defence committees, including many prominent republicans, travelled to Dublin to demand aid, which often meant military training and guns.[134]

In the cabinet, a group led by Charles Haughey, Minister of Finance and Neil Blaney, Minister of Agriculture, pressed for a more decisive response than that favoured by Lynch. Despite this, when the government decided to create a distress fund for the victims of northern violence, it was left to Haughey to decide on the size of the fund, and he was given effective autonomy in allocating these resources. Haughey and Blaney were also key members of a committee set up to improve the government's profoundly inadequate knowledge of what was going on in Northern Ireland. In May 1970, Lynch sacked Haughey and Blaney, who were subsequently tried and acquitted on charges of attempting to import arms illegally. The evidence from their trial, a subsequent investigation by the Dail Public Accounts Committee and the impressions of some of the participants in the crisis, indicate the development of a para-state apparatus for involvement in Northern Ireland through an attempt to influence the main lines of development of Catholic insurgency.[135]

This approach involved military intelligence officers, public employees on secondment, businessmen allies of Fianna Fáil and at least one prominent Irish journalist. A major aim was to ensure that the various defence committees were led by reliable people, so that they would be single-minded in their role as a Catholic defence force and as insulated as possible from some of the more radical currents which were perceived to have developed in the civil rights movement. One cause for concern here was the degree to which northern republicans had been infected by the new politics of the IRA national leadership. The cabinet, through the Justice Department and the Special Branch, had been given an exaggerated version of the supposed threats of radical subversion which existed in the south. While much of this concerned the 'Marxist' takeover of the Labour Party, there was serious disquiet about the influence of 'communists' on the IRA leadership.[136] If arms and military training were to be provided for members of the defence committees, it was necessary to ensure that northern republicans who would be at the core of any 'defence' activity were not under the influence of the 'reds' in Dublin.

Neil Blaney, who as a Donegal TD was closely in touch with the situation in Northern Ireland, had made an approach to Francie Donnelly, the IRA commander in South Derry, in the spring of 1969. The contact was renewed after August when, at a meeting in Donegal, Blaney sounded him out on the numbers available to defend the area and the number of weapons available. A car and a weekly wage were also offered if Donnelly would act as an organizer.[137] The contacts were reported to Goulding, who encouraged their continuation, for by now it was clear that there was a likelihood of substantial resources being channeled to forces hostile to his leadership. In early October Donnelly attended a meeting in the Shelbourne Hotel, Dublin. Two prominent businessmen and supporters of Fianna Fáil attended, one of them an ex-member of Saor Uladh. Others in attendance were a journalist who was to play an active role in the Fianna Fáil intervention in the north, and a recently elected civil rights MP. The possibility of acquiring arms and moving them into the north was discussed but there was a condition: that the IRA in the north set up a separate northern command, independent of the 'communists' in the southern leadership.[138] Soon after this Donnelly, whose farm was in Maghera, County Derry, was visited by Charles Haughey's brother Padraig and others. In his struggle to win the leadership of Fianna Fáil Haughey would make much of the northern roots of his republicanism. His father's family were from Swatragh in south Derry, a few miles from Maghera. They discussed the situation and left £200 'to help you out'.[139]

In Belfast the various defence groups created in the barricaded Catholic ghettoes in the aftermath of the violence were often led by republicans who had resisted the new direction or dropped out in disgust. It was to people like these that the Haughey/Blaney group looked for the basis of their intervention in Northern Ireland. Captain James Kelly, the military intelligence officer who played a central role in the affair, had made contact in September with a number of crucial figures in Belfast, including the Republican Labour MP for a Stormont constituency which included the New Lodge Road, Paddy Kennedy. Kennedy was on friendly terms with many leading Belfast republicans, particularly of the traditional variety. After the violence there was a scramble by the various republican factions for southern support. Goulding's supporters in the leadership of the Belfast IRA, asked a Belfast Catholic politician to make contact with Blaney about their pressing need for arms 'for the defence of the people'.[140] The politician met Blaney and returned with promises of an arms shipment and offers of men, including an explosives expert.[141] Like much else that would be promised, none of this materialized and it gradually became clear to the Goulding loyalists that assistance from the south was being directed elsewhere. Initially, some money was channeled their way, including £1,000 of a promised £3,000 from some prominent businessmen in county Louth who had been contacted by a friend of Blaney. But within a month or so of the August violence it was being made clear to the leadership of the Belfast IRA that a condition for assistance was a break with the Dublin leadership. By then the Blaney/Haughey group had direct representation on the Central Citizens' Defence Committee (the body with representatives from all the areas which had barricaded themselves in August) in the person of Hugh Kennedy, an employee of Bórd Báinne, the Irish Milk Marketing Board, which was a responsibility of Blaney's ministry of agriculture.[142] Kennedy became 'public relations officer' for the CCDC. He worked in close liaison with two prominent republican brothers from the New Lodge area, John and Billy Kelly. Both had been imprisoned during the 1956 campaign and had drifted out of active involvement after 1963. Now both would play a key role in mobilizing anti-Goulding sentiment in Belfast.

Initially, an attempt was made to win over the existing leadership. Hugh Kennedy arranged a meeting between Jim Sullivan – representing the Belfast 'brigade staff' – and an *Irish Press* journalist in a Belfast hotel. The journalist told Sullivan that resources would be available and set up a meeting in the Republic involving Sullivan, Captain Kelly, Haughey and Blaney. Here it was agreed that a bank account would be opened in Dundalk to allow the transfer of money for guns to begin.[143] Goulding himself was approached by Captain Kelly who informed him that he was still regarded as a 'sound' republican who had been fooled by a clique who were basically loyal to the Communist Party of Great Britain, which was in fact itself infiltrated by British intelligence agencies. He was asked to break with this group and concentrate his movement's resources on the north. If this was done, it was promised, he would receive aid and assistance, including the training of northerners in Army bases in the Republic.[144]

Faced with the strong possibility that such assistance would go to his opponent, Goulding did not rebuff the overture. Soon after this he was contacted by a priest working in the Irish Centre in London who told him that money could be made available for the purchase of arms if it could be guaranteed that they would only be used in the north. Goulding travelled to London where the priest's contact turned out to be Padraig Haughey. Goulding asked for £50,000 and was given £1,500 on account.[145]

But the animosity towards Goulding's leadership in Belfast was so great that the original attempts to negotiate with McMillen and his supporters soon gave way to a decision to overthrow the local leadership. In late September, a meeting of the Belfast staff of the IRA was broken up by the intervention of a group of armed men. It included some of the most prominent older critics of the new policies – Jimmy Steele, Billy McKee, Joe Cahill and Jimmy Drumm – and the Kelly brothers. McMillen, while making it clear that he would not accede to their demand that he resign as commander of the Belfast IRA, did formally accept their other demands: for representation in the Belfast leadership and for a break with the Dublin leadership.[146] From September there was a de facto split in the IRA in Belfast. McMillen and his supporters maintained a secret affiliation with Goulding and entered into prolonged negotiations with Captain Kelly to try and extract resources for arms. It was becoming clear, however, that Fianna Fáil support was being directed towards areas where their opponents were increasingly dominant. In October, a new paper began publication, funded directly from the money the Lynch government had decided to make available for relief of distress. The *Voice of the North* was edited by Seamus Brady, a former speech writer for Blaney and an employee of the Propaganda Unit established by Lynch's government to put the Irish case on the north internationally.[147] Its board of management included Hugh Kennedy, John Kelly and the veteran Derry republican Sean Keenan.[148] Its ideology was bitterly anti-communist, its accent traditionally Catholic and nationalist. In the New Lodge area, where the Kelly brothers increasingly dominated the IRA, the house of a younger brother became the centre for the distribution of the *Voice* in the city.[149] In areas like the New Lodge and Ardoyne, where the small units of the IRA were swamped by a wave of young Catholics eager for military training, a strong nucleus for the Provisional IRA was in existence by December 1969. The Goulding loyalists in Belfast were aware that a combination of the large influx into the IRA after August and the new assertiveness of their critics, behind whom stood powerful backers, represented a threat. However, a certain complacent contempt for many of the people involved in the 'coup' in September – because of their having dropped out after 1962 – contributed to a tendency to underestimate the seriousness of what was involved. One illustration of problems faced was the discovery that although no money had been paid into the bank account opened in Dundalk, a substantial sum of money from the government's distress fund had been paid into an account in Clones in the Republic. Money could be drawn from this account on cheques signed by one of three prominent Belfast Catholics, including a Belfast politician. One of the others informed McMillen about the account and also about a decision to exclude those in the IRA leadership who were still suspected of supporting Goulding. As a result the politician was 'arrested' by the IRA and made to sign a cheque for £2,000 which was then cashed by a volunteer. He was made to repeat the operation a week later. It was perhaps because of this that the Clones account was closed in November and the money transferred to a Dublin bank.[150] Money would continue to find its way into the hands of Goulding loyalists in Belfast until January 1970. But it was usually sums of considerably less value – £200 at the end of January 1970, for example – and they were convinced that their rivals were receiving the bulk of the 'relief' money.[151]

Bishop and Mallie dismiss too categorically the role of Fianna Fáil in the events which led to the formation of the Provisional IRA. Later statements about the role of Fianna Fáil from the Officials may well have exaggerated the threat to the political system in the Republic which the intervention was supposedly designed to head off; and it is true that the August events would inevitably have provoked a communalist up-surge beyond the bounds of the IRA's existing strategy. Ruairi O'Bradaigh, a leading anti-Goulding figure and the first president of Provisional Sinn Féin, would subsequently play down the Fianna Fáil connection – 'Their split with the IRA was not the result of Blaney intrigue, but of rank and file exasperation for the IRA Executive's unpreparedness last summer.'[152] It is undoubtedly the case, however, that the vigour and self-confidence of Goulding's challengers was stimulated by the knowledge that they, and not the discredited 'reds', had a serious prospect of material and ideological assistance.

5

The Officials:
Regression and Development
1970–77

An extraordinary IRA 'General Army Convention' was held in early December 1969 to take decisions on the report of the Structure Commission. Those opposed to the ending of abstentionism later complained of the failure to pick up delegates known to be opposed to change. Even some of those in support had doubts about the wisdom of pushing on with the abstention debate after the exacerbation of divisions within the IRA by the violence in the north. The vote in favour of ending abstentionism was 39 to 12 and when the result became clear Sean MacStiofain, soon to be Provisional Chief of Staff, burst into tears declaring 'this is the end of the IRA'.

MacStiofain – who as John Stephenson, an English-born IRA man, had been jailed with Goulding in 1953 for a failed raid on the armoury of an English public school – had been appointed Director of Intelligence in 1966. Goulding had admired his energy and his disciplined and systematic approach to work while scorning his traditionalist attitude to politics – MacStiofain, a vehement critic of Roy Johnston's role, had been suspended for six months in 1964 for refusing to circulate an edition of the *United Irishman* in which Johnston criticized the practice of reciting the Rosary at republican commemorations. After the December convention he had immediately set about organizing an alternative 'Provisional Army Council'. It could look for support to the very substantial dissident elements in Belfast and to many prominent traditionalists throughout Ireland. At this level its most crucial members were Daithi O'Connaill and Ruairi O'Bradaigh. Both had been active in the 1956 campaign –

O'Connaill had been on the Brookeborough raid – and served on the Army Council in 1962. At that time O'Connaill had been in favour of ending abstentionism but then he had drifted out of the movement, disillusioned by its 'communist' links. A carpentry instructor with the Republic's Board of Works he had been in Donegal in 1969 and had approached Goulding with an offer to become active again. He was made O.C. in Donegal, a decision Goulding was to regret bitterly. O'Bradaigh had been Chief of Staff for the last two years of the 1956 campaign. A school teacher, his devout Catholicism produced a marked distrust of the 'extreme socialism' which he thought Johnston was pushing and he was a fierce opponent of moves to end abstentionism. O'Bradaigh and O'Connaill would provide the core of Provisional ideology and strategy down to the late 1970s.

Both the Provisional and what was now being referred to as the 'Official' IRA under Goulding mobilized their supporters for the forthcoming Sinn Féin Árd Fheis. As an Official pamphlet would later describe it, in the interval between the IRA convention and the Árd Fheis 'the scramble for delegates was only equalled by the scramble for dumps [of arms]'. On Saturday, 10 January 1970, the largest Sinn Féin Árd Fheis since the 1920s met at the Intercontinental Hotel in Dublin. The first major debate centred on the proposal for a National Liberation Front which was carried by a large majority. The debate on a resolution to remove 'all embargoes on political participation in parliament' from the constitution of Sinn Féin was bitterly polarized. For those like O'Bradaigh and the veteran republican from Leitrim, John Joe McGirl, who had been a Sinn Féin abstentionist TD between 1957 and 1961 and a close friend of Goulding and Sean Garland down to the late 1960s, the case was a moral, almost theological one. Two generations of republicans had made sacrifices and some had died in the struggle to defend the 'legitimacy' of the Second Dail against the Treaty settlement and the 'Partition statelets' which had emerged from it. 'Politicization' would mean gradual absorption into the state structures based on this settlement – Sinn Féin would go the way of Fianna Fáil and Clann na Poblachta. For their opponents such arguments simply condemned republicanism to a declining existence on the margins of Irish political life. Although the resolution was passed, it failed by 19 votes to get the two thirds majority necessary for an amendment to the constitution. However, by the end of an emotional and charged four hour debate many on the majority side were determined to press the issue to breaking point. Thus, when a northern delegate proposed a vote of confidence in the leadership of the IRA – which had already accepted the proposal for an ending of abstentionism – MacStiofain and a third of the delegates walked out to found an alternative Sinn Féin.[1]

The first statement by the Provisionals after their split at the Sinn Féin Árd Fheis on 11 January 1970 gave five major reasons for their walk-out. The first was the prospect of recognition of the three parliaments, which would 'change a National Movement into yet another political party seeking votes at all costs'. This was linked to the proposal for a National Liberation Front with other radical groups, which was portrayed as the product of the influence of 'infiltration and take-over' by those who had joined the movement from the Irish Workers' Party to push 'an extreme form of socialism'. They attacked 'repressive' internal methods, which included expelling branches in North Kerry and Sligo which opposed the new line, disbanding the Cumann na mBan organization for the same reason, and expelling leading veteran republicans like Jimmy Steele and Sean Keenan. The Goulding leadership had 'let down' the north: 'The leadership of the Movement was obsessed with the "Commission" . . . preparations for the defence of our people did not receive the necessary attention'. There was criticism of the opposition to the abolition of Stormont: 'We find absolutely incomprehensible from any Republican stand-point the campaigning in favour of retaining the Stormont parliament. . . . In any future struggle for freedom it would surely be preferable to have a direct confrontation with the British Government on Irish soil without the Stormont junta being imposed. In any event, the taking away of the Orange Order's power block would surely be a step forward rather than backward.'

The new organization dismissed any notion of healing the split: 'there can be no question of rapprochement or of meetings with those who are opposed to us.'[2] However, in the issue of the *United Irishman* which dealt with the Árd Fheis, the editor took a much more conciliatory attitude towards those who had walked out. He had warned those most militantly in favour of getting rid of abstentionism that 'a two-thirds majority [necessary for such a constitutional issue as the removal of the ban on participation in existing parliamentary institutions], instead of isolating the reluctant third might eventually isolate the two-thirds from the mainstream of Republican opinion, that the vote of the Árd Fheis might not reflect the real state of opinion on this issue.'[3] In fact, after a bitter four-hour debate, the resolution favouring participation did not obtain the necessary two-thirds majority – the vote was 153 to 104 in favour of participation. The walk-out was precipitated by the proposal for a vote of confidence in the Army Council which had in December voted in favour of participation, a decision subsequently endorsed by an IRA convention at which the Belfast IRA, in a semi-detached relation since the 'coup', was not represented.

The editor's 'personal view' was critical of younger delegates, particularly those who had been active in the civil rights movement in the north, who 'could see no virtue in marking time to avoid a split' and who needlessly antagonized those with doubts about participation by labelling them as inactive reactionaries. This reflected the concerns of some in the leadership, including Goulding and Garland, who had favoured a more gradualist approach to the abstention issue and who resented the abrasiveness of people like Seamus Costello and the former editor of the *United Irishman*, Tony Meade. The latter, in canvassing for the new policies, had not hesitated to label all signs of equivocation as evidence of 'constipated thinking'.[4] Garland and Goulding would continue to believe that many sincere republicans had been pushed into the Provisionals by what Garland would subsequently term a 'combination of unfortunate errors on the part of some people.'[5]

The Official leadership was convinced that many of the dissidents could be won back, that they were the unwitting dupes of an alliance between a group of superannuated reactionaries stimulated by the August violence and the Blaney-Haughey faction of Fianna Fáil. The January issue of the *United Irishman* had warned of 'the most determined attempt in recent years by the *Sunday Press* and the *Irish Press* to cause disruption within the ranks of the Movement'. As the then editor of the *Irish Press*, Tim Pat Coogan, admits in his own history of the IRA (produced just after the split), the news of the IRA Convention vote against abstentionism had been leaked to the *Sunday Press*, and both papers gave the issue, and divisions in the Republican movement, much coverage as the Árd Fheis approached. This coverage reflected the established concern of sections of the Fianna Fáil leadership about communist influence on the Army Council. Coogan symptomatically described the NLF proposal as coming very close 'to giving Moscow a voice in the Irish national movement for the first time in history'.[6] The *United Irishman* had warned that the press campaign was all part of the Fianna Fáil strategy of 'binding this country closer to British Imperialism, only a united, alert and growing Republican movement in the 1970s can save the Irish nation from a future worse than that which followed the Act of Union.'[7] The Official IRA's Easter statement in 1970 continued to emphasize the need to end the division in the face of the 'real' enemy: 'A division in Republican ranks helps only Ireland's enemies: British Imperialism, Unionism and Free Statism. This decade may well decide the future of the Irish Nation for decades to come. It may well decide whether or not there will be an Irish nation. In this perspective, our internal difficulties on tactical questions are of small importance, however large they may seem in people's minds at present.'[8] The Army Council called for the utmost efforts to 'achieve unity in our ranks', claimed that the Officials would continue to avoid controversies that might deepen divisions and would 'direct all our shafts at the enemy'. If immediate unity was impossible, there should at least be 'maximum co-operation in the struggle for the emancipation of our people. . . .' Such calls continued to be made into 1971. In February, MacGiolla, in response to 'British Army provocation' and growing violent conflict between Officials and Provisionals in Belfast, called on all those opposed to 'the British Army and British rule' to unite 'or at least cooperate with each other'. He made it clear that he was calling not for organizational fusion but 'cooperation and unity of action where possible'.[9] At the Official Easter Commemoration parade in Belfast in 1971, Garland made another appeal to his 'former colleagues' to unite 'in the attempt to restore the land of Ireland to the people of Ireland'.[10]

The lack of response to such appeals reflected in part the intense competition between the two organizations in Belfast; despite the fact that a post-August influx soon ensured the Provisionals an easy numerical predominance, the Officials also began to recruit substantially in a number of areas, particularly the Lower Falls where the preeminence of McMillen and Sullivan was unshaken by the split. The *United Irishman* was to claim that the loss of membership due to the split was made up in six months and that by the end of 1970 the membership had increased by 40%.[11] Certainly the northern crisis provoked a broad, if inchoate, republican sentiment throughout Catholic Ireland, which resulted, among other things, in large crowds marching on the Official headquarters in Gardiner Place demanding guns and transport to the North.[12] Sales of the *United Irishman* soared to 70,000 in the early 1970s.[13] In Belfast, the bulk of the membership had stayed with the Officials, although it was now clearly dwarfed by the Provisionals' 'pogrom' levy. The Belfast leadership of the Officials regarded the Provisionals with a mixture of contempt and bitter animosity. The role of 'ex-members' like the Kelly brothers and Joe Cahill defined the nature of the Provisionals for Officials like Jim Sullivan. Although he was unable to persuade McMillen of the need to eliminate physically the leadership of the Provisionals in the city, Sullivan lost no opportunity in attempting to establish the Officials' military credentials in as many areas as possible. The pre-August Officials did not take the Provisionals seriously as potential competitors. They were seen as 'a collection of Glasgow Celtic supporters, backward nationalists, people on the make and general ne'er-do-wells'.[14] The Officials would pride themselves on maintaining a serious attempt to screen and educate the increasing numbers who applied to join the IRA, and would compare this with the Provisionals' promiscuous intake of those infused with a Catholic defender mentality.[15] Subsequent evaluations of the period, however, stressed the many negative effects of the Officials' northern expansion in the two to three years after August 1969. In 1975 Sean Garland gave a stringent assessment of the effects of the northern crisis: '. . . the six County situation has, since 1969 dominated the attention of the movement despite many efforts on our part to bring the struggle back to basics, by attempting to raise issues which require the involvement of the mass of the people, we have been unable to do so. . . . The imbalance that the six County situation creates in the entire country has been one of the greatest difficulties we have had to face and fight. After internment we found ourselves gradually getting involved in military activities, as a reaction to the British Army and also, in some cases, as competition with the Provisionals. . . . Without doubt over the past years we attracted many unreliable elements to our movement, opportunists, ultra leftists, criminals and plain unadulterated madmen. It has taken us much effort to retain our fundamental struggle and to shake off these unstable elements.'[16] These reflections on the undesirable effects of the shift in the strategic axis of the Official movement brought on by the northern crisis and its militarizing consequences, need to be amplified by a consideration of the central defects of the Officials' analysis of the crisis, which made creeping militarization difficult to contain.

The Freedom Manifesto – Social Republicanism in Crisis

The 1970 Árd Fheis adopted a 'Freedom Manifesto' which was supposed to be the strategic basis for the creation of the National Liberation Front. For all the charges of 'extreme socialism' and 'communism' which the Provisionals were to level at the Officials, the most striking characteristic of the manifesto is its emphasis on the centrality of the national question. All reforms and advances, whether in the area of civil rights or economic and social conditions must help to 'weaken imperial control. . . . The need to reunify the nation dominates the immediate horizon. No demand should be formulated without this in mind.'[17] Despite the importance accorded to the national question, the section on the Six

Counties continued to put the civil rights issue at the centre of demands. The relationship of civil rights to the Protestant working class was the source of major problems for the manifesto. It recognized that support for civil rights demands was confined to a 'tiny politically conscious minority' of Protestants in the trade union movement. Support for the 'national demand for unity' was recognized to be even slighter although the startling claim was made that there was still less support for social demands amongst Protestant workers. This was because of the 'elite position' in the job market which Unionist Party patronage had given Protestant workers. There could be no progress on social issues until this patronage system was destroyed. The process of destruction was identified with the campaign to force the British government to reform the political system in Northern Ireland. However, so fixated was the Official analysis on the supposed British 'master-plan' to reintegrate the Irish Republic into the United Kingdom that the very radical import of a demand for the destruction of the existing sectarian state apparatuses was neutralized by the insistence that this could only be accomplished through the reform of the Stormont system and not by its abolition. Direct rule was passionately opposed on the grounds that it brought the north under tighter 'imperial' control – at least Stormont was run by Irishmen.

The strategy of pushing for the reform of the Stormont regime and opposing demands for its abolition was a difficult one to explain to many northern Officials, let alone to the Catholic communities in which they operated. Even those with least regrets about the split with the Provisionals found it difficult not to see the plausibility of the Provisional charge that they were attempting to reform the irreformable.[18] Goulding, who had had his own difficulties with the strategy, was ultimately convinced by Coughlan and Johnston. As in the past, it was tempting to explain the failure of strategic calculations in Dublin by referring to the recalcitrant material that had to be worked on in the north – in an interview in 1972 Goulding mentioned as one of the problems the Officials faced the fact that '. . . in the North every Catholic youth is a Provo at heart'.[19]

At the heart of the Official analysis was an implicit

recognition of the depth of communal polarization, the implication of which was certainly that only gradual incremental change was possible. This allowed some realistic counterpoints to be made to the Provisional contention that once the 'puppet regime' at Stormont was gone, the 'Irish people' would quickly resolve the basic conflict with the British state. It was pointed out, for instance, that the abolition of Stormont would not shatter the Unionist 'power-base': '. . . is not the real Unionist power base the determination of one million Protestant Irishmen not to enter a united Ireland?'[20] The Officials had consistently portrayed the essence of the civil rights movement as one of creating conditions which would allow for political differentiation within Unionism. While it was admitted that winning over Protestants, 'even some of them, may seem improbable at the present time,' it was pointed out that the civil rights movement has shattered the unity of the Unionist Party and that 'if proportional representation can be won, divisions in the ranks of Unionism may become institutionalized and can be exploited even further.'[21]

However, the very positive aspects of an analysis which recognized the realities of massive internal opposition to a united Ireland, and the consequent need to pursue a process of political development within Northern Ireland, were ultimately nullified by the basic strategic framework of the National Liberation Front, which valued reforms and political development only if they assisted in developing 'a more Irish-orientated framework in the Six Counties within which some of the one million Protestants can be won in time to stand for a United Ireland'.[22] Direct rule was opposed not essentially, as the Provisionals claimed, because of the 'reformism' of the Officials – after all direct rule was arguably a better framework for the introduction of reforms than a crisis-ridden and divided Unionist regime – but rather because of a fundamental concern about its effects on the 'Irish nation' as a whole. The abolition of Stormont would represent an important shift towards fulfilment of Britain's new strategy towards Ireland. A speech by Quintin Hogg calling for the institutionalization of relations between Dublin, Belfast and London and arguing that Fianna Fáil was the best party to institute detente in Anglo-Irish relations was seen as of great revelatory significance: 'People who take the political independence of the 26 Counties for granted are in for a shock. The 26 Counties is economically far more dependent on Britain now than it was 10 years ago. . . . Political dependence follows economic dependence as night follows day.'[23] A subsequent article in the *Economist* supporting direct rule was used as further evidence of the grand design: 'The Catholics would be guaranteed civil rights, the Protestants would be more secure within the United Kingdom than ever, the "wild men" on both sides would be isolated. Northern Catholics would have no say in a UK parliament of 640 MPs and Lynch and the British would begin discussions about the Anglo-Irish federation.'[24] The concern with evaluating every specific proposal for change in the north in relation to the Official depiction of 'Imperialist' strategy enabled some remarkable resistance to reality to be maintained. When Paisley's Protestant Unionist Party won its first seats at Stormont, Sinn Féin issued a statement pointing out that the development of Paisleyism should not be used to justify arguments for direct rule. It alleged a British plan to replace Stormont with interim rule by a commission and to establish a Council of Ireland in which Belfast, Dublin and London governments were to be represented.[25] Such moves would be presented as moves towards a united Ireland but were in fact aimed at giving Britain greater political control over Ireland as a whole.

In fact, as I have argued at greater length elsewhere, the British state's relationship to Ireland was the reverse of the one posited by the Official analysis. Rather than thirsting to impose direct rule on Northern Ireland as part of a strategy to bring Ireland as a whole further into its sphere of interest, the Wilson and Heath governments resisted the pressure which the unfolding crisis in Northern Ireland imposed for greater direct involvement. It was precisely this reluctance to remove the convenient buffer of the Unionist government, even after the sending of troops in August 1969, that created the best possible conditions for the development of the Provisionals. In the eyes of Northern Ireland Catholics, the reforms introduced in late 1969 were the hostage of a Unionist government under increasing pressure from its own ultras and the Paisleyites to backtrack. British troops would very soon be easily depicted as defenders of a corrupt and disintegrating Unionist regime. Such developments could have been avoided if, as the Wilson government had threatened, Stormont had been abolished at the time the troops were sent in. It was precisely because the dominant policy current in the British state was deeply averse to being sucked back into the 'Irish bog' that a series of disastrous expedients were adopted to keep the Unionists in power, expedients which contributed powerfully to an upsurge of militant republicanism.[26]

For all its undoubted struggle to modernize its politics and ideology, Official republicanism still suffered from that congenital nationalist belief in an unchanging substratum of British interest in Ireland. This resulted in a reading of recent economic history which was the exact reverse of the truth. The Lemassian break with protectionism and the opening of the Irish economy to foreign capital was a result of the bankruptcy of traditional Sinn Féin economic philosophy in the face of an economic crisis of mammoth proportions in the 1950s. Liberalization of the Republic's economy was no doubt welcome to Britain and sections of its industry, but it implied no concomitant need for a reordering of constitutional relations between Britain and the Republic. The new economic policies were impelled by the crisis of the Republic's economy and although they were profoundly disturbing for traditional nationalist ideology, they did little to affect the British ruling elite's fundamental lack of interest in Ireland. By presuming a British ruling class with changeless outlook and interests, Official republicanism produced an analysis of the northern situation which at times verged on the exotic,[27] and, more fundamentally, was not able to restrain the creeping militarization of its supporters in Northern Ireland.

Militarization

As Chief of Staff of the Official IRA, Goulding faced a major dilemma after August 1969 and the subsequent split. But the roots of the dilemma were in the conflict which implicitly existed between politicization of the republican movement and the continuing existence of the IRA. As Goulding described it, one facet of the problem was that many of those attracted to the republican movement were drawn by its military mystique, but most people who wanted guns 'had no politics, or bad politics'.[28] The existence of the IRA as the dominant wing of the movement had many negative effects: in particular, it created permanent pressure for 'action'. Goulding used a prosaic metaphor in internal debates: 'It was like a greyhound who is trained to race – you have to let it race or it goes bad.'[29] Prior to the northern crisis, the solution of the dilemma had been seen in developing Sinn Féin, involving members in social, economic and civil rights campaigns and, most importantly, taking a very selective and restrictive approach to recruitment to the IRA, which would only take the most 'politically conscious' members of the movement. Revolution would be redefined away from a fixation on armed struggle towards notions of a popular mass movement which might ultimately need force to defend its gains. In the interim, this view enabled important individuals like McMillen to stay loyal, since for all its upgrading of politics and emphasis that there was more to 'anti-imperialist' activity than action against British troops in Northern Ireland,[30] it reserved the implicit leading role for the IRA, filled as it would be with the politically conscious elite of the movement. But it was very much a transitional view of the respective roles of politics and force and it would ultimately prove unsustainable.

By the end of 1971, it was clear that developments in Northern Ireland had disrupted any plans for a change in the nature and role of the IRA. Within four months of the split the Provisionals were involved in a bombing campaign against commercial targets which were often owned by prominent Unionist businessmen. The Provisionals correctly calculated that the bombings would lead to increased pressure on the Unionist government and the British state for a policy of repression. British government acquiescence in the more repressive measures which the Unionist cabinet declared were necessary to prevent a drain of support to the Protestant ultras, and increasingly hostile relations between British troops and the Catholic communities from which the Provisionals operated, allowed the Provisionals to intensify their campaign. They killed a British soldier in February 1971 and launched an intensive bombing campaign in the summer of that year. Under great pressure from the Unionist government Edward Heath's Conservative government sanctioned the introduction of mass internment in August 1971. The results were disastrous – in 1971 prior to internment there had been 34 deaths; between internment and the end of the year there were 139. An atmosphere of fevered resentment and anticipation developed in many Catholic ghettoes. The dynamics of communal expectations and competition with the Provisionals drew the Officials into attacks on the British Army and, after internment, even more indiscriminate violence.

The British Army's imposition of an arms search and curfew on the Lower Falls soon after the Conservative election victory in 1970 gave the local Officials the opportunity to establish their military credentials in a major gunbattle which entered Official mythology as the 'Battle of the Lower Falls' and encouraged McMillen and Sullivan to believe that forceful assertion of the defensive role of the IRA would soon recuperate any ground that had been lost to the Provisionals. This inevitably caused friction with the Provisionals, as, for example, when Sullivan brought a group of Officials into Ballymurphy to respond to local complaints of army harassment, to the chagrin of the local Provisionals – among them Gerry Adams – who regarded Ballymurphy as their territory.[31] Such territorial disputes over issues like fundraising and paper-selling as well as military action, soon resulted in violent and brutal conflicts and killings. At the same time the Officials appeared to be happy to justify a 'defensive' role for the IRA while attributing any polarizing effects of violence to the Provisionals' bombing campaign.

As the Provisional bombing campaign intensified in the spring and summer of 1971, with the predictable Army response – saturating Catholic areas, massive house searches, large-scale screenings of the population etc. – the Officials moved from 'defensive' to 'retaliatory' action. In its 'New Year Statement' in January 1972, the Official IRA blamed the escalation of its own activities on the 'sectarian bombing campaign' of the Provisionals, 'people who are blinded by bigotry and unable to see who the real enemies of the Irish people are'. This had allowed the British Army to 'escalate their terror tactics', which in turn were held to justify the new 'defence and retaliation' doctrine. At the same time, the statement was at pains to emphasize that 'it has never been and is not now our intention to build a movement to launch a purely military campaign against British forces in the North' and to deny that it was engaged in a military campaign in Northern Ireland. This denial sounded hollow, set against other lines in the statement that boasted of the 'many casualties inflicted on the forces of Imperialism' by the IRA.[32] Armed struggle 'on its own, or as an end in itself', was declared to be doomed to failure. The problem for the Officials was that as the impetus of the civil rights movement disintegrated and their agitational strategies in the Republic made only limited progress, there was a real danger that their political comple-ment to IRA activities would seem increasingly formal and gestural.

Internment in August 1971, and the substantial increase in violence which it caused, greatly intensified these negative tendencies. While many prominent Officials were interned, the ranks were swelled by new recruits. By the end of 1972 the Officials' membership in Belfast, though still substantially less than that of the Provisionals, was around 800.[33] the distinction between 'retaliatory' and 'offensive' action was always a dubious one and increasingly IRA attacks also clearly contradicted its claim that it had 'consistently eschewed all sectarian actions . . . our units will not take action designed to alienate any section of the working class.'[34] In December 1971, the homes of prominent Unionists in the Malone Road area of Belfast were attacked and, in 'reprisal for the destruc-tion of working-class homes by the British forces' the Derry brigade admitted responsibility for the murder of a prominent Unionist politician, Senator Barnhill, shot dead by IRA men who had planned to blow up his home.[35] In the aftermath of the Bloody Sunday killing of thirteen civilians by British paratroopers, Official militarism reached its nadir. In February 1972 a car bomb attack on the Officers' Mess of the Parachute Regiment at Aldershot killed seven including five women canteen workers and a Catholic priest. Soon after this an attempt was made to murder the prominent Unionist minister John Taylor in Armagh, and an RUC sergeant was shot dead by the 'South Down–South Armagh' Official IRA. In Derry, the Officials, whose numbers had increased substantially since 1969, combined impatience with the national leadership's emphasis on civil rights with a ready belief in the revolutionary significance of 'armed struggle'.[36] In March they 'executed' a local Catholic accused of 'spying' and in April murdered another Catholic home on leave from the British army.[37] By this time the disastrous implications of militarism were apparent. Roy Johnstone resigned from Sinn Féin after the Barnhill shooting, which he portrayed as the culmination of a process in which the balance in the movement had been unhealthily tilted towards a northern fixation with competing with the Provisionals: 'there has always been a difference in the points of view between both areas of the Republican movement. The national movement sees Ireland as a whole. . . . the northern section only sees one end of it and their feelings are sharp at the moment . . . they will tend to think of a purely military campaign.'[38]

The problems which Johnston's resignation highlighted were increasingly obvious to most people in the national leadership of the IRA and Sinn Féin. Most worrying was the threat posed to the political development of Sinn Féin in the Republic by IRA military activity in Northern Ireland. August 1969, internment and Bloody Sunday had all provoked spasms of emotional nationalism, but these quickly subsided with little evidence of any significant effects on the main lines of political affiliation in the south. As Provisional violence intensified and Protestant paramilitary groups in Belfast launched a horrifying brand of counter-terror, the Officials' own involvement in northern violence was threatening marginalization in the Republic. There were real fears of internment[39], but even more significant was the growing fear that the organization's preoccupation with the northern crisis was distracting attention from what an IRA statement defined as 'the central and most important issue facing the Irish people today', the proposed referendum on membership of the EEC.[40] EEC membership was portrayed as the culmination of the 'anti-national' economic policies pursued by Fianna Fáil since 1958, the result of which was depicted in apocalyptic terms: 'the loss of employment and livelihoods that would result from entry, would mean the final devastation of a devastated people. North and South would face economic ruin and national extinction.'[41]

The anti-EEC campaign saw the Officials and Provisionals united with the Irish Labour Party and the left fringe. The result was a major blow to the whole republican project. The people of the Republic voted by five to one for membership.[42] The *United Irishman* had to admit that the result was 'a kick in the stomach for the Republican movement. . . . The Irish people have rejected the proclamation of 1916 and the principles of national independence and sovereignty. . . .' It drew the reasonable if pessimistic conclusion: 'what happened proves how much hard and patient work there is to be done before we will have convinced the people of either the necessity or more importantly the possibility of socialism.'[43]

Throughout 1971 and 1972, leading Officials continued to reiterate the need for mass support for an 'anti-imperialist' strategy based on conditions in Ireland as a whole. As Garland put it 'the North is not the only battleground'.[44] But attacks on elitism ('the doctrine which sets aside the wishes of the people with the expectation that where militants lead the people are bound to follow') and the emerging theme of 'the revolutionary party of the Irish people'[45] sat uneasily with the actualities of northern military emphases. In one of the earliest speeches canvassing the notion of a 'revolutionary party', Sean Garland also emphasized the need to widen radically the scope of republican activity: 'the struggle is everywhere, in the schools, in factories, in the fields, in the churches. . . .'.[46] Of course this was not new; it had been at the heart of the post-1962 rethinking. That it had to be reiterated in such an emphatic way was a sign of the degree to which the movement had regressed under the pressure of the north.

A prolonged and bitter debate in the Official Army Council in May 1972 resulted in the declaration of a ceasefire. There was much opposition from representatives from Belfast; McMillen argued that it would be extremely difficult to impose on the rank and file. His resistance was largely responsible for conditions attached to the ceasefire; the IRA reserved the right to undertake 'defensive' and 'retaliatory' actions.[47] Delegations of Belfast Officials, particularly in areas like Ardoyne where the Officials were a small minority, came to Dublin to protest that the ceasefire would destroy any remaining credibility they had in competing with the Provisionals.[48] In Derry, where the militancy of the local Officials had checked the growth of the Provisionals, there was bitter opposition to the ceasefire and, in particular response to the intensification of Loyalist killings of Catholics, there was pressure for an end to the ceasefire or at the very least for a liberal interpretation of 'retaliatory' action. Such pressure was resisted, but the fact that the ceasefire was not unconditional and that the IRA continued to exist would lead to increasingly bitter internal wranglings over the next three years. At the core of the conflict was the ever more obvious incapacity of the strategic framework set out in *Ireland Today* to relate to politics and society in either of the Irish states.

Civil Rights Versus the National Question

The imposition of Direct Rule was a major blow to the Officials, who continued to argue that it was a retrograde step though there was an increasingly clear formalism in their criticisms. Once the familiar charge that it was all part of Britain's broader aim of 'a false unity without independence'[49] had been repeated, the substance of Official demands – ending of internment, anti-discrimination legislation, 'fair and free elections under proportional representation' – could all be reasserted within the new framework. These were defined as 'interim democratic demands' and commitment was still maintained to 'full national unity and social freedom', but there was no mistaking the essential gradualism of the perspective. The major problem for the Officials was the lack of evidence that political reforms would prompt significant numbers of Protestants to the necessary reassessment of national identity. The lack of credibility of gradualist republicanism, together with the fevered expectations aroused by the crisis in Northern Ireland, created the conditions for a major assault on the civil rights component of the *Ireland Today* strategy.

The two key figures were Sean Garland and Seamus Costello. As early as May 1971, Garland had warned of the dangers of playing down the national question. Referring back to the Republican Congress, he claimed that it had failed because of its concentration on 'social questions' and its separation of these from the national question. In fact this was the exact opposite of what the dominant, O'Donnellite, position had been, but Garland was obviously rewriting history with a purpose. He concluded, in strong implicit contrast with the *Ireland Today* analysis: 'the centuries-old struggle of the Irish people to establish an independent nation is still today one of the most potent weapons in the revolutionary arsenal, is in fact the one single issue on which all Irishmen can come together.'[50] In marked contrast to this would be the continuing emphasis on the centrality of civil rights in the *United Irishman*, where statements like this were typical: 'the foremost issue for the people of the North is not the national question, but a democratic question of peace, justice and security.'[51]

The editor of the time, Eoin Ó'Murchú, has given an account of the tensions of the period. A strong supporter of the civil rights emphasis, he subsequently left Sinn Féin to join the Communist Party. Despite the ceasefire, the continued emphasis on civil rights was not popular: 'there was a growing feeling among many of the rank and file that there was a third way – neither militarist nor alliancist, but an individual, and indeed, exclusivist, political republicanism.'[52] He explains this in terms of three factors: a residual anti-communism in the Officials, which saw the NLF strategy and the civil rights emphasis as Communist inspired, traditional republican isolationism and distrust of working with other groups, and the continued pressure for military action from the north which, given the ceasefire, made it all the more important to emphasize the specifically Republican aspect of the movement's strategy.

There was certainly some resentment among the Officials that the Communists tended to see themselves as the hegemonic group in the NLF – providing theoretical leadership and 'experience of working-class struggles'.[53] Johnston's decision to join the CP on resigning from Sinn Féin may have intensified this. But such feelings, and also the desire to ensure Official hegemony in campaigns, would have been shared by people on both sides of the debate over civil rights. The crucial source of the conflict lay in the different responses to the increasing evidence that, contrary to the expectations of the late 1960s, prospects for radical change in Ireland were dim indeed. Part of the necessary ideological baggage which the post-1962 transformation had carried along was a nebulous notion of a coming 'Irish revolution' in which a revamped Republican movement would play a central role. Since little serious thought was given to what such a revolution would entail, it was not surprising that for some members, particularly in the north, the disintegration of the Unionist state and the continuing disorder and unrest appeared to create a potentially revolutionary situation.

It was to Seamus Costello, Director of Operations of the Official IRA, that such people increasingly looked for direction. A man whose bitterest opponents would admit had qualities of energy, efficiency and practical intelligence, he was fundamentally committed to the notion that 'armed struggle' could create revolutionary situations. Although his various proposals for joint action with the Provisionals and for various Official 'spectaculars' in Northern Ireland got little support either at Army Conventions or in the Army Council, the increasing disarray over political strategy provided a favourable environment in which he could continue to press for a return to militarism. In the IRA Convention in October 1972 the issue of whether the emphasis on civil rights was too 'reformist' was raised and, after clear evidence of divided opinions, was referred back to the local units of the IRA for discussion. In the interim, Garland had drafted a document calling for a reassertion of the national issue, and at the reconvened Convention and the subsequent Sinn Féin Árd Fheis, the new emphasis was accepted.[54] This produced unprecedented internal confusion and disarray. The bulk of the IRA and Sinn Féin leadership opposed the change, on the basis that a renewed emphasis on the 'national struggle' would be read as meaning a return to militarism. This was not Garland's intention, but he failed to specify what means were available to raise the 'national question', apart from those being currently used by the Provisionals. Simply to reemphasize traditional republican values while practically engaging in agitations and electoral activity which the Provisionals denounced as reformist seemed insufficient for those Officials who emerged as Costello's supporters.

In 1973 and 1974 questions of strategy were intertwined with increasing concern for the basic structure of the Official movement. Participation in electoral activity was expanded in both states at local and parliamentary levels. This increased political work raised again the question of the respective roles of Sinn Féin (in the north, the Republican Clubs) and the IRA. Prior to August 1969, it had been possible to hope that the increased involvement in agitations and electoral activity would, of itself, lead to a gradual diminution in the significance of the military organization. By the time of direct rule such hopes were clearly over-optimistic. In Northern Ireland at least, the IRA still dominated, and the high level of dual membership meant that the Republican Clubs were clearly and practically subordinate organizations. Even after the ceasefire, there was considerable resistance to electoral activity. In the 1973 local government elections the Republican Clubs had ten of their eighty candidates elected with an average of 10% of the poll in constituencies contested.[55] The results were hailed as a victory for 'the development of genuine non-sectarian working class politics', but there was little evidence to support this; the fact was that the victories were obtained on an abstentionist platform because of continuing internment in predominantly Catholic constituencies.[56] And despite the traditionalist aspects of the campaign, there was clear resistance to involvement from some Officials. The United Irishman complained that some areas had played little or no part in the campaign: 'this displays a total misunderstanding of the opportunity the elections provided to publicize Republican policy, and is dangerously close to elitism . . . it is felt that the goal of a Socialist Republic can be won without the cooperation and understanding of the people.'[57] The resistance was not lessened by the results of the subsequent Assembly elections where, still fighting on an abstentionist platform, the Republican Clubs had no candidates elected and got a mere 1.9% of the total poll.[58] The undoubtedly attractive and positive note in the Officials' propaganda, stressing the need to reach the Protestant working class, was undermined by the fact that the stated project was to win them to Republicanism – albeit of a 'progressive' and class-conscious sort.[59] The unreality of this approach made it more difficult to challenge the idea, common amongst the supporters of Costello, that the Protestant working class was a privileged stratum that could only be won away from its reactionary politics by the destruction of the northern state.

The nationalism of the *Ireland Today* programme acted increasingly as a major ideological obstacle to the clarification of perspectives necessary for a fundamental break with militarism. For people like Garland, MacGiolla and Goulding, the activities of the Provisionals were anathema, as were Costello's proposals for alliances with them and for an intensified aggressive posture for the Official IRA.[60] However, ideological dependence on the *Ireland Today* analysis would continue into the mid-seventies,[61] and it would be only slowly undermined. In this process it would be the unresolved question of the role of the IRA which would prove decisive in forcing a fundamental reassessment of the whole republican tradition.

By the beginning of 1973, in part because of the ceasefire which had led to the release of many Official internees and also because of the successes of the security forces in actions against the Provisionals, the Officials were for the first time since the split almost as strong as the Provisionals in Northern Ireland.[62] This raised the question of their purpose, particularly given the restraint imposed by the ceasefire. The national leadership might complain of 'a dangerous tendency . . . in some areas to equate the national question with the border and British troops . . . we must continuously re-emphasize that the national question . . . is all about the ownership of the wealth of this country;'[63] but the movement's military presence in Northern Ireland was functioning to reproduce the tendency which Garland was criticizing.[64] Garland's 1972 intervention had opened the way for those who wished to read the renewed emphasis on the national question as meaning a break with what a chief supporter of Costello referred to as 'the bourgeois reforms' of the civil rights movement. It was now argued that the support for the civil rights strategy meant that 'the republican movement had fallen behind the people in their revolutionary demands'.[65] The critic, the prominent Derry republican Johnnie White, was proposing an amendment to the main political resolution, which restated the commitment to the NLF strategy, and its emphasis on the fight for reforms. This was seen as a deliberate backtracking on the decision the year before to upgrade the priority of the national question.[66] The supporters of the amendment claimed that the effect of the resolution would be to turn the republican movement into a 'reformist' organization, ignoring the obstacle that partition represented to progress in Ireland as a whole. As in 1972, the critics of the civil rights strategy also implied that it had led to the failure of the IRA to defend Catholics against the British Army and Loyalist assassins.[67] Little hope was held out for developing relations with the Protestant working class until partition was ended. Many of these criticisms echoed those the Provisionals had been making since 1969, as did the claim that the leadership of Sinn Féin was 'simply another facet of the Communist Party of Ireland'.[68]

By 1973 key figures in Official Sinn Féin and the Army Council had moved towards new organizational principles as part of a desperate search for the means of disciplining and marginalizing Official militarism without provoking another split. Some of these means were the predictable resources of a conspiratorial organization, like the denial of weapons and training to units of the IRA suspected of 'disloyalty'. However, as Director of Operations, Costello, the centre of resistance to the dominant line, was well-placed to create an alternative infrastructure.[69] More significant was the attempt to reconstruct the relationship between the IRA and Sinn Féin. In his Bodenstown speech in 1972, Garland had spoken of the need to build a 'revolutionary party' and this was a notion that was increasingly voiced by leading members of Sinn Féin. It was very unclear, however, what relationship this party would have with the IRA. While denouncing Provisional 'terrorism' and its sectarian effects, Garland had added that repudiation of terrorism did not mean there would be no role for the IRA, 'the army of the people', in 'defending the interests of the working class'.[70] For those in favour of the Costello approach, talk of a revolutionary party was seen as disguising a turn to 'social democracy', and there had been substantial opposition to the idea at the 1972 Árd Fheis.[71] A Structure Commission was established and produced a report in August 1973. According to Ó'Murchú, three positions were argued: 'One, the IRA should be abolished forthwith. While this had extensive support, it was felt too blunt, too likely to provoke the split which subsequently happened. . . . Two, that the IRA's authority as the prime revolutionary force be reasserted. Three, that the IRA be removed entirely from political affairs and Sinn Féin developed as the sole Republican political voice with the implied understanding . . . that the IRA would in fact wither away and disappear without formal abolition.'[72]

He claims that no formal position was adopted – the events of the Costello split in 1974–75 intervening – but that 'it is reasonable to assume that the third strategy was adopted.'[73] In fact there was serious resistance to the third proposal and substantial figures, particularly McMillen, asserted themselves in favour of the second position. The Report of the Structure Commission had noted the 'feeling of many people in the movement that failure to maintain Group B (the documents referred to the IRA as Group B and Sinn Féin as Group A) would create a dangerous vacuum which possibly would be filled by the Provos or some other group.'[74] The strength of the resistance only persuaded the leadership to pursue a more gradualist approach. The pressure to maintain the IRA as the leading core was recognized but a majority of the Army Council was persuaded to support a strategy substituting a form of Leninist for military vanguardism.

To the chagrin of the Derry Officials, influenced by the Trotskyism which affected much of the student and labourist left in Northern Ireland from 1968, the 1973 Árd Fheis had passed a resolution committing the Officials to a concept of 'Irish freedom' like that 'presently being built in the Socialist countries.'[75] The Officials would be represented at the 'World Congress of Peace Forces' in Moscow in October 1973, and although the message was a traditional one,[76] the visit symbolized the increasing desire of the Official leadership to adopt Leninist (Stalinist, as their opponents labelled them) forms of organization. In 1973, a meeting of the Army Council passed a resolution committed to transforming the movement into a party, the philosophy of which would be Marxist and whose organizational principles would be Leninist.[77] Such commitments, particularly that to the creation of a 'revolutionary party' based on democratic centralism represented in part the feeling of Goulding and Garland that the phase of ideological apprenticeship to the Communists was over and that the Officials needed to assert their independence. At the same time, the recognition of the very uneven results of the process of internal education, especially given the 'distractions' of northern violence, meant that the major immediate concern was with organizational rather than philosophical questions.

An Extraordinary Árd Fheis was supposed to be held to discuss the issues raised in the Structure Commission Report, but by the time of the 1974 Árd Fheis this had still not occurred.[78] As in 1969, it appears that Goulding and others who favoured quite radical changes were unsure about the likely response emerging from an immediate and open debate. One major consideration was Costello, who had been suspended from Sinn Féin for allegedly promoting a secret list of supporters for election to the National Executive at the 1973 Árd Fheis. He was subsequently 'court-martialled' and dismissed from the IRA for undermining the organization and misappropriation of funds.[79] It was feared that, as in 1969, 'ordinary decent' Officials would be swayed by Costello, because of the radical implications of the 'revolutionary party' proposal for the existence of the IRA. During 1974 a leadership committee carried out a programme of visits to branches throughout Ireland to explain the implications of the 'revolutionary party' concept and to minimize support for Costello.[80] The subsequent decision, ratified at the 1974 Árd Fheis, to expel Costello from Sinn Féin, represented more a reaction of the majority of Officials against any activities that threatened another split than a clear decision on the future organizational and political direction of the movement. The difficulties of transforming a movement with militarist and commandist traditions were immense and often entailed using very traditional methods to achieve modernizing objectives.

If the organization which Costello's supporters established in December 1974 – the Irish Republican Socialist Party – had been simply a new ultra-left nationalist grouping, the Officials would probably have ignored it. But Costello was a substantial figure in his own right, and had used his considerable organizational abilities to produce the infrastructure for a new military formation. How the arrival of a new, more 'revolutionary' armed competitor would have been treated by the Provisionals, had they not been on terms of truce with the British government through most of 1975, can only be speculated upon. Costello's abrasive role prior to the 1969 split had made him many Provisional enemies.[81] However, it was the Officials in Belfast who attempted to eliminate the new organization's military capacity before it became established. McMillen, who had been criticized for not acting against the Provisionals in 1969, was determined to ensure that Costello's supporters in Belfast did not use training and weapons acquired in the Officials to set up a rival organization. He had initially proposed a series of beatings and punishment shootings which he thought would be sufficient to deter the main Costello supporters and particularly their leader in Belfast, the former student radical Ronnie Bunting. However, the view of most of the leading younger Officials who dominated the 'command staff' in Belfast was that more drastic action was needed. Although McMillen successfully opposed a proposal for the killing of Costello, it was decided that those who attempted to take weapons would be killed. The result was a vicious conflict initiated by the Officials in which seven of their members were killed and many others injured. McMillen himself died and Garland was seriously injured. Over a hundred Officials in Belfast joined the IRSP including the whole IRA unit in Divis Flats.

As the conflict with the IRSP and its military wing erupted, the Republican Clubs were preparing for elections to the Northern Ireland Convention (the British government's proposed forum in which local parties would discuss possible arrangements for the future internal government of Northern Ireland). On the day of a planned press conference on the organization's proposals for reform of policing, the Official IRA killed its first leading IRSP member.[82] The killings continued throughout the election campaign and culminated in the death of McMillen three days before polling. Leading members of Official Sinn Féin would subsequently complain at press portrayal of the conflict as a 'feud' or 'gang warfare' at a time when the public image of the party was crucial in electoral terms.[83] Yet it was clear that a fundamental source of the problem lay not with the 'capitalist press' but with the Officials' still unresolved conception of the IRA's role.

The problem returned in October 1975 when the Provisionals launched a concerted series of armed attacks on prominent Officials. When they ended in November, eight members, supporters and relatives had been killed. As Bishop and Mallie note, the Officials 'were efficient at fighting back': seven Provisionals were killed, as was the chairman of the Falls Road Taxi Association, which was a major source of revenue for the Provisionals.[84] The Provisional attack was undoubtedly partly motivated, as the Officials alleged, by the growing unpopularity of the ceasefire their leadership had negotiated with the British: militancy was siphoned off against the Officials.[85] Aggression may have been encouraged by the fact of McMillen's death and his replacement by a much younger and relatively inexperienced Official. Yet although the Officials clearly felt the aggrieved party, popular perception of the conflict was that it was little different from that with the IRSP. The days of relatively indiscriminate woundings and killings were widely seen in both Catholic and Protestant communities as an internecine Republican conflict, and any distinctiveness which the Officials' political strategy sought to establish was correspondingly weakened.

It was this year of violence that provoked the crucial shift in the internal balance in the Officials. McMillen's death removed the last major figure who wanted to maintain the IRA as the vanguard of the movement. A decision symbolic of the shift was the disbanding of Fianna Éireann in 1976. The dominant role of this organization had been to prepare adolescents for future membership of the IRA. In practical terms, in 1976, it meant nearly 250 youngsters, in Belfast alone, with military training and the build-up of energy and expectation that accompanied it.[86] The replacement of the Fianna with a new wholly political youth movement proved less than successful; many of the Fianna would not join the new organization and some joined the IRSP. It nevertheless indicated that an era had ended, making clear to all members that the IRA had had its day as an organization capable of replacing itself across the generations. The break with republican military continuity would not be open or without some lingering resonances in subsequent incidents. This was particularly the case in Belfast where the years of bitter co-existence with the Provisionals had left their mark: the outlook of many people in the organization and among its supporters was dominated by the memories of physical clashes with Provisionals and IRSP/INLA members. Loyalty was visceral and deeply overlain with local and familial ties. The arms of the Official IRA were never handed in: in 1977 they were used in the last serious confrontation with the Provisionals in which a number of lives were lost. In the same year Seamus Costello was shot dead in Dublin. In 1982 the INLA killed the man who they claimed was Official IRA commander in Dublin at the time of Costello's death and had carried out the killing. Allegations of the continuing existence of the Official IRA continued to be made down into the 1980s but even the substance of the charges gave evidence of the fundamental break with a tradition which placed the 'army' at the directing centre. For such charges have centred on the role of what appear to be vestiges of the IRA in the intra-ghetto conflicts and rackets – there has been no suggestion that the political direction of the Officials from the late 1970s has come from anywhere but its developing political organization.[88] If the break with militarism was not a clean one, it was decisive for all that. It was followed by increasing evidence of a substantial ideological break with the main tenets of republican ideology as well.

The Officials and the 'Hidden Ireland'

In his talk on strategy in 1975, Garland had referred to the 'imbalance that the Six County situation creates in the entire country'[89] as one of the major problems facing the movement. In a lecture to the Boston Irish Forum, Tomás MacGiolla depicted the situation in Northern Ireland as a major obstacle to progress in Ireland as a whole. It had served to 'smother all progressive ideas, to weaken the forces of the left and strengthen the right-wing parties to the extent that they are now dominant in both North and South.'[90] The Officials' perspective on Northern Ireland now implicitly accepted the closure of the broader perspectives of the *Ireland Today* document: civil rights leading to the dissolution of Unionism, in turn leading to a section of the Protestant working class reassessing their fundamental political allegiances. The positions adopted in 1969 had been reiterated as late as 1974. The British government's proposal's for a powersharing Executive were opposed. The Sunningdale Agreement signed by the British and Irish Governments and the recently formed Executive was denounced as 'a British imposed solution . . . the beginning of the political integration of the whole of Ireland under a Federal Government in London'.[91] However, the overthrow of the Executive by the Ulster Workers' Council strike in May 1974 ushered in a period of intensifying sectarian violence and by 1975 it was being argued that the major priority in Northern Ireland was to check the growth of a 'civil war psychosis among a fairly widespread section of the population'.[92] It was necessary to judge all political questions according to the criterion 'do they encourage or distort class politics?'[93] Thus, if the Unionists and the SDLP could come to some arrangement leading to an internal settlement within the framework set out by the British government, this should be supported because it would lead to lessening of sectarian animosities.[94] This was a sharp break with the previous approach, which had judged all political developments in Northern Ireland according to whether they aided or resisted 'imperialism's' master plan for Ireland as a whole. Increasingly, the whole concept of imperialism which had underlain the Officials' analysis and their continuing fealty to the social republican tradition was put in question.

In February 1977, the *United Irishman* announced the publication of a major document, 'The Irish Industrial Revolution', (IIR) produced by the Research Section of Sinn Féin's Department of Economic Affairs. The IIR, and in particular its first part, 'The Road to Underdevelopment', which provided a broad sweep over the economic history of Ireland from the Penal Laws of the eighteenth century to the 1960s, represented a forceful repudiation of the canon of Irish nationalist history. As Michael O'Riordan, the general secretary of the Communist Party of Ireland, put it in a letter of denunciation sent to all 'fraternal Communist and Workers' Parties', it demonstrated a 'volte-face' by Sinn Féin, which had now repudiated its membership of the 'Irish anti-Imperialist movement.'[95] O'Riordan was particularly annoyed by a reference in the IIR to the 'mythical national question'.[96]

Other critics have seen the IIR as the culmination of the 'denationalizing' influence of the Economic Affairs Department of Sinn Féin and its Research Section.[97] This Department had been created in 1973, after the disintegration of an earlier attempt to develop Sinn Féin's influence in the trade union movement, the Republican Industrial Department. Goulding, who was the prime mover behind both efforts, had brought back an IRA veteran of the 1940s to set up the Economic Affairs Department.[98] Eamonn Smullen had served five years in Portlaoise during the Second World War. On his release he had rejoined the IRA in Dublin and had been close to Goulding, sharing a commitment to the idea of the need for political development of a leftist sort. He had been a member of the Dublin Connolly Group, composed mainly of republican ex-prisoners, and in the late 1940s they had often been involved in discussions with communists and a smattering of leftist students including Roy Johnston. In the early 1950s, Smullen had been forced to go to England to get work. There he joined the Communist Party and became a trade-union activist in the building industry. He maintained his commitment to republicanism and when the northern crisis developed offered his services to Goulding. He was arrested and jailed in England in 1969 after attempting to buy arms.

Smullen set about the task of building up a trade union presence in a single-minded way which soon brought him into competition and conflict with the Communist Party, who resented what was seen as a republican intrusion. Others criticized what was seen as a secretive and conspiratorial style of work. Yet it is doubtful whether the success of the Economic Affairs Department in expanding Official influence in some key unions could have been achieved by such methods on their own. Smullen's major achievement was effectively to harness the resources of a small but growing group of intellectuals in the Research section. At the core of this group was former member of the Wolfe Tone Society Eoghan Harris, who was by then a producer with the Republic's broadcasting authority, RTE. He and a small group of Official sympathizers in the media and the civil service made the first serious attempt to take stock of the massive changes in the economic and social structure of the Republic since the 1950s. They argued that the new economic policies of Lemass which republicans had denounced had in fact produced a major shift towards urbanization and industrial development which held out new possibilities for advance.

However, for Harris and a number of other key intellectuals, such an advance was predicated on a fundamental reassessment of the traditional republican view of Irish history. Harris was undoubtedly a major influence on the development of the Officials in this period. His own massive energy, coupled with a forceful and dominant personality and the Research Section's penchant for secrecy which often bordered on parody, has ensured that analyses of the ideological transformation of the organization have focussed on personalities to the almost total neglect of broader reasons for change.[99] One sympathetic professional historian noted of the controversial first section of the IIR that it was 'best interpreted as an explanation in socialist terms of some "revisionist" findings by the younger generation of Irish economic historians'.[100] Harris had been a student of the important revisionist historian John A. Murphy at University College Cork, and the historical section of the IIR is replete with references to the work of the most important modern Irish historians.

At the core of the vehement response from social republican and nationalist traditionalists was the charge that the IIR had eliminated the role of 'British imperialism' in causing Irish economic backwardness and blamed instead the Irish Catholic bourgeoisie for 'refusing' to create an industrial revolution.

There is certainly a tendency to polemical exaggeration, a bending of the stick too far back in an effort to break with the traditional nationalist focus on 'British imperialism' as the source of all Irish problems.[101] Nevertheless, the essential contribution of the IIR and its real and positive significance was to provide, for the first time, a serious intellectual basis for a break with the *Ireland Today* analysis. It was clear in a brutal and practical sense that the notion of a National Liberation Front and a 'progressive' struggle against British imperialism was a road to nowhere. But in ideological and theoretical terms there had been no decisive break with a framework which still tied the Officials to a critique of the Provisionals and IRSP which was concerned to prove that they were not 'real' republicans, a criticism which for all its internal resonance had no wider appeal, whether to Protestants or, even more critically, to the urban masses in the Republic.

The IIR emphasized that the Irish national revolution was a profoundly Catholic and conservative affair with a rural bourgeoisie as its leading class. It demythologized the Land War of the 1880s, long romanticized by left republicans as a heroic struggle of a poverty-stricken peasantry against greedy landlords, and instead emphasized the dominant role played in the Land League by a strong rural bourgeoisie which had emerged in the post-Famine years. More disturbing to the whole focus of social republican 'class analysis' since the 1920s was the degree to which the IIR depicted the small farmers as the effective allies of the rural bourgeoisie, tied to them by their own intense aspirations for more land and livestock. As the economic historian, Cormac O'Gráda, pointed out, such an analysis cut the ground from under the core class alliance between workers and small farmers posited by social republicanism down to *Ireland Today*.[102]

At the same time as the IIR decisively shifted the focus of radical aspiration to the working class, it challenged the fundamental assumption about Ireland's domination by 'British Imperialism'. Again, the rethinking represented the appropriation of an expanding body of academic and serious journalistic analysis of the Irish economy since the 1950s. Such analysis demonstrated that the new economic policies were tending, contrary to the Johnston-Coughlan theses, to lessen the Republic's economic dependence on Britain. The expanding foreign-controlled manufacturing sector, a source of very rapid economic growth in the 1960s and 1970s, was dominated by US, European and Japanese companies. If 'imperialist' domination of the economy of the Republic was still a central concern, it now became disassociated from the 'national question' in a way that was fraught with implications for traditional republican strategy. Imperialism was now acknowledged to have had certain positive characteristics – the influx of multinationals had created a larger working class. 'What happened in the period 1958–75 was that international capitalism had created what 73 years of native capitalist rule had failed to create – a highly organized and militant industrial working class.'[103] Previous attacks on multinational investment were dismissed as reactionary, as was opposition to the EEC.

The 1977 Sinn Féin Árd Fheis, which voted to change the name of the party to Sinn Féin – The Workers' Party, also adopted a political resolution stressing the change in the nature of Imperialism: 'the centre of Imperialism has moved from Britain to the USA and where British Imperialism has declined and lost control it was replaced by American Economic and Cultural Imperialism.'[104] While the exact 'scientific' value of this characterization may be questioned, its political implication for the republican project was immense. From the social republicans of the inter-war period to the Official Republicans in the early 1970s, all the diverse struggles and activities of the movement had been given a fundamental unity by the belief that they were responses to one common enemy which opposed the small farmer in the west and the shipyard worker in East Belfast. The IIR and the new emphasis on US imperialism effectively destroyed such assumptions of the basic unity of all issues, north and south. The criticism of British government policies in Northern Ireland would cease to be based on the a priori assumption that they were an attempt to defend some fundamental 'Imperialist' interest in Ireland as a whole. Instead they would centre on specific economic and political reforms whose basic objective was the lessening of division inside the working class.

Although the formal commitment to a 32-county 'secular socialist republic' remained, it would increasingly assume the role of an ultimate aspiration. If at the centre of republicanism as an ideological tradition there is the assumption of an essential 'national being' assaulted and distorted by external intervention, its fundamental incompatibility with Marxism is obvious. For many social republicans 'Marxism' was a way of tapping new popular constituencies for the national struggle. Increasingly in the 1970s, Marxism was attractive to leading Officials as a way of justifying in 'revolutionary' terms what were policies of demilitarization and gradualism in Northern Ireland. Marxism's emphasis on the central role of the organized working class in revolutions in capitalist countries could be used as an antidote to the frantic and fevered claims that 'armed struggle' in the north had a revolutionary significance. This functional use of Marxism was, for a while, compatible with an analysis of the Irish situation as a whole which was still fundamentally influenced by nationalist assumptions. However, as the north moved towards an ever more obvious sectarian impasse, it became of prime importance for the very survival of the movement that it redirect its resources to the Republic, where the only possibility of substantial political advance lay. The political prioritization of the Republic then demanded an analysis which took account of the fact that there was very little evidence that urban workers would welcome any attempt to link agitations on economic and social issues with the 'national question'.

The increasing importance attached to work on a range of economic and social issues in the Republic, and the attempt to develop a trade union presence, was particularly welcome in the Dublin area where, in the aftermath of the EEC defeat, an internal document complained of 'a general malaise and apathy within the movement'.[105] Another complained of 'attempts to escape from the realities of life which the working class of Dublin faced by continually bawling about the "North" or indulging in fantasies of "instant revolution".'[106] In 1972 some Dublin members who were not convinced that the Officials were capable of moving decisively in a socialist direction had resigned and formed the Socialist Party of Ireland. However, many who remained in the Dublin organization shared some of the impatience and criticisms of those few who had left. They recognized the possibilities for expansion created by the Irish Labour Party's decision to return to the strategy of coalition – one forsaken in its period of 1960s radicalization. Even in 1973 – the year which saw the Labour Party enter government as a coalition partner of the traditionally right-wing Fine Gael party – the Sinn Féin organization in Dublin, after 'one of the most bankrupt years in its history'[107] with 300 members in twenty-five branches (just over half the members were active), had received 300 applications for membership. [108] The Coalition had to face the major implications of the post-1973 international recession. Unemployment increased from 7.9% in 1973 to 12.5% in 1977, the year it was defeated. EEC membership ushered in a period of major crisis for the Republic's traditional industries in a new competitive environment. The Industrial Development Association had estimated that there would be 17,000 job losses in the 1973–77 period. The actual figure was 57,000 in the first three years.[109] In Dublin in particular the Officials were able to emerge as the hegemonic group in the left's response to the economic crisis. This was in part the product of the movement's ability to channel its membership in a disciplined way into a number of significant campaigns on high visibility issues, particularly those of resources protection and housing. In the Resources Protection Campaign the issue was the proposal of the Labour Minister for Industry and Commerce, Justin Keating, to allow a multinational to develop the large zinc and lead deposits at Navan, County Meath. Sinn Féin's Research Section had produced a large amount of material linking the issue to that of the exploitation of off-shore oil and gas reserves and proposing an alternative statist development strategy with greater job-creating capacity.[110] On issues like this and the economic crisis, Sinn Féin members worked with members of the Communist Party and the Liaison Committee of the Labour Left. However, such cooperation was shortlived as Sinn Féin became more and more convinced that it was providing the serious intellectual and research capacity and should be in a position to reap the greatest political benefit from this work.[111] It was certainly the case that the contributions of people like Harris and other Sinn Féin members impressed even their critics[112] and that in this period the Officials emerged with a distinct persona in Dublin as the talented and articulate defenders of a statist strategy of economic development. At a time when the post-1959 policies of economic liberalization and attraction of foreign capital were faltering in a hostile international environment, there was scope for such an approach. It was particularly attractive to workers in the Republic's large public sector at a time when prominent Fine Gael members of the government were complaining of the 'parasitic' role that the public sector was playing. Defence of the public sector, and demands for its expansion into areas like energy and construction, ensured a growing audience for Sinn Féin's ideas in the public sector unions.[113]

Throughout this period of Dublin expansion in the mid-1970s the movement retained the secretive and conspiratorial side that was a legacy of its history. The input of intellectuals was organized through two 'secret' branches distinct from the ordinary, geographically based ones. Members of these branches were not open members of the organization and had little if anything to do with the activities of its ordinary members. Justified by reference to the possible victimization of individuals who had jobs in the media and the civil service, the 'secret' branches tended to constrict serious discussion of major revisions of party policy by the bulk of the membership. At the same time the very traditional republican self-designation of the movement as composed of a dedicated, self-sacrificing elite was now expressed in the transformed terms of the 'revolutionary vanguard' contemptuous of the 'social democrats' in the Labour Party and increasingly determined to displace the Communist Party. The dominant role which Sinn Féin, through its Research Section, played in the mobilization of a left critique of the Coalition's response to the economic crisis, allowed it to attract a substantial number of disillusioned Labour Party supporters.[114] The real, if limited prospects for political advance in Dublin which opened up after 1973 were a major reason for the consolidation of ideological revisionism in the Official movement.

The IIR was the first major documentary evidence that a part of the 'republican tradition' was willing to accept popular opinion when it violated a central tenet of republican faith. The clear evidence of mass support for economic liberalization, particularly the decisive vote for EEC membership, was a major blow to the social republican project in the Republic. The IIR was the belated recognition of this fact, and in an important sense it marks the departure of the Officials from the social republican tradition.

6

The Provisionals and the Rediscovery of Social Republicanism

In 1977 Jimmy Drumm, one of the group of older republicans who had played a central role in the emergence of the Provisionals in Belfast after August 1969, gave the annual address to the Wolfe Tone commemoration at Bodenstown. A traditionalist had been chosen to read out what was a withering critique of the main lines of Provisional strategy since 1970 and would publicly inaugurate a prolonged, contradictory and ultimately unresolved engagement with some of the central themes of social republicanism. Drumm complained of attacks on the Provisionals which accused them of 'having been devoid of political thinking, dependent entirely upon the bomb and the bullet'. At the core of the speech was a major reassessment of the 'armed struggle': 'We find that a successful war of liberation cannot be fought exclusively on the backs of the oppressed in the six counties, nor around the physical presence of the British Army. Hatred and resentment of this army cannot sustain the war, and the isolation of socialist republicans around the armed struggle is dangerous and has produced at least in some circles, the reformist notion that "Ulster" is the issue, which can somehow be resolved without the mobilization of the working-class in the 26 Counties. We need a positive tie in with the mass of the Irish people who have little or no idea of the suffering in the North because of media censorship and the consolidation of conservatism throughout the country. We need to make a stand on economic issues and on the everyday struggles of people. The forging of the strong links between the Republican movement and the workers of Ireland and radical trade unionists will create an irrepressible mass movement and will ensure mass support for the continuing armed struggle in the

North.'[1] The speech was notable precisely because the
'reformist' notion that 'Ulster is the issue' had been at the
centre of Provisional strategy since 1969. The Provisionals'
major policy statement, *Eire Nua* (1971), had, it is true,
provided for a four-province federal Ireland, and Ruairí
O'Brádaigh, president of Provisional Sinn Féin, had assured
Ulster Protestants that 'We would never ask you to join the
26-County state – we are trying to escape from it ourselves.'[2]
But as increasing northern disquiet with central aspects of *Eire
Nua* would soon make clear, it had never been more than a
constitutional froth on an armed struggle that had its own
dynamics, and increasingly these appeared to demand a
significant strategic reappraisal.

The immediate pressure for change came as a result of the
truce between the Provisionals and the Army and RUC,
which had lasted for most of 1975. This had left the
Provisionals severely weakened, and militarily and politically
divided and demoralized. This was the second time the
Provisionals had entered into negotiations with the British
government. In 1972 the first secretary of state for Northern
Ireland, William Whitelaw, had had six leading Provisionals,
including Gerry Adams, secretly flown to England for
negotiations.[3] These negotiations had come to nothing and
the associated truce had been brief, with no harmful effects on
the Provisionals' military capacity. But in 1975 the disruptive
effect of the truce flowed in large part from the analysis which
the leadership group – still largely Dublin based – made of the
British interest in negotiations. As one sympathetic observer
has described it: 'The leadership then, and in particular Daithi
O'Connaill (IRA Chief of Staff) believed that the British could
be negotiated into a settlement or at least that the appearance of
negotiations with the IRA would so destabilize the British
position in the eyes of Northern Unionists, and indeed of
established politicians North and South of the border, that
they would have no option but to disengage.'[4] The disruption
of British-sponsored reforms by the Ulster Workers' Council
strike was believed to have brought about a fundamental
reassessment of the link with Northern Ireland. This notion
was encouraged by the Northern Ireland Office negotiators,
who needed a truce to create the requisite atmosphere for the

release of internees. This was designed to allow the inauguration of a shift in security policy towards 'criminalization' and
away from those aspects of previous policy, like internment
and reliance on the British Army, which were seen as allowing
the Provisionals to represent their activities as part of a
legitimate national liberation struggle.[5] The coincidental
effects of economic recession on industry in Northern Ireland
were seen as evidence of an 'economic withdrawal'. Well after
the collapse of the truce, it was still being argued that 'the
rundown of the six counties, commercially and industrially,
has already begun, and this rundown is also taking place
coincidentally with military withdrawal.'[6] The wishful
thinking involved in such predictions was forcefully repudiated in Drumm's speech: 'The British Government is NOT
[emphasis in original] withdrawing from the Six Counties and
the substantial pull-out of businesses and the closing down of
factories in 1975 and 1976 were due to world economic
recession though mistakenly attributed to symptoms of
withdrawal. Indeed the British government is committed to
stabilising the Six Counties and is pouring in vast sums of
money to improve the area and assure loyalists.'[7] Drumm had
been involved, with his wife Maura, in the negotiations with
the NIO and long remained convinced of the correctness of
the strategy embodied in the truce.[8] The critique in his speech
represented a reassessment, the core ideas of which came from
Gerry Adams, in a series of contributions to *Republican News*
under the pen-name 'Brownie', written in Long Kesh between
1975 and 1977.

Adams, who had joined the republican movement in 1964,
had few of the reservations that led older republicans like
Drumm and Joe Cahill to drop out of the movement. With
other young IRA members like Joe McCann he had been
involved in housing and civil rights agitation which he later
wrote about in positive terms: 'We were also enjoying the
breakdown of republican isolation, the political exchanges and
interchanges, the pooling of resources and experiences arising
from the informal alliances which were being developed in the
"thick of the battle" between the different elements of the civil
rights movement. The traditional internalization of republican activities and their restriction to a chosen few now

seemed a thing of the past.'[9] The deinsulation of republicanism referred in Adams's case to the emerging common ground
– in analysis at least – with the main left ideologists of the
student-based People's Democracy organization, who saw in
the civil rights campaign a way of hastening a crisis of the
Northern state with a potentially revolutionary outcome.[10]
For Adams, the fundamental reason for opposition to the
national leadership was the 'reformism' of its position on
Northern Ireland, not the concept of the National Liberation
Front or the commitment to socialism. He dissociated himself
from those parts of the first major Provisional statement of
policy, which denounced the Officials for their 'extreme
socialism' and the NLF position, and for a number of months
after the split he and other IRA members in his Ballymurphy
area maintained a degree of independence from both Officials
and Provisionals.[11] Although he felt a degree of alienation
from the more traditional elements in Belfast and in the
national leadership, such differences were soon far out-
weighed by the common commitment to force a major crisis
in the northern state through aggressive military action. But
the impasse of the Provisional military campaign created the
conditions for Adams to reassert some of his 'lessons of 1968'.

The bankruptcy of the dominant military line was clearly
revealed in a defence of the Provisionals' campaign of
commercial bombings – a central component of the military
campaign since 1970 – written in 1976. It bluntly proclaimed
that its key purpose was to polarize political forces in
Northern Ireland and make British-sponsored reform impossible: 'It has disrupted parliamentary practice, helping to
topple Stormont and polarized the electorate to the extent that
the professional politicians are the victims of mutually in-
congruous manifestoes. Therefore it has forced British direct
rule into being and clarified that Westminster rule is imperialist: their army an army of occupation. The growth of reaction
isn't to be frowned upon. We can inflate its importance and at
our own leisure burst its credibility. As George Jackson, that
great Black revolutionary, once said. "What would help us, is
to allow as many right wing elements as possible to assume
political power".'[12] There was no mention of the Republic in a
portrayal of strategy which was content to label itself as a

'Ghetto Peoples' War'. It proclaimed that the biggest achievement of the bombing campaign was within the Catholic ghettoes themselves: 'behind those bombers, is a massive structure based on streets and districts, whose existence is dependent upon the active support and mandate of the people.'[13] (In fact, the article made clear that such support was limited to a minority in the ghettoes, focussing only on those who actively assisted or identified with the 'armed struggle'.) The degree of self-deception involved in this type of analysis – it also predicted imminent British withdrawal – was not shared by all leading Provisionals. In Long Kesh, a strain of leftist Provisionalism was emerging, with Adams at its centre. This displayed a much more realistic appreciation of the extent of popular identification with the 'armed struggle' and of British government intentions.

With some irony, conscious or unconscious, Adams chose an article on Mellows's *Jail Notes* to put forward a more realistic assessment of the limits of current Provisional strategy. Mellows had been a central figure in the ideological reorientation after 1962, and his reappearance in internal Provisional debates had to be treated delicately. Adams was careful to point out that the *Notes* had been labelled 'Communist' by the anti-Treatyites, thus establishing at the beginning the lack of credibility of such charges. The message of Mellows was 'the need to show an effective alternative to Brit/Free State institutions'. This was all the more necessary since the British government was seen as desiring, not withdrawal, but some internal accommodation between 'Orange and Green politicians' which could be foisted on a 'war-weary people'. The current resources of the Provisionals were realistically and critically assessed. The 'republican war machine' had survived 'despite attrition', but this was clearly insufficient as it countered only one facet of British involvement in Ireland: 'We need to counter the Brit economic, political, cultural, national and military fronts.' What was needed was a programme of 'active abstentionism' to win popular support for the Provisionals in the northern ghettoes and, just as important, to break the isolation of the 'anti-imperialist struggle' in Northern Ireland. Far from nearing its end, the building of a 'National Alternative' to 'Brit and Free State institutions' had not yet begun.[14]

In his prison contributions, Adams repeatedly stressed the need to avoid narrowing down the republican struggle to a military campaign in the north: 'We need to expand our struggle onto a Thirty-Two County basis. We are fighting for National Freedom but one major drawback appears to be that we are restricting ourselves a great deal to the North.'[15] Much of this approach demonstrated how extensively the *Ireland Today* analysis was appropriable by the Provisionals. This extended to the verbatim, but unacknowledged, reproduction of the analysis of the nature of imperialism and the characterization of the south as a 'neo-colony' of Britain.[16] As the Officials moved to jettison the legacy of Johnston and Coughlan, part of it was taken up by Adams and his supporters.

But the declaration of the need for an 'economic resistance' campaign encountered all the problems that had arisen a decade earlier. Adams sought to mobilize the masses in the Republic against their 'Vichy-type' government by exposing its various 'sell-out' policies, from foreign exploitation of mineral resources to the whole direction of post-1958 economic strategy, 'which offered Irish resources and Irish labour for exploitation on a joint-partnership basis between Irish and American capital'.[17] The economic 'sell-out' was linked to the 'collaboration' of southern governments with the British government's campaign against the 'Resistance Struggle'. Adams was prepared to admit that the national question was not at the top of the political agenda in the Republic: 'The overriding question is of course the National Question but there are many, many issues affecting people in the Free State in which we should be showing a lead – issues which are linked to the national question, and which can only be solved when it is solved, but issues which people do not relate as relevant to that issue.'[18] He instanced wages, equal pay for women, regressive taxation structures, capitulation to foreign mining companies and lack of resources in higher education. That all these were real issues was undeniable. The problem for the Provisionals was that there was no structural link between any of them and the 'national question', unlike the situation in Northern Ireland, where the deep-rooted structures of economic and occupational inequality between the Catholic and Protestant communities provided a material substratum for the reproduction of a communal nationalism of grievance. In the Republic, as the Officials had gradually perceived, any attempt to link agitation on economic and social issues to a nationalism bent on 'completing' the agenda of 1921 was doomed to popular repulsion if it went beyond the passionate pieties of Fianna Fáil. By the mid-1970s the undoubted reserves of sympathy for northern Catholics and sentimental support for the ideal of a united Ireland were counteracted by a recoil from the seemingly endless violence in the north. Any organization which sought to link economic or any other domestic issue to support for 'armed struggle' was doomed to perpetual marginality in the Republic.[19]

Predictably, the resistance to these themes came from those for whom it raised the spectre of the earlier dispute with the Officials. At the Sinn Féin Árd Fheis in 1977, one Donegal delegate urged the movement not to become entangled with international socialism or communism: 'we are not engaged in a class struggle.'[20] At the time, Ruairí Ó'Brádaigh disagreed: 'whatever one liked to call it we were struggling against a corrupt system in which 70% of the wealth was owned by 5% of the people.' The Provisionals were committed, he claimed, to 'revolution across the board – to the Socialist Republic'.[21] In fact his conception of socialism, defined at the Árd Fheis as the redistribution of wealth, was one developed precisely to counteract the 'extremist' class-struggle ideas which he and others believed Goulding had attempted to introduce in the 1960s. As Richard Davis has shown, *Eire Nua* had its origin in a programme of moderate socialism put forward in the first issue of the Provisional *An Phoblacht*. It was based on the Comhar na gComharsan (Neighbours' Cooperation) philosophy, traced by Ó'Brádaigh and Seamus Ó'Mongain to ideas developed by the IRA in the 1940s. In a situation of some similarity in so far as in both cases the 'philosophy' was a self-conscious attempt to distance the IRA from 'Communism', the emphasis was on 'Irish and Christian values'. In the 1940s there had been a discussion, clearly based on the papal encyclical *Quadragesimo Anno*, on 'distributive ownership', the duty of the state to protect a limited private property and the power of the community to appropriate the excess. As Davis sums it up: 'In its specific ideas, Comhar na gComharsan did not stray very far from the ideas of the great popes. Emphasis was laid on the nationalization of the monetary system through the commercial banks and the insurance companies. . . . It also followed the Douglas Credit movement, popular in the Great Depression, which appealed to many wishing to change the economic system without upsetting the class balance. In their suggestion for nationalizing key industries, mines, building land and fishing rights, the Provisionals fell well within Catholic guidelines which permitted government ownership of particular enterprises where such could be demonstrated to be in the public interest.'[22] The problem with *Eire Nua* for its critics arose precisely because its main purpose was to demonstrate that the Provisionals were not just reactionary militarists. Having accomplished this, it then assumed an increasingly formulaic existence. Critics of the lack of political development of the Provisionals focused on the rank and file's lack of clarity about its purpose – was it, for instance, 'a programme for action or an election manifesto'.[23] Its concrete proposals for 'Economic Resistance' consisted of little more than a list of heterogeneous and often conflicting components: 'the elements of resistance are farming co-ops, producer and consumer co-ops, credit unions and trade unions'.[24] The problem was not, as Bishop and Mallie claim, that it was 'a document written by Southerners from a Southern perspective': its chief critics, particularly Adams, were concerned because the Provisionals had made so little political progress in the Republic.[25] It was precisely because the programme was written by people who were convinced that the 'war in the north' would be won relatively quickly that it had so little to say to those increasingly sure that the prospect was of a 'long war' in which southern political advance would be of crucial importance.

Nevertheless despite the major opportunity which the 'anti-national' coalition government of Fine Gael and the Labour Party was held to offer – '. . . the Coalition has failed to provide safety valves by which the instinctive Irish urge for freedom can be tapped and controlled by the Government'[26] – there remained the major unspoken problem of the Provisionals' commitment to abstentionism in Dáil elections. Ruairí Ó'Brádaigh told the 1977 Árd Fheis that Sinn Féin was the fourth largest political party in the Republic, basing this calculation on the number of Sinn Féin seats in local authorities. Limits on progress were blamed on the 'Establishment's' censorship of Sinn Féin views through the recently toughened ban on radio and television interviews with party members.[27] But for some of those listening to him, the obvious limit was abstentionism itself: after all, the policy was not applied to candidates for local government in the Republic, the one area where there was some evidence of limited electoral support. The issue of political advance in the Republic was all the more pressing because of the anticipation that the despised Officials, now Sinn Féin – The Workers' Party, might make significant progress, unconstrained by abstentionism. Thus one of the most vituperatively anti-Official commentators in *Republican News*, after dismissing them as a serious force in the north, admitted that the situation was different in the Republic: 'The situation in the South is different. For there is a possible place for their type of reformist policies in the South. They are trying to take over the spot previously held by the Labour Party before it openly sided with reaction. While rejecting the national liberation struggle the Sticks are taking up in a militant fashion, a struggle against wage restraint, against cuts in social expenditure, against misuse of natural resources and curbs on civil liberties. Given no other credible reformist party such a campaign could make an impact. It should come as no surprise if the Sticks were to grow in the South. This could be a sticky problem for republicans and socialists.'[28] ('Stickies' or 'Sticks': a nickname for the Officials which grew out of early Official – Provisional competition. In this case the issue was sales of the republican emblem, the 'Easter Lily', sold for display on the annual commemoration of the 1916 Rising. The Official version was attached by adhesive, the Provisional by a pin. Of the two resulting nicknames, 'Stickies' and 'Pinheads', only one has lasted.)

Although the problem was recognized, there was little evidence of a capacity to deal with it, beyond the assertion of the need for Sinn Féin in the Republic to take up all 'popular social and economic struggles . . . within the revolutionary

framework of the national struggle.'[29] The 'Sticks' might be a
despised minority in the north but their potential in the
Republic demanded regular and intense denunciation: 'we
need to continue to pick up the Sticks, chew them over, and
spit them out into the gutter where they belong.'[30] But
although such tirades against the 'treacherous', 'pro–Brit' and
'Loyalist' Officials had a ready audience in northern ghettoes,
their effect in the Republic was severely limited. If the strength
of traditionalism made it impossible to raise the issue of
abstentionism, the radicals were reduced to exhortations, an
increasingly ultra-left rhetoric and complaints about the need
to break down 'partitionism' in the movement.

This latter problem was defined as 'the common Southern
view that the "Black North" is somewhere apart and that the
Brits are not a problem which directly affects the twenty-six
Counties'.[31] This mentality, which was admitted to affect not
only the broad mass of the population in the Republic but
traditional republican supporters as well, could be broken
down only by recognizing that 'in many cases in the south the
national question isn't of central importance' and that this
dictated republican involvement in issues that were of
immediate significance: 'unemployment, low wages, bad
housing, high prices . . . .'[32] It was hoped that the merger in
1979 of *An Phoblacht*, the Dublin-produced and more traditionalist paper and *Republican News*, under the editorship of
Danny Morrison in Belfast, would give a major impetus to the
radicalization of the movement and its progress in the
Republic. The first issue of the merged paper emphasized that
the struggle was a 32-county one and that it would result in a
very different 'Rising' from that in 1916: '. . . it will not occur
some Easter morning. It will be the coalescence of sympathy
and support in the south (which we shall have earned) with the
Resistance of northern Republicans to British Imperialism and
Loyalism.'[33] It focused on recent industrial unrest in the two
Irish states and claimed that the 'Labour situation' in the
Republic had a great revolutionary potential. However, it was
admitted that the republican movement in the Republic had
not demonstrated a capacity to work in these 'hitherto twilight
areas', and responded to the obvious rank-and-file apathy by
emphasizing that coverage of 'working class struggles . . .

doesn't mean we are going "sticky".'[34] The problem remained that the only way to maintain a distinctive Provisional approach to social and economic issues was to emphasize constantly that there could be no 'real' answer to the problems of working-class existence as long as partition remained, and that for all their significance these issues were secondary in 'the Revolution which consists primarily of the armed struggle and resistance in the ungovernable north'.[35] Thus although by the end of the 1970s the Provisionals' analysis and rhetoric had been radicalized, the change entailed a variant of social republicanism even more patently out of tune with key realities than the 1930s and 1960s versions.

In a speech at Bodenstown in 1979, Gerry Adams gave an assessment of the Provisionals' position after a decade of 'war'. It was a view which mixed a sober assessment of the limits of 'armed struggle' with an essentially unrealistic view of how this could be complemented by southern strategy. He claimed that the IRA was winning, but that this was insufficient, for British withdrawal could lead to 'the establishment of a thirty-two county neo-colonial Free State'. This would be prevented only by 'more than a military alternative to the establishment'. Once again he emphasized the need for an agitational struggle in the Republic, 'linking up republicans with other sections of the working class'. But he acknowledged that 'our most glaring weakness to date lies in our failure to develop revolutionary politics and to build a strong political alternative to so-called constitutional politics'.[36] The main obstacle to such a development was identified as lack of commitment and discipline, a typically republican focus on will rather than circumstance. That the problem was deeper than this would gradually become apparent, and the question of the role of abstentionism would emerge. When it did, it was overshadowed by developments in the north which led to a major increase in the Provisionals' political involvement.

'Active' Republicanism and Politics

One of Adams's major concerns about the situation of the Provisionals in the post-truce period was their growing isolation from the majority of people in the Catholic ghettoes. The demoralization amongst republicans caused by the failure of the truce and predictions of British withdrawal was complemented by a more wide-spread 'war-weariness', partly manifest in the widespread support for the temporary spasm of the Peace Movement in 1976. Adams commented from Long Kesh: 'the rate of attrition is increasing in Republican areas and the Brit news media is spreading stories to increase the confusion within the ghettoes. . . . The Brit intends to isolate us from the people.'[37] His answer was a vaguely defined 'Active Republicanism' that took up all the issues of the 'people's struggle for survival'. At that time it was clear that the main priority was reinvigorating the republican hard core by putting more resources into the institutions which had emerged in the ghettoes as a result of the prolonged violence and resultant communal involution. The 'war machine' needed to be surrounded by a popular infrastructure of 'very necessary things like housing committees, street committees, defence groups, advice centres, local policing, people's taxis etc.'[38] Concern for the isolation of the IRA was exacerbated by the serious inroads which a modernized and reorganized RUC, now assuming a role of primacy over the army under a new security strategy, was making. At the end of 1976, the head of the RUC could report that complete Provisional units had been eliminated in various parts of the north, and that charges against IRA members had more than doubled compared with 1975.[39] In 1977, the Labour secretary of state for Northern Ireland, Roy Mason, was claiming that the 'tide had turned against the terrorists'.[40] In fact, 1978 brought clear signs that the Provisionals had been able to regroup and reorganize, moving to augment the traditional geographically based structure of brigades and battalions with a cellular structure designed to be much less penetrable by the security forces. The British Army's mislaid intelligence document *Northern Ireland: Future Terrorist Trends* (November 1978) commented admiringly that 'there is a stratum of intelligent, astute and experienced terrorists who provide the backbone of the organization . . . our evidence of the calibre of rank-and-file terrorists does not support the view that they are merely mindless hooligans. . . .' The report did note a political weakness – 'there is seldom much support even for traditional protest marches' – but downplayed its significance: 'by reorganizing on cellular lines, PIRA has become much less dependent on public support than in the past and is less vulnerable to penetration by informers.'[41]

Adams publicly quoted the report, particularly the part which claimed that 'the campaign of violence is likely to continue while the British remain', as a 'projection of the inevitable and final defeat of British Imperialism'.[42] Despite this, the Provisionals were profoundly disturbed by their apparent political weakness, even in the supposed heartlands of northern militancy. Since the abolition in 1976 of 'political status' for people sentenced for terrorist offences, the Provisionals had put the issue of 'Prisoners of War' at the centre of attempts to build a popular 'anti-imperialist' alliance. Most IRA members convicted in the non-jury Diplock Courts after 1976 refused to wear ordinary prison clothes or to work as directed. When they were refused their own clothes they went 'on the blanket', and when the prison authorities attempted to pressurize them by refusing exercise and other facilities, they retaliated by adopting the 'dirty protest' – smearing their cells with excrement.[43] But by the end of 1979 the attempts of the Provisionals to mobilize support for the 360 'blanket men' in the H Blocks at Long Kesh had been noticeably unsuccessful. Thus Anthony Cronin, a journalist with strong republican sympathies noted of the position in the Republic: 'the fact is that response to the Provisionals' appeals on any issue whatsoever, H-Block included is really dead in the south. Even if the old civil strife and massacre of the Catholics situation were to come about at last, the south would not respond'.[44] Gerry Foley, an American Trotskyist who had fervently supported the Officials in their militarist period and then transferred his loyalties to the Provisionals, was moved to admit: 'the limitations of the Provisionals' campaign had become evident. It was now seen by larger and larger sections of the ghetto population as getting nowhere, more and more out of control and a source of unnecessary hardship.'[45]

At an internal conference of Sinn Féin on the prisoners' issue similar points were made. Joe Cahill, head of the 'POW Department' admitted that 'with a couple of notable exceptions, the main demonstrations on the H-Blocks issue have remained within the nationalist ghetto areas of the six counties and have only mobilized republican supporters'. Little support had been developed in the Republic and Adams concluded that 'the movement has to recognize that so far, in mobilizing on the H-Blocks, it has failed to fully realize its potential'.[46] He blamed the political exclusivism of Sinn Féin, which had insisted that it would only work in cooperation with groups and individuals who not only supported the prisoners but also the 'armed struggle'. Certainly the Provisionals' exclusivism had long been complained about by the various tiny 'anti-imperialist' left groups like the People's Democracy. In the European Elections in 1979 the former student activist and ex-MP for Mid-Ulster, Bernadette McAliskey (previously Devlin), stood as an 'anti-repression' candidate focusing on the H-Blocks issues. Sinn Féin boycotted the election and denounced McAliskey: 'an anti-repression ticket which will bring along to the polling booths those otherwise disillusioned with such procedures, or hostile to the EEC, is just what the Brussels bureaucrats desire.'[47] Although McAliskey obtained fewer than 40,000 votes, the result encouraged some to raise the issue of whether better use could not have been made of the European and Westminster elections in 1979 by running prisoners as candidates. In an interview, a member of the IRA Army Council would admit: 'perhaps we could have made more propaganda than we did. . . . Certainly this question of standing candidates is one of continued dialogue within the movement. There is no principle involved in the question of whether or not to stand candidates.'[48] In fact, even the most militant supporters of 'active' republicanism shrank from the possibility of electoral rejection. It took the unwelcome initiative of the prisoners in starting a hunger strike for political status to force a reluctant leadership into electoral politics.[49]

The first wave of hunger strikes petered out before the end of 1980. A second, more determined wave led by Bobby Sands, the Provisionals' commanding officer in the H-Blocks, began in March 1981. As early as November 1980, the H-Block committees were turning out parades comparable in size to the great civil rights marches. The hunger strikers and their supporters, as Richard Kearney put it, 'articulated a tribal voice of martyrdom, deeply embedded in the Gaelic, Catholic nationalist tradition'.[50] The death of the MP for Fermanagh–South Tyrone (a strong republican sympathiser and semi-abstentionist) shortly after Sands went on the hunger strike created a major opportunity. Again the Sinn Féin leadership was extremely nervous about a prisoners' candidate, and was precipitated into the election by McAliskey's declaration of interest in running. Sands's election was a major propaganda victory soon to be augmented by the election of two other hunger strikers in the Republic's general election in June 1981 and, after Sands's death, of his election agent, Owen Carron, as MP for the Fermanagh – South Tyrone constituency.[51] The Provisionals' relationship to the Catholic masses in the north was transformed by the hunger strikes and the resultant ten deaths. By October 1981, they had to accept Thatcher's determination not to concede political status, though they won substantial concessions on clothing and association. However, they enjoyed a major boost to their self-confidence and electoral fortunes, revealed after their decision to contest the Northern Ireland Assembly elections in 1982 and the Westminster election in 1983. In the first they got 10.1% of the poll to the SDLP's 18.8%; in the second they cut even further into the SDLP's support with 13.4% of the poll to the SDLP's 17.9%; and Adams was returned as MP for West Belfast.

Sinn Féin's ambitions in Northern Ireland were encouraged by the obvious disquiet which the 64,191 first preference votes in the Assembly elections had caused in the Irish and British governments. The Irish prime minister, Garret Fitzgerald, gave an interview on BBC television in which he spoke in anxious terms of the need for talks with the British government to prevent 'destabilization' in Northern Ireland. The republican newspaper commented: 'any further advance by Sinn Féin, Fitzgerald correctly construes as a fatal blow to the SDLP. And Sinn Féin emerging as the majority voice of Northern Nationalists would obviously turn traditional Dublin policy on its head.'[52] In March 1983 the Dublin government, under pressure from the SDLP leadership, announced the establishment of the New Ireland Forum, designed to produce a consensus among the 'democratic' parties on 'the manner in which lasting peace and stability can be achieved in a new Ireland through the democratic process'. Adams denounced it as a 'life-line for a party under threat from Sinn Féin'.[53] Increasingly, the SDLP would be portrayed as an effete, declining party of the Catholic middle class, facing imminent extinction due to their 'collaborationist' role. Although the dominant emphasis was placed on the 'revolutionary nationalism' of Sinn Féin, the 'class nature' of the struggle was also frequently referred to. Thus in the campaign for the 1983 Westminster election, it was claimed that 'the class divisions between the SDLP and Sinn Féin are becoming clearly defined . . . as the nationalist middle class attempts to maintain its electoral sway and influence over the increasingly radicalized nationalist people, the bulk of whom are working class.'[54] The Catholic Hierarchy was denounced for its support for the SDLP and its fear of 'the growing independent-mindedness of its flock'.[55] Such militant optimism was encouraged by the substantial increase in electoral support in the Westminster election. Ruairí Ó'Brádaigh hailed the results as 'a turning point . . . the Sinn Féin vote increased from 64,000 to 103,000 and its share of the Nationalist vote has increased from 35% to 42%. . . . In the 1985 local elections in the Six Counties Sinn Féin will finally overtake the SDLP and nationalist politics will undergo their most radical and significant change since 1918'.[56]

It was now presumed in many quarters that the surge for Sinn Féin was irresistible. It was not to be; Adams and his forces were soon checked. Danny Morrison was heavily outpolled by the SDLP's leader John Hume in the European election of June 1984 (91,476 votes to 151,399). Hume fought a subtle campaign which effectively surrendered much nationalist territory to the Provisionals and sought instead to win moderate Catholic support away from other parties and thus swell his total. Even the normally cautious Adams had portrayed the election as part 'of the work of supplanting the SDLP as the party representing the Nationalist people in the Six Counties . . . the smashing of the SDLP is an ongoing process.'[57] In the aftermath of the setback, Adams consoled supporters with the claim that the vote was a 'principled, republican vote, as opposed to a nationalist or Catholic vote

. . . it is ideologically sound. . . .'[58] He also obliquely criticized the IRA; 'there is a number of people who while they voted for us in June 1983, may not have been able to tolerate some aspects of IRA operations . . . in which civilians were killed or injured'. He referred to his statement at the 1983 Árd Fheis 'that revolutionary force must be controlled and disciplined so that it is clearly seen as a symbol of our people's resistance'.[59] In fact 1983 had seen the first of a string of 'fraternal' calls from the expanding Sinn Féin political organization for a 'refinement' of IRA activity to minimize adverse electoral repercussions.[60] Although Adams publicly welcomed the setback as 'an injection of reality', he still claimed that Sinn Féin had not hit an electoral ceiling in Northern Ireland: 'I think that if we work hard, if we pitch our campaign right, if Republicans refine their tactics that we can win a majority of the nationalist electorate.'[61] The 'real battle between the SDLP and Sinn Féin', which he had predicted in the 1985 local government elections, while resulting in a substantial new Sinn Féin presence on Northern Ireland's local authorities (59 councillors) still left the organization with electoral support at 11.8%, a substantial vote but indicating little progress in the struggle to supplant the SDLP.

Sinn Féin and the Anglo-Irish Agreement

Despite the evidence of a possible 'peaking' in Sinn Féin's electoral surge, the Thatcher government was soon to initiate a major shift in policy which would radically change the political context in which the Provisionals operated. In December 1980 after the failure of her secretary of state for Northern Ireland, Humphrey Atkins, to get an inter-party agreement on devolution, Margaret Thatcher had met the Irish prime minister, Charles Haughey, for discussions in Dublin. In the joint communiqué, Thatcher acknowledged Britain's 'unique relationship' with Ireland; she permitted the establishment of joint study groups to find ways of expressing this uniqueness in 'new institutional structures', and committed herself to future discussions on 'the totality of relationships within these islands'. The Sinn Féin response came in a substantial analysis which emphasized that a major shift in British policy was possible. Arguing that the main British interest in partition was a strategic one, it accepted that this might now be better defended by a shift away from reliance on the 'Loyalist veto': 'the policy shift involves, at the very minimum, acknowledging that an all-Ireland dimension is necessary to satisfy nationalist aspirations whilst maintaining the Union (at least for the time being) to satisfy Unionist aspirations . . . this shift could lead in the direction of a new constitutional – or as the summit communiqué put it (to avoid drawing too much Unionist fire) "institutional" arrangement between Britain and the Free State, even, at its maximum limit, meaning a thirty-two county, partitioned neo-colonial state.'[62] There were three possible variations on this 'dangerous option': devolution plus an institutionalization of the 'unique relationship'; a condominium where the north would be jointly ruled by Britain and the Republic; and a new 32-county confederal arrangement. All variants were rejected as maintaining the 'six-county state' and not really challenging British domination, but it was recognized that any of them could have a powerful appeal to at least sections of the Catholic population in Northern Ireland.

The deterioration in Anglo-Irish relations brought about by the hunger strikes and Haughey's refusal to support Britain during the Falklands War ensured that little more was heard of such possibilities until the electoral gains of Sinn Féin had resulted in the setting up of the New Ireland Forum. The Forum Report, when it was published, put forward three options: a unitary Irish state, a federal Ireland and joint authority. Each was brusquely dismissed by Thatcher when she met Garret Fitzgerald in November 1984. The subsequent developments were perceptively summed up by Danny Morrison: 'At the Chequers London/Dublin summit in November 1984 Thatcher made her infamous "Out, Out, Out" reply. Dublin and the SDLP were shattered. Republicans were proved correct. However, there were allowances made in the comuniqué issued at the time for further intergovernmental developments, which went virtually unnoticed by republicans and most others. Sometime afterwards (and probably as a delayed reaction to the October Brighton bomb), Thatcher realised the damage that her "Out, Out, Out" remarks had done to the cause of "constitutional nationalism". Dublin also recruited intense political lobbying from the US Senate and Congress for a British change of heart.'[63] The Anglo-Irish Agreement signed by Thatcher and Fitzgerald at Hillsborough in November 1985 was described by Adams as 'a coming-together of the various British strategies on an all-Ireland basis, with the Dublin government acting as the new guarantor of partition'.[64] It was also recognized that the creation of structures like the Inter-Governmental Conference and the permanent secretariat staffed by British and Irish civil servants and situated at Maryfield in the Belfast suburbs, were developments of major significance: 'Dublin has been granted a consultative role in Northern Ireland affairs far short of the least demand of the three Forum options – but a big step forward as far as Dublin and the SDLP are concerned, as it represents a significant recognition of them from Britain.'[65]

The Sinn Féin leadership was seriously concerned about the various possible effects of the Agreement: 'it is an attempt to isolate and draw popular support away from the republican struggle while putting a diplomatic veneer on British rule, injecting a credibility into establishment 'nationalism'. . . and insulating the British from international criticism of their involvement in Irish affairs.'[66] An earlier consideration of the possible implication of such a major shift in British policy had warned: 'the increasingly sophisticated approach of the enemy means that good 'old-fashioned' nationalism and 'pure' militarism will be an insufficient republican response.'[67] The previous tendencies to denounce the 'middle class' and collaborationist role of the SDLP might have been expected to intensify in the aftermath of the Agreement. In fact, increasingly Adams and his supporters would distance themselves from their previous 'ultra-leftism'. Thus in his *Politics of Irish Freedom*, Adams noted that the emergence of Sinn Féin 'may have unnecessarily brought out some of the class differences between ourselves and the SDLP leadership'. The differences, while real, should not be emphasized too much: '. . . it might have been better in this phase of the independence struggle if there could have been some kind of general unity, in which both parties would agree to disagree on social and economic issues and maximize pressure on points of agreement.'[68] Clearly, it was increasingly perceived that just as the Hillsborough Agreement was aimed at isolating and marginalizing Sinn Féin, so some of the policy positions and rhetoric adopted by that organization were achieving the same result.

Adams, who had earlier encouraged the movement to take up social and economic issues, was now anxious to stress the dangers of pushing such 'leftism' too far. He was particularly concerned with those in Sinn Féin who wanted the republican movement to style itself 'socialist republican': 'this must narrow the potential support-base of the republican movement and enable other movements to claim that they are "republican" though they are not socialist; for example, Fianna Fáil or the SDLP. This carries the danger of letting these parties off the hook, for their leaders will be able to claim that they are the real republicans and that what the "republicans" are offering is some foreign importation called socialism.'[69] The encouragement of a new radical note in Sinn Féin's repertoire in the early 1980s had led to the creation of trade-union and womens' departments, and the cultivation of the left fringe of the British Labour Party and the small number of sympathetic Labour MPs. Sinn Féin gained many new members as a result of the hunger strike mobilization, most with no 'military' background, and some of the influx were from left sects like the PD. The modernization of the organization's profile associated with this influx now appeared to have gone too far. In 1985, against the advice of the leadership, the Árd Fheis voted to support 'a woman's right to choose', hardly a vote catcher in the Catholic ghettoes. Adams, always careful to protect Sinn Féin from charges that it was a 'Marxist' organization, was by 1986 seriously concerned that certain aspects of the organization's public persona were dangerously extreme.[70]

Rather than attacks on the SDLP's class nature, Sinn Féin began to issue calls for talks to 'maximize not fracture Nationalist unity'. Such calls had been made before 1985 but had sat incongruously with the bitter denunciations of the constitutional nationalists in the republican press. Unlike some of the 'greener elements' in the SDLP, who had periodically expressed an interest in talks,[71] Hume had refused on the basis that the real power in the republican movement lay with the IRA's Army Council. This position was maintained for as long as it seemed possible that the Hillsborough Agreement would seriously erode Sinn Féin's support base. However, as some of the more extravagant hopes raised in the nationalist population by the Agreement were dissipated, new possibilities opened up for Sinn Féin.

Hume had always insisted that if the British 'faced down' Unionist opposition – 'lanced the Protestant boil' was his vivid phrase – Unionists would be forced to reassess their position and reach an accommodation with nationalist Ireland. He confidently predicted such a breakthrough before the end of 1986 and continued with this optimism in the early months of 1987:[72] 'the consequences of [the Agreement] for the Unionist community are that they have to consider the choice, either they continue to live apart, only now they are not being underpinned by a British government and they no longer have a veto on policy in Northern Ireland, or they decide to live together with us.'[73] However, Unionist acquiescence in the Agreement was occasioned largely by the economic benefits of the Union: it did not presage any reassessment of relations with nationalist Ireland. Hume gradually came to realize throughout the course of 1987 that his earlier assessments had been over-sanguine. He also had to take into account the balance of forces within the nationalist community. The Westminster election in 1987 produced little evidence of a Sinn Féin electoral decline: the party won 11.4% of the vote and Adams kept his seat with an increased majority. By early 1988 Hume and some of his senior colleagues were involved in a series of discussions with Sinn Féin which went on from March to September and represented the only serious dialogue between physical force and constitutional nationalism since the onset of the present 'Troubles'.

The heart of the difference between the parties was the SDLP's contention that the Anglo-Irish Agreement demonstrated that 'Britain has no interest of her own in remaining in Ireland, that she has no military or economic interests and that if Irish people reached agreement among themselves on, for

example Irish unity, that Britain would facilitate it, legislate
for it and leave the Irish to govern themselves.'[74] Sinn Féin
denied that Britain was neutral, but its list of interests that
supposedly impelled Britain to maintain partition was not
impressive; the key interests were strategic and economic.
Ironically, Danny Morrison had earlier accepted that 'the
occupation of the North is a net financial loss to, and a
considerable drain on, British revenue.'[75] Now, although the
British annual subvention to the north was admitted to be £1.6
billion, it was denied that this negated any British economic
interest in Ireland. This however, turned out to be the defence
of British investment and that of its 'multinational capitalist
allies' from 'the potential or perceived threat posed by an
independent Irish state'. Such preemptive ruling-class calculation was also supposed to determine Britain's other interest,
which was strategic: 'strategic interests are now the most
important consideration in Britain's interference in Ireland.
Quite apart from the very real, if somewhat exaggerated fear
among the British establishment, that an Ireland freed from
British influence could become a European "Cuba", even the
prospect of a neutral Ireland is regarded as a serious threat to
British and NATO's strategic interests.'[76] As Paul Bew and I
have argued at greater length elsewhere, the strategic interest
of Ireland for Britain is much less than it was in the 1940s,
when British thinking was dominated by the maritime losses
of World War Two, and it has also become clear that Irish
governments are prepared to undertake to join NATO if the
partition question is solved.[77] Even more significantly, there
is evidence that Sinn Féin's leadership is itself less than
convinced of these 'explanations'. Clearly, they imply that a
British withdrawal will lead to a united Ireland where radical
forces will be in the ascendant. However, Adams had earlier
explained to a British audience the unlikelihood of such an
eventuality: 'certainly it is Sinn Féin's policy to see established
in Ireland a democratic, socialist republic based upon the 1916
Proclamation. We would prefer that such a non-aligned nation
would evolve fairly immediately from a British withdrawal. . . . Regrettably our organization, particularly in the
26 Counties is presently too small and lacking in influence to
capitalize on the potential dividends accruing to the Repub-

lican movement as the organization which finally ended eight centuries of British interference in Ireland. Notwithstanding this state of play, one finds the "Ireland another Cuba" scenario often being propounded by right-wingers as an excuse for maintaining partition.'[78] In the talks, Hume argued for an IRA ceasefire to facilitate a 'powerful response within Britain itself',[79] while Sinn Féin and the IRA leadership made it clear that this was out of the question. Despite this gulf, the talks ended with both sides claiming that the 'dialogue' would continue and Sinn Féin emphasizing its view of their import-ance. While the talks were taking place, Adams issued a call for Fianna Fáil and other political parties in the Republic to join in a 'national consensus on Irish reunification', adopting a joint strategy to achieve it: 'such a strategy must involve primarily a consensus of the clear national majority on Irish reunification as a policy objective and an international and diplomatic offensive to bring political pressure to bear on the British government to concede to the Irish people their national rights. . . .'[81] Although he repeated the standard anathema against the Anglo-Irish Agreement – its objective was 'the maintenance of Partition' there were signs that the Sinn Féin leadership saw very positive, if unintended, results flowing from some aspects of the Agreement.

Adams has referred more than once to the 'educational' nature of the Agreement: 'one of the shocks for loyalists in recent years has been the educational nature of Hillsborough. We have been saying to loyalists for decades the British government will use and abuse them. There is no British loyalty. The British government have interests. When the British government want to dump them they will do so. Some loyalists have already started to take that on board.'[82] Thus, the disorienting effect of Hillsborough upon sections of Unionist opinion has been a positive one. Further, the Agreement has deepened the division between British and Unionist opinion: 'the British public watched loyalist oppo-sition to what very many people see as a very mediocre treaty. Their response and behaviour alerted a lot of people to the fascist nature of loyalism.'[83] Adams also discerned signs that useful changes are emerging in constitutional national-ism. Hume, convinced that the failure of the Unionists to dislodge the Agreement demonstrated a fundamental shift in the balance of forces, argued that the next stage was for the Unionist leadership to 'sort out' its relationship with Dublin through an all-Ireland constitutional conference. Although one of the stated objectives of the Hillsborough Agreement was the creation of devolved institutions of government in Northern Ireland, Adams was pleased to note that Sinn Féin's bitter opposition to 'diversions like internal devolutionary Stormont arrangements' was increasingly mirrored in the SDLP.[84] Important also was the return of Fianna Fáil to power in the Republic's general election in 1987. Charles Haughey had criticized the Hillsborough Agreement on the predictable nationalist grounds that the 'majority consent' clause in the Agreement was an acceptance in principle of the northern Unionist majority's right to refuse to join a united Ireland. It was a renunciation of the claim to unity embodied in the Irish constitution.[85] This position, while initially unpopular with public opinion, allowed Fianna Fáil to define itself as 'the lone party with the nationalist forces'.[86] Once in office however, Haughey gave a guarded commitment to working the Agreement to extract reforms for northern nationalists while continuing to reiterate that the only way forward was an all-party conference to discuss a possible federal Ireland. Sinn Féin would be invited to such a conference if IRA violence ceased.[87] The Anglo-Irish Agreement, which had been seen as a measure to marginalize and isolate Sinn Féin had come, in less than three years, to produce radically different results. Most crucially, it had shifted the ideological balance in nationalist Ireland in a direction which Sinn Féin could only welcome.

The SDLP's case was that an IRA ceasefire would allow a united approach by all the nationalist parties in Ireland to the British government with a 'peaceful and comprehensive approach to achieving self-determination in Ireland'.[88] Sinn Féin had always poured scorn on the SDLP's desire to attain unity with the consent of Unionists, on the not unrealistic assumption that consent was unlikely to be forthcoming. The 1988 talks did little to persuade them of the redundancy of the 'armed struggle' and had they been persuaded there is little evidence that the IRA would have listened to them. It is unlikely that Adams and his colleagues failed to be impressed by Hume's very concrete vision of fundamental constitutional change. Such optimism, baseless though it may have seemed to more dispassionate observers, was nonetheless an increasing ideological reality. It brought Sinn Féin dramatically in from the cold, as the SDLP declared that 'politically the positions of the SDLP and Sinn Féin are not unduly removed from one another and are bridgeable'.[89] In response, Sinn Féin leaders explained to their activists the errors of past 'ultra-leftism'. At a conference of Sinn Féin activists held during the talks with the SDLP, Tom Hartley, the general secretary of Sinn Féin, explained the need for a 'more structured and political way' of relating to the SDLP: 'since the beginning of its electoral strategy, Sinn Féin has been in confrontation with the SDLP. . . . As a party we have tended to see the SDLP as collaborators. Because of this we have a blinkered view of the SDLP. The Sinn Féin view has always allowed for a well-defined ideological separation to take place. The SDLP have now emerged as our class enemy. As a result we have found it more difficult to bring broader sections of the Nationalist population into struggle. We are now thrust into a full headlong clash with the SDLP which restricts our development into wider areas of the Nationalist community.'[90] Already the call by some IRA prisoners for the 'upgrading of the socialist content of the party'[91] had been sidelined; as Danny Morrison explained: 'Sinn Féin, as its leadership maintains, is not a Marxist organisation, and indeed many of its members and leaders, including Gerry Adams and Martin McGuinness are committed Catholics.'[92] In 1986, Adams had disabused a journalist who had claimed that Sinn Féin asked people to vote for socialist and republican policies: 'I don't think socialism is on the agenda at all at this stage except for political activists of the left. What's on the agenda now is an end to Partition. You won't even get near socialism until you have national independence.'[93] This was in stark contrast to the positions taken up in the early phase of the 'long war' strategy. In an earlier critique of the movement's lack of political development, Adams had castigated those who thought the armed struggle by itself could establish a 'Democratic Socialist Republic'. The best conditions for a British withdrawal would be created by the IRA in alliance with a radical popular movement 'capable of articulating not only the Republican Movement's position but also of being representative of all those with the commitment to a socialist republic'.[94]

In 1986 the Sinn Féin Árd Fheis voted to remove the ban on attendance in the Republic's parliament from the constitution. A minority of traditionalists led by Ó'Brádaigh and O'Connell walked out and created a new organization, Republican Sinn Féin. In his presidential address, Adams upbraided those who identified politics with 'constitutionalism' and the 'stickies' as having 'little concept of the class nature of the struggle'.[95] Again he reiterated that the most important task was to develop an all-Ireland political struggle: 'while consolidating our base in the 6 Counties, we must develop a popular struggle in the 26 Counties to complement the struggle in the 6 County area.' Sinn Féin was still an isolated organization, particularly in the Republic, where it was 'a party apart from the people, proud of our past but with little involvement in the present and only dreams for the future'.[96] The way out of isolation was by 'approaching people at the level they understand. This is the sad and unfortunate reality of the dilemma facing us. . . . This means Sinn Féin getting among people in the basic ways which people accept.'[97] The implication was in many ways similar to the social republicanism of the 1960s – 'projects of economic, social or cultural resistance'.[98] But this time there was to be no downplaying of 'our republican gut': 'while developing the struggle in the 26 Counties we must never lose sight of our national objectives.'[98] Strong support for the 'armed struggle' would be maintained and delegates doubtful of the new direction may have been encouraged by a previous decision of the General Army Convention – the first for 16 years – to support the ending of abstention from the Dáil.[99]

Adams warned delegates not to expect a breakthrough in the next election – the election after that would be the first major test of Sinn Féin's ability to win major support.[100] But even he may have been shocked by the miserable performance of Sinn Féin in the 1987 general election for the Dáil, when it got a mere 1.9% of the poll. An article in Sinn Féin's journal

Iris noted that 'for all complaints about Section 31 [the legislative ban on Sinn Féin appearing on radio or TV in the Republic], garda harassment, etc., most of them [Sinn Féin members] knew it was a fairly accurate reflection of how ordinary people viewed Sinn Féin'. Although anticipating that the new Fianna Fáil government would introduce major public expenditure cuts, creating the conditions for a 'modest swing to the left', it admitted that this would most likely benefit the Workers' Party, as Official Sinn Féin had become, and the Labour Party. It would take a long time for Sinn Féin to shake off the 'burden of history. . . . Southern workers see Sinn Féin as a party that avoided domestic class issues by concentrating on the national question' and this could only be compensated for by 'the long and sometimes painfully slow effort of involving itself in working class and community struggles'.[101]

Adams, perhaps too influenced by the irruption of Sinn Féin in northern elections, was dangerously exposed in the adoption of this southern strategy. His grasp of southern politics is less than sure. His hopes for the expansion of the Sinn Féin vote have been expressed in terms of winning working-class support from the Workers' Party and the Labour Party on the basis that they are both 'reformist', and the former 'two-nationist' as well. This implies a heavy emphasis on the 'revolutionary' nationalism of Sinn Féin, the raising of just that syndrome of issues which he also recognizes the mass of the working class in the Republic is not 'ready' for.[102] In fact, the major party from which Sinn Féin might hope to take support is Fianna Fáil. As Peter Mair puts it: '. . . the increased profile of Sinn Féin, both North and South, inevitably stimulates a more militant position among those voters who would welcome unity almost regardless of the cost . . . history and tradition suggest that these are more likely to be inclined towards Fianna Fáil.[103] Mair's important analysis of surveys of popular attitudes to Northern Ireland in the Irish Republic registers the continued existence of a 'sea of territorial nationalist commitment'. The proportion of survey respondents approving of Irish unity was 74% in the year the Forum reported.[104] Within this sea, Adams would be encouraged by the increase in levels of sympathy for the IRA.

Thus, those reporting actual approval for the IRA rose from 2% in 1978 to 5% in 1984 – just slightly above their share of the poll in the 1984 European election.[105] More significant was the group of respondents who indicated an admiration for the motives or ideals of the IRA, while disapproving of their methods; this rose from 32% in 1978 to 41% in 1980, falling to 39% in 1984. The long years of Fianna Fáil control of the state had produced a calcified irredentist political culture which increasingly formed the main basis of Sinn Féin aspiration in the Republic. As Adams puts it, quoting a *bête noir* of Sinn Féin:'In all the different walks of Irish life there is a grudging respect for the concept of republicanism. As Conor Cruise O'Brien has pointed out, republicanism is in a sense the conscience of the Irish people. There is a feeling that if the Rising of 1916 was . . . right, then the resistance in 1969 was right and in 1986 is right as well. There is a tolerance and an ambivalence because in the back of people's minds is the notion that there is some logic and rectitude to what republicans are saying.'[106] As it became increasingly clear that the appeal of Sinn Féin on economic and social issues was rebuffed by some sections of the working class because of their association with northern violence, the only hope of the Adams strategy lay in an appeal to the undoubtedly large reservoirs of nationalist sentiment in the southern electorate. The problem here is that outside of a few border constituencies in a time of major crisis in the north, southern nationalism is what O'Brien has called a 'low-intensity aspiration'. Thus in 1980 only 29% found paying more taxes an acceptable price for unity while 63% found it unacceptable. As Mair sums up his review, 'support for the aspiration for unity is quite pervasive . . . there is little support for anything beyond this.'[107] Such national self-deception is a shaky basis for a project of southern expansion. Yet it is increasingly what Adams is reduced to with repeated calls for a broad 'anti-imperialist' alliance to include the SDLP and Fianna Fàil: a bathetic reprise of the 1930s, when O'Donnell and his supporters sought such an alliance to prove to the masses the 'compromising' nature of middle class leaderships of the 'national struggle'. The dominant position in Congress was that the struggle for the Republic would have to be transformed into a class struggle to be successful. In the late 1970s and early 1980s this approach was temporarily influential in the Provisional leadership, but the apparent opportunities offered by developments since Hillsborough have produced a significant shift in emphasis. By the end of 1988 Adams had returned to the position of Sinn Féin in 1919 – one subsequently bitterly criticized by left republicans like O'Donnell. The issue is now declared to be self-determination, not the social content of 'freedom': 'the choice of the type of society chosen in that context is a matter for an Irish nation freed from outside interference.'[108] The emphasis is no longer on a 'Scenario for a Socialist Republic' but rather on building a new mass movement on an all-Ireland basis, 'open to everyone committed to the principle and objective of Irish self-determination'.[109] This movement, which would include non-republicans and non-socialists, could, Adams suggests, be built around a 'Freedom Charter' similar to that of the ANC.[110] The purpose of such a movement would be to expose the merely 'verbal nationalism' of the main constitutional nationalist parties, the SDLP and Fianna Fáil: 'Since at this stage the majority of nationalists look to constitutional nationalism for their political leadership, this requires placing pressure on constitutional politicians to take up and defend the interests of the people they claim to represent . . . either they get involved for fear of being discredited with their own base, in which case there will be a dynamic which will bring wider sections of the people into the struggle, or they will refuse, in which case they will be exposed. . . .'[111] This new strategic emphasis is very clearly influenced by the Sinn Féin leadership's positive evaluation of the talks with the SDLP. As Richard McAuley, a key Sinn Féin propagandist told the delegates to the 1989 Árd Fheis, 'the talks with Hume were extremely important and beneficial'.[112] Adams had earlier specified their importance in terms of narrowing the British state's options in Northern Ireland: 'It was a welcome sign, perhaps, that the SDLP recently said that they have no ideological adherence to devolution. The SDLP are a very important part of the equation in the Six Counties. The British need to have a party or an element which is nationalist or at least non-Unionist.'[113] The 'verbal commitment' given by the

SDLP leadership during the talks to the republican view – 'an internal Six County settlement is no solution and that the real question is how do we end the British presence in Ireland. . . .' – was seen as a major shift favouring Sinn Féin and representing a 'marker against which their activity can be judged . . . future involvement by the SDLP in a British Six County arrangement would be examined against the above.'[114]

The failure of the Anglo-Irish Agreement significantly to erode electoral support for Sinn Féin, the unlikelihood of any internal accommodation between constitutional nationalism and Unionism, and the increasingly all-Ireland flavour of the Fianna Fáil-SDLP discussions of the future development of the Agreement, encouraged the Sinn Féin leadership in their hopes of a quicker resolution of the conflict than had been envisaged at the beginning of the eighties. A central problem that emerged in this context was the IRA's 'armed struggle'.

As the Northern editor of the *Irish Times* commented on Adams's call for a 'national consensus', 'the logic of his demand for a broad nationalist front, including most of the political parties in the Republic, is the abandonment of violence by the IRA, but there is no indication that this is likely in anything Mr Adams has said. . . . He has always insisted that he has no influence over the activities of the IRA.'[115] There is some evidence of an appreciation by some Sinn Féin councillors of the existence of 'contradictions between the armed struggle and our political work', and even of a willingness to argue that the IRA is an electoral liability.[116] But the most that Adams could call for was a 'refining' of the armed struggle. He faced a major dilemma. Convinced that the politicization of the movement since the hunger strikes has produced major gains, including the unintended effects of the Anglo-Irish Agreement in increasing the profile of the 'national question', he also realized that Sinn Féin's participation in such a pan-nationalist consensus was precluded by the continuation of the IRA's violence. His responses have ranged from increasingly open criticism of IRA 'mistakes' like the Enniskillen Remembrance Day atrocity and the killings of Protestant 'civilians' by a unit which the IRA subsequently disbanded, to calls for a mass 'non-armed political movement' to work for national self-determination. Individuals within such a movement could have their own different positions on 'armed struggle' but the movement itself would not 'support or oppose' it.[117] The Sinn Féin leadership was as concerned with the danger of political isolation at the end of the 1980s as it was in 1977–78. There was, at the same time, no doubting their belief that only the continuation of the IRA's campaign would ensure British withdrawal. As Adams put it in an interview with *Playboy*, the British 'will leave only when they are forced to leave'.[118] By 1988, the military organization was better equipped than at any time in its history.[119] In September 1988, after a summer in which two Semtex bombs had killed fourteen British soldiers in Northern Ireland, a senior republican claimed: 'this is the final phase. The next eighteen months to two years will be critical because the IRA has the resources and will know then if it has the capacity to end it.'[120] It is unlikely that the calculations of Adams and other Sinn Féin leaders were so categorical. For not only could an intensified IRA campaign lead to attrition in the organization's own membership;[121] the response of the state in activities like house searches for arms could produce increasing war-weariness and resentment even in the strongest areas of support. It would also undermine Adams's public calls to the IRA for a 'refining' of its violence. At the 1989 Árd Fheis a substantial number of IRA 'mistakes' in previous months led Adams to inform the IRA publicly: 'you have to be careful and careful again'. The 'mistakes' were thought not to harm the 'republican base' but it was possible that the 'wider nationalist support base' would become demoralized and confused.[122] An intensified campaign also created difficulties for the Sinn Féin objective of building a broader anti-imperialist movement. In Tom Hartley's words, 'we need to break out of our narrowness and have the confidence to acknowledge that we do not hold the holy grail on the anti-imperialist question'.[123]

The attempt to build up Sinn Féin as a relatively independent political organization allowed its leadership to establish a degree of distance from the IRA, deemed essential for the maintenance and expansion of electoral support. At the same time, if IRA violence did bring about any significant shifts in British policy, Sinn Féin could benefit directly from it. It was a strategy whose obvious contradictions needed careful handling. One attempt to deal with them was Adams's declared hope that IRA violence would increasingly focus on British soldiers in Northern Ireland, Britain and Europe. Such deaths, it was hoped, would have more influence on British opinion as the twentieth anniversary of the arrival of British troops in August 1969 approached. Such a campaign was 'vastly preferable' to killing Ulster Protestants in the RUC and UDR: 'both communities here have suffered enough. It also diffuses the sectarian aspects of the conflict. . . .'[124] But an IRA campaign that restricted itself to British targets would be extremely difficult to organize and maintain, while pressure to continue killing local and softer targets has been irresistible.[125]

Adams has been at the centre of a relatively successful attempt to build up Sinn Féin as a substantial political organization, with some degree of distance from the IRA. Its councillors, advice centre workers, trade-union, women's and cultural organizations have created a broad infrastructure with a significant presence in many of the major concentrations of Catholic population in Northern Ireland. Nonetheless, if substantial progress outside the republican hard core is not made, major dangers become apparent. One is that warned of by its more traditional republican critics: effective incorporation through the pressure of electoral considerations and clientelist expectations.[126] In the 1985 local government elections, the Sinn Féin candidates' literature laid an overwhelming emphasis on issues like road improvements, housing, DHSS benefits and related resource demands on the state.[127] Adams is a major sponsor of Obair – The Campaign for Employment in West Belfast – which has produced a substantial analysis of the local economy and its massive problems of unemployment and poverty. A serious critique of the limits of current state policies is combined with a set of proposals for state-funded activity to create employment in the area.[128] It was not a member of the SDLP or Workers' Party who pointed out the 'contradictions', but a prominent Sinn Féin councillor at a meeting of party activists who argued that the IRA was becoming an electoral liability and that many people 'believe we can't call for jobs to be created while the IRA campaign continues'.[129] On one hand, there is the recognition of the fundamental reality of Sinn Féin's limited support, and on the other, the resolution not to give up on an 'armed struggle' which, if it can be suitably modulated, at least helps to maintain the hope of some future violently engendered crisis in British commitment to Northern Ireland. If the possibilities opened up by the Anglo-Irish Agreement prove ultimately barren, the question of the long-term value of the politicization process could be pregnant with major disruptive possibilities for the republican movement.

Conclusion

Eamonn McCann, one of the most articulate leftist sympathizers with the Provisionals, remained critical of their
subordination of political development to military concerns.
Writing at the end of the 1970s, he quoted the self-abnegating
lines of the secretary of Sinn Féin in 1975: 'Sinn Féin is the
political wing of the Republican Movement . . . the allegiance
we give does not allow for haggling or hankering after other
political groups, be they large or small. . . . There can be no
room for dissidents or those at variance with the Leadership.
The Árd Comhairle of Sinn Féin supports all actions taken by
the Leadership [IRA Army Council].'[1] By then, however,
McCann detected hopeful signs in a speech made by Adams at
the Wolfe Tone commemoration in June 1979. Adams
referred to the need for links with those 'oppressed by
economic and social pressures' and for an agitational struggle
in the Irish Republic centring on 'an economic resistance
movement, linking up Republicans with other sections of the
working class'. He called for the development of 'revolutionary politics' and for Sinn Féin to 'encourage the independent
mobilization of workers. . . . We must ensure that the cause
of Labour becomes the cause of Ireland, a task neglected since
Connolly's time.'[2]

In the decade since his speech Adams has been the pivot of a
major shift in the respective weights of politics and 'armed
struggle' in the republican movement that by 1986 had led
some of the more traditionally minded in Sinn Féin and the
IRA to fear a creeping 'Stickie' trend in his leadership. No
longer was it possible to write, as Seán Cronin had in 1980,
that 'The Provisionals have no political organization worthy
of the name in the North.'[3] Ten years after the British Army
Intelligence document had commented that the IRA had a
'strata of intelligent, astute and experienced terrorists who

provide the backbone of the organization',[4] a knowledgeable commentator on the republican movement noted: 'It is no secret that since 1982 Sinn Féin has attracted most of the best that the Provisional movement has had to offer – in terms of brains, ability, understanding of and commitment to the armalite and ballot-box strategy. Sinn Féin has taken and continues to take talent away from the IRA.'[5] Danny Morrison, in the atmosphere of euphoric optimism produced by the hunger strike election victories, had justified a commitment to a serious and continuous electoral strategy in a speech to the 1981 Árd Fheis: 'Who here really believes that we can win the war through the ballot-box? But will anyone here object if with a ballot paper in this hand and an Armalite in this hand we take power in Ireland?'[6]

By the end of the 1980s Sinn Féin had consolidated its position as a political organization representing about 11% of the Northern Ireland electorate and a substantial minority of the Catholic population.[7] But it had not shaken the grip of constitutional nationalism on a majority of northern Catholics, and despite the removal of the ban on participation in the Republic's parliament in 1986 there is little evidence of its being able to make a significant breakthrough. The latter is a failure with major implications for Adams's modernizing project.

In his presidential address to the 1986 Árd Fheis, Adams defined the development of a '32-County-wide political struggle' as the most important task facing the republican movement.[8] Of course, such an emphasis had featured in his writings and speeches since the late 1970s. Not until the mid-1980s, however, did Adams and his supporters feel confident enough to push against the ban on participation in Leinster House. He justified the new direction partly in terms drawn from the social republican tradition – 'The Reconquest of Ireland, much less a British withdrawal, cannot be completed without the support of more of these people [population of the Irish Republic].'[9] To some, this smacked too much of the arguments of previous modernizers. Adams criticized those who associated 'politicization' with degeneration into constitutionalism and particularly with the detested Officials, now the Workers' Party: 'The great and the most recent example of the corrupting nature of "politics" which is often quoted by some of our membership is the Sticks. Indeed, in the past few weeks some republicans who should know better have actually referred to some people on this platform as Stickies. . . .To compare us with the Stickies is an obscenity. To talk of 'only the personalities being changed" and of "some people believing that the British can be talked out of Ireland" is contemptible.'[10] His riposte to such critics was the assertion that whereas the then leadership of the republican movement had by 1969 abandoned armed struggle, the current leadership made clear its support for the IRA.[11] Joe Cahill and other veterans of the 1969–70 split like John Joe McGirl spoke in support of Adams and proclaimed the completely different conditions that supposedly allowed them to support the step that they had denounced 16 years before. Cahill's contribution, however, exemplified the problems that the leadership's strategy would soon face. Commenting on Adams's claim that it would be the election after next in the Republic which would give some indication of their political progress, he claimed that by that time 'the freedom fighters of the IRA will have forced the Brits to the conference table'.[12] This harking back to the perspectives of the early 1970s, when the stock-in-trade of the Provisionals had been the repetition of claims that the 'armed struggle' was about to force the British to withdraw, demonstrated some of the incongruities in Adams's attempt to win support for the 'long war' approach.

According to the new Provisional analysis developed after the crisis of the mid-1970s the 'struggle' could never succeed as long as it was waged on the backs of a 'minority of a minority'. As Adams made clear in 1986 Sinn Féin was still a tiny force in the politics of the Republic. Promises of the type made by Cahill – whatever their short-term effects on easing the passage of the anti-abstentionist resolution – were unlikely to be kept and only indicated the extent of the problems faced by Adams and his supporters. While the consolidation of their electoral support, demonstrated in the 1989 local government elections in Northern Ireland, has clearly confirmed the existence of a core republican vote, there is little evidence of Sinn Féin's capacity to erode the support for the SDLP, whose vote in fact increased in the election.[13] The limited survey evidence available seems to support the conclusion of two political scientists that 'The gap between Sinn Féin and the SDLP reflects two largely different electorates – only to a limited extent are they fishing for votes in the same pond.'[13] Most Sinn Féin voters are drawn from the manual and semi-skilled working class and the unemployed – a third of Sinn Féin voters are unemployed compared to 13% for the SDLP. Sinn Féin is also disproportionately strong among the young – about half its voters are under 34 compared to a third for the SDLP, and it is over-represented in the 18–24 age group.[14] Such evidence would seem to support the image of the party encouraged by the Sinn Féin leadership in the early 1980s as the vanguard of a young and impatient Catholic working class. It does not encourage much confidence in the increasing concern of Adams since 1986 to develop a broader 'anti-imperialist' alliance to include at least sections of the SDLP. This strategic initiative produced a predictable response from sections of the 'anti-imperialist' left who had welcomed the leftist noises of the organization in the early 1980s. Thus, when the documents of the internal party conference in Belfast in June 1988 were leaked to the press, Eamonn McCann proclaimed that they signified a crisis in republicanism: 'Their thrust was that Sinn Féin should seek cooperation not conflict with the SDLP, that there was a contradiction to be recognized between the armed struggle and the party's electoral activities, and that Sinn Féin should be careful about castigating the Catholic Church since this risked isolating the movement within the Catholic community. . . . The fact that the presentations were made and by senior members of the party, were clear indications of the drift of thinking at the top of Sinn Féin. And this drift is clearly towards the right.'[15] In fact, building a broad front of the 'anti-imperialist' population and in the process demonstrating that Sinn Féin was the only serious 'anti-imperialist' force was quite compatible with the social republican tradition from which Adams and other leading northern republicans had drawn inspiration. From Mellows through O'Donnell and Gilmore to Goulding in the early 1960s, class was significant as a resource to be mobilized behind a pre-existing objective. It did not imply a new and distinctive view of the world which could put into question the very nature of the republican project. Adams was quite consistent with this tradition when he developed a set of populist and class-based themes to bring republicanism out of the militarized ghetto of the mid-1970s. Certainly the republican movement included a serious attempt by some to synthesize republicanism and socialism, and a minority of republican prisoners seem to have been very seriously influenced by Marxism.[16] In response to the 1986 decision on abstentionism, approximately thirty prisoners in Long Kesh resigned from the republican movement and established a League of Communist Republicans. The prisoners stated that the abstention decision, while it influenced their resignation, was not the only or the main reason. This they claimed was the fact that the leadership of Sinn Féin had no desire to move beyond a vague Catholic nationalist populism – 'Sinn Féin's desire to "appear all things to all men" meant that the struggle for socialism within the Movement was finally lost.'[17] People like Adams, Morrison and Tom Hartley were under no illusion about the likely effect of a more principled leftism on Sinn Féin's electoral support in many parts of the north, particularly the rural areas and smaller towns. Although they were prepared to admit that the development of Sinn Féin as a substantial political force would have major implications for republicanism, and that there was a need for debate and discussion to develop a 'republican politics',[18] there would be strict limits to such restructuring. Thus when in 1986 Sinn Féin began to circulate an internal discussion sheet to deal with questions of politics and theory, Morrison warned that it should not become a 'Marxist esperanto club'.[19] The traditionalists who left in 1986 and some who remained had been concerned with the influx during the Hunger Strikes of new members drawn from various leftist groupuscules like the Peoples Democracy. The fear was that these people who were identified as the most committed opponents of abstentionism and who were 'purely political' would soon call for a reconsideration of the 'armed struggle' itself as an obstacle to electoral progress.[20]

It was certainly the case that Adams, while maintaining a very traditional republican contempt for 'armchair theoreticians' who lectured the Provisionals on their political backwardness, was quite influenced by some facets of the writings of 'green' marxists, particularly the most formidable Peoples Democracy intellectual, Michael Farrell, author of the classic 'anti-imperialist' history of the northern state.[21] But Adams had a typically republican and instrumental attitude to such writings. In the construction of his composite radical persona for the Provisionals, a core component would be the notion of 'labour aristocracy' – a crucial element in Farrell's analysis – to put a modernizing gloss on a bitter northern assault on the federalism which O'Bradaigh and O'Connaill had written into the Eire Nua proposals. Federalism, which would have offered the Protestants the 'reassurance' of their control of a provincial legislature, was the last of a long line of republican attempts to maintain a vestigial fealty to the stirring, if ultimately barren, declaration by Wolfe Tone that the freedom of Ireland could only be won through a unity of 'Protestant, Catholic and Dissenter'.[22] By the late 1970s the northern republican participants in the bitter sectarian polarization of the period were impatient that such a 'sop' to Protestant sensibilities was written into Sinn Féin's constitution. It was quite clear that the strategy of trying to interest various Loyalist leaders in the Eire Nua proposals had got nowhere; increasingly, the southerners who had developed the policy were criticized for naiveté and ignorance of northern realities – in terms that ironically echoed similar charges against Goulding and Roy Johnston in the late 1960s.[23] There could be no serious expectation of significant political and ideological change until the Northern Ireland state was destroyed. The O'Bradaigh/O'Connaill axis was guilty of encouraging illusory possibilities of winning Protestant support, just as the Officials/Workers' Party had allegedly sold out the national struggle because they were in thrall to the utopian idea of uniting the working class whilst in fact the Protestants were a 'labour aristocracy' committed to a 'pro-imperialist' position by the privileged economic position they enjoyed inside the Northern Ireland state. As the security policies of the British state shifted towards a large reduction in the numbers of British troops and their replacement by an expanded RUC and the locally recruited Ulster Defence Regiment, the IRA's attacks increasingly focused on Ulster

Protestants in and out of uniform. 'Ulsterization' gave the Provisional campaign a pronounced sectarian character at odds with the conciliationist logic of federalism and simultaneously made it more difficult to present as a progressive anti-imperialist struggle. The value of the labour aristocracy notion was twofold. First, it provided a plausible argument to counterpose to the airy implausibility of federalism. In 1982 federalism was dropped from the constitution in a major reverse for the rapidly declining southern leadership group – in 1983 O'Bradaigh would resign from the presidency of Sinn Féin. Second, it allowed the Adams axis to provide an internationally appealing version of their struggle. Just as the IRA and Sinn Féin were presented as the equivalents of the ANC and the PLO, the very substantial obstacle to a united Ireland represented by the Protestant community was identified with 'privileged colon' reaction from Algeria to Israel and South Africa.

The increasing dominance within the Adams group of young, plausible, radical-sounding Belfast Provisionals did much, in the early 1980s, to enlarge the republican movement's constituency on the left of the British Labour Party. It is hard to say how much Provisional leftism in the early 1980s – the emphasis on its working-class roots, socialist inclinations and even its feminism – was determined by a calculated wager on a hoped-for future Labour government in which the left would have significant influence. It seems clear that the brief leftist phase owed something to the upsurge of constituency leftism and municipal socialism in Britain. Even then it was impossible to protect Adams's blossoming relationship with Ken Livingstone and the Labour left from the irrupting logic of an 'armed struggle' which demanded periodic shocks to the 'imperialist heartland' like the Harrods bombing at Christmas 1983 which killed eight people. The consolidation of Thatcherism and the resultant substantial strengthening of a revisionist centrism in the Labour Party which has consigned Sinn Féin's allies to the protesting margins has removed one of the pressures for a leftist persona from the Adams leadership. The transition from the pursuit of the British left to calls for a muting of abrasive class rhetoric in the interests of alliances with SDLP and Fianna Fáil supporters clearly stemmed from new possibilities detected by the Sinn Féin leadership since the Anglo-Irish Agreement. While demonstrating the essentially instrumentalist approach to socialist themes and emphases, it should not be allowed to detract from the skill with which the Sinn Féin leadership can shift from 'left' to 'right' idioms to suit changing circumstances. As Adams pointed out during the debate on abstentionism, 'Our experience teaches us that, as a group, we are often successful when we have a flexible approach. We are at our weakest when we are forced into a static political position.'[24] If recent election results demonstrate a strengthening of the SDLP and the reduction of Sinn Féin to reliance on its urban heartlands of support, then we might expect a return to a sharper and more 'socialist' tone as the possibilities which were detected in the period of talks with the SDLP disappear. But a return to a more radical rhetoric would not disguise the formidable problems that face this final spasm of social republicanism.

Here a final comparison of the two currents separated in the schism of the late 1960s is helpful. At the level of a progressive anti-imperialist rhetoric there is not much that separates the Official analysis of the late 1960s and the Sinn Féin leftism of the 1980s. This is unsurprising given that their ideological origins are in the social republican project of Mellows and O'Donnell. For social republicans the central objective has been the uprooting of the 1921 partition settlement. The settlement was blamed on the interventions of 'British Imperialism' and the betrayal of the national revolution by the Irish bourgeoisie. Republicanism's defeat in the Civil War was attributed to its failure to appeal to the masses by linking the national question to the demand for radical economic and social change. The trajectory of social republicanism was, down to the mid-1970s, a consistent search for the issues that would link the republicans to the vital concerns of the small farmers and workers. However, it was never conceived that such a connection with the needs and interests of the masses would hold any implications for basic republican objectives. As long as the fundamental sources of support and aspiration lay in the largely agrarian south, as was the case down to the mid-1960s, it was possible to maintain this combination of social radicalism and unquestioned republican objectives. The growing weight of the urban working class and the rise in support for the Irish Labour Party in the Dublin area in the 1960s pushed the Goulding leadership to remove the most obvious obstacle to political development – abstention from the Dáil. At the same time as this issue was provoking severe internal conflict, the developing crisis in Northern Ireland added a new dimension of bitterness to the battle between modernizers and traditionalists. However, in the case of Northern Ireland the modernizers were severely handicapped by their ill-judged reliance on the civil rights movements as a political solvent of the Unionism of the Protestant working class. Misunder standing the roots of popular Unionism, they severely underestimated the possibilities that the disintegration of the Unionist state from 1969 onwards held for communal polarization.

The intellectual progenitors of Official Republicanism, like Desmond Greaves and Anthony Coughlan, had rightly perceived the capacity of a mass civil rights movement to undermine the northern state, but they had grossly exaggerated its capacity to create the conditions for winning the Protestant working class to an 'anti-imperialist' position. In one sense they remained true to the more exalted perspectives of a Wolfe Tone republicanism which argued that the only 'real' republican struggle was an expansive and secular one which mirrored the ultimate objective in current strategies to produce a unification of Protestant and Catholic workers. Cathal Goulding summed such a perspective up in 1971: 'There can be no Ireland in Wolfe Tone's sense without the Protestant working class. They must be reached. We believe we are on the right road. The 1919 Dáil Eireann Democratic Programme was buried and ignored and now we are going to the root of the Irish question.'[25] While it would be to the Officials' ultimate and lasting credit that they repudiated the Catholic 'defenderism' which fuelled the initial development of the Provisionals they were unable to provide any coherent justification of such abstinence. As Goulding's statement shows, they maintained for some time the social republican dream of the 1930s of winning the Protestant workers – or at least a section of them – to their anti-imperialist alliance. But it was increasingly easy for their critics – first the Provisionals and then the supporters of Seamus Costello – to point out that it was extremely unlikely that the support of any section of the Protestant population would be forthcoming. To continue to prosecute the 'anti-imperialist' struggle in the north meant, in effect, jettisoning any hope of reaching sections of the Protestant working class until after the 'armed struggle' had forced a British withdrawal. In an interview in 1979, Gerry Adams also returned to the Democratic Programme of 1919 as a defining document of radical republicanism.[26] However, unlike Goulding he had no illusions that such an ideological tradition would appeal to Protestants. The development of the Provisionals would ultimately force the Officials to jettison many of the defining themes of the radical republican tradition. The result has been the emphasis from the mid-1970s on the need to reduce divisions in the north through demilitarization and internal political development. This has led to a focus on the need for a 'democratic devolved government' which their nationalist critics have dubbed a plan for the return of the discredited Stormont administration. Certainly the emphasis on the need to develop 'class politics' has often seemed exotic in the conditions of communal polarization and the traditions and common-sense assumptions of Protestant and Catholic working class life. Strident attacks by the Republican Clubs and the Workers' Party on the Provisional IRA, and their robust defence of the RUC, have produced a favourable response in quarters like the main Unionist daily, the *Belfast Newsletter*. But inevitably they have led to charges of betrayal, pro-Unionism and, more brutally, of being 'Prod lovers'. The de facto exit from anything that is recognizably a republican/nationalist ideological tradition has meant a marginalization in many Catholic areas whilst at the same time the continuing institutional links with the 32-county aspiration in a party that has an all-Ireland structure and a 'national' leadership which is largely based in Dublin, has placed a strict limit on the extent of Protestant support. The result is a basis of support, according to the latest local government election results, of 2.1% in Northern Ireland and 5.3% in Belfast compared with Sinn Féin's substantial support base of 11.3% and 18.7% respectively.[27]

Although the break with the anti-imperialist and nationalist perspective may have created many problems in Northern Ireland, it appears to have been a prerequisite for political progress in the Irish Republic where the protagonists of the Official tradition have made real, if limited, gains – while neither the recent history of Sinn Féin nor its political prospects appear promising. Without the combustible material of an economically marginalized proletariat with a strong sense of communal oppression – as in its northern heartlands – Sinn Féin faces all the problems of a late arrival in a crowded and competitive political space: the struggle for the support of the Republic's urban working class. By the 1987 general election over a decade's work as a hard-left scourge of the Irish Labour Party, and the advantage afforded by its tradition of single-minded discipline in the clientelist political culture of the south, had produced a real but limited increase of support for the Workers' Party: four TDs were elected with 3.8% of the national vote compared to the Labour Party's twelve TDs and 6.4% of the vote.[28]. The party was clearly a significant political force in Dublin, where it had drawn level with the Labour Party in terms of electoral support. The party was the dominant left-wing group on Dublin Corporation and three of its TDs were from city constituencies. Whether the Labour Party – now that is has forsaken a coalition strategy and returned to the role of a party of opposition – can regain the ground lost to the Workers' Party must remain an open question. Certainly the latter's limited electoral gains have contributed to a debate about whether it is 'Marxist', euro-communist' or 'social-democratic'.[29] Whether it can replace the Labour Party as the leading force on the left – a clear, if usually unarticulated, ambition since the 1970s – remains unresolved and poses major questions about the party's structures and ideology. What is clear is that it maintains a sharp critical edge against the more nationalist and irredentist aspects of the political culture of the Republic.[30]

In its first participationist electoral intervention Sinn Féin got less than 2% of the vote and had no one elected. Gerry Adams argued that the 1987 election came too soon after the anti-abstentionist decision at the 1986 Árd Fheis and that the party still suffers from the severe restrictions imposed by Section 31 of the Republic's Broadcasting Act which excludes

Sinn Féin from radio and television. He rejected the argument that points to the low level of support for the left in the Republic as an index of the problems facing Sinn Féin by arguing that the Labour Party is 'reformist' and the Workers' Party 'two nationist', i.e. effectively Unionist: thus, there is a future for a new 'republican-labour' party like Sinn Féin.[31]

But the thesis that there is a substantial constituency for a militantly republican party more radical than the Labour Party is implausible. Outside of some major crisis in the north the constituency for militant republicanism is safely corralled inside Fianna Fáil and there is little evidence that it can be prised loose by the 'class nature of this struggle' referred to by Adams in his outline of current Sinn Féin strategy.[32] That a constituency for social radicalism does exist in urban Ireland is, to a limited extent at least, demonstrated by the development of the Workers' Party. Yet its evolution would seem to indicate that a prerequisite for progress is that southern workers are not alienated by the feeling that their conditions and grievances are being used as the raw material to mobilize support for a different struggle entirely. Yet this is precisely what the modernized Sinn Féin commitment to electoral intervention in the Republic amounts to. An editorial in *An Phoblacht/Republican News* defending the decision to jettison abstentionism made it clear that the role of Sinn Féin was to move working-class consciousness in the Republic from a trade union to a 'republican' level. This entailed enlisting popular support for the 'armed struggle' in the north – 'rather than compromise or be evasive, republicans must explain the origins of the war and the justification and correctness of physical force'. It added uncompromisingly: 'We can then learn to live without the support of those to whom armed struggle is an insuperable difficulty.'[33] Only those who were suffering from the myopia of northern ghetto vision could see in such continuing intransigence anything other than a recipe for continuing marginalization. Yet only the existence of the 'armed struggle' gives the vague social populism of Sinn Féin any distinctiveness in the Republic. The Officials' earlier evolution blocks the possibility of an exit into a more substantial socialist radicalism. The very existence of the Workers' Party forces Sinn Féin into emphasizing the things that separate it from the 'Stickies' – the national question, the north, and the 'struggle', identifications that leave the masses in the south largely cold and indifferent.

In an interview with a Dublin journalist, Danny Morrison provided a typically strident but ironically poignant illustration of the dilemma of the current republican leadership, struggling to come to terms with realities in a state where anti-partitionism is largely an affair of piety and bad conscience.

Question: In terms of a political solution, what about those who don't want a United Ireland?
Morrison: Tell us. People of the 26 Counties that don't want the Six Counties, *let us know*. If they're telling us to fuck off, telling us they're happy with the state they've got and fuck 1916, then tell us. Because, if they don't want us then I would have to look again at the situation . . . if they think they've got an Irish nation inside the 26 Counties they should build a wall and lock us out. [emphasis in the original].[34]

The 'armalite and the ballot-box' strategy justified itself to those suspicious of increasing political involvement by holding out the prospect of political advance in both states which would complement the 'cutting edge' of the IRA. The unlikelihood of anything more than incremental progress in the Irish Republic appears to be confirmed by recent evidence that Sinn Féin's electoral support in Northern Ireland, while still substantial, has been subject to some erosion in rural areas and relies heavily on the urban working class of Belfast and Derry.[35] Though anchored there, contemporary republicanism is still a long way from being able to shake the hegemony of constitutional nationalism.

Some commentators speculate on an increasing tension between the two poles of the armalite and ballot-box strategy, culminating in a conflict between the IRA and Sinn Féin over funds.[36] While it mirrors the criticism of those prominent ex-Provisionals now in Republican Sinn Féin like Ruairi O'Bradaigh and Seán MacStiofain,[37] and undoubtedly reflects real tensions, such speculation is probably over-optimistic. Firstly, Adams and his colleagues have become relatively skilled at handling the conflicts and contradictions between politics and force. Secondly, they have consistently emphasized their commitment to the 'armed struggle' and stressed their own history of involvement in 'the longest phase of resistance to the British presence'.[38] Thirdly, it is not necessary for Sinn Féin to realize Danny Morrison's grandiose ambition of 1981 – 'to take power in Ireland'. All they need to do is remain a formidable force in Northern Ireland, relying on the combination of a limited but substantial electoral presence and the IRA's military capacity to sap the commitment of the British state to stay in Northern Ireland.

Of course, this represents a marked retraction of ambition and a narrowing of the social, regional and political project of contemporary republicanism. Now leading members of Sinn Féin will unabashedly explain that in a united Ireland created by British withdrawal conservative forces are most likely to be dominant. This admission of the social void at the centre of Sinn Féin's strategic objectives is not necessarily damaging in Northern Ireland where one acerbic local commentator noted: 'Provoism is now a deeply-embedded sub-culture in the urban ghettoes . . . a sub-culture which subsists on a diet of economic marginalization, political-cum-cultural exclusion and state authoritarianism.'[39] This lack of a hegemonic capacity in the strategy of the current Sinn Féin leadership – its ghetto corporatism, to use a vulgarized concept from Gramsci – has been criticized by some who maintain an allegiance to a 'principled' social republican tradition. A 'communist republican' analysis of the impasse of the republican tradition gave an impressive depiction of the real but ambiguous nature of Sinn Féin's bedrock of support: 'In Northern Ireland, a section of the Catholic population views republicanism almost as a threat to hold over the heads of British authority in lieu of improvements in social conditions. . . . It is a sad but harsh reality that where long-term unemployment is endemic, there is a tendency to view the state as a source of income rather than as an organ of control. . . this tends to produce a section of society with more of the characteristics of the old Roman plebs. In a modern context this leads to reformist demands for increased state benefits and improved leisure facilities. Support for republicanism therefore can be analysed as a means to forcing concessions from a mean government. When these concessions are achieved, there is a noticeable cooling in republican ardour.'[40] A left republican critique of Sinn Féin could also be found in the statements of some survivors of the IRSP/INLA tradition. Marginalized by the politicization of the Provisionals after 1977[41] and wracked by increasingly murderous internal feuds, one of the surviving strands has labelled itself 'Marxist-Leninist' and hopes to provide a 'socialist alternative' to Sinn Féin.[42] Yet such critiques are based on the clearly unfounded premiss that a constituency for an all-Ireland socialist 'anti-imperialist' strategy exists. It founders on the rock of the popular legitimacy of the southern state. Such purist social republicanism, while it may make intellectually convincing criticisms of Sinn Féin, has little hope of undermining its strong northern support which is based precisely on the overdetermination of class by communal identifications. Adams recognizes that the only realistic future for republicanism lies, not in movement in a socialist direction, but in continuing to express and exploit the grievances of large sections of the Catholic working class.

Sinn Féin's and the IRA's support is largely impervious to the government's depiction of them as 'terrorists' or 'mafia'. The problems created for them by reactive authoritarian spasms like the Home Secretary's ban on media interviews in October 1988, while serious, do not impinge much on their dense presence in crucial areas like West Belfast. They can rely on the British government's disinclination to develop a serious reformist strategy for Northern Ireland. The republican movement's presence – military, 'policing', economic, social and political – is so entwined in the fabric of everyday existence in large parts of Catholic Belfast and Derry that only a veritable economic and social 'revolution from above' (creating the conditions of effective citizenship for what is, in effect, a Catholic under-class) could hope to undermine it. A leading republican admitted to a local journalist: 'Repression we can cope with, reform we can't.'[43] Ten years of Thatcherism have both exacerbated the problem of unemployment and made a reformist agenda seem less likely. The Anglo-Irish Agreement represented, for the British government at least, an alternative to the ideologically distasteful and costly strategy of dealing with the material bases of Catholic grievance.

In a late-capitalist state exhibiting many of the polarizing effects of a neo-liberal regime happy to consign millions to the position of those effectively excluded from citizenship by a combination of region and class, sections of Northern Ireland's marginalized working class use Sinn Féin as a political voice. The message of this voice is equivocal despite Sinn Féin's claim that, at its core at least, it represents 'principled republican' support. In fact much of the propaganda of modernized republicanism focuses on the proclaimed 'irreformability' of the Northern Ireland state. At its core this is its historic and current inability to offer employment to a substantial section, disproportionately Catholic, of its working class. As two British sympathizers put the case, 'in 1981, Northern Ireland male Catholic unemployment was 30.2%, while in the worst region on the mainland, Merseyside, it was 19.1% (the Protestant male unemployment figure was 12.4% and the UK average was 11.3%).'[44] In some of the areas of Belfast most associated with hard-core Sinn Féin support, male unemployment rates varied between 50 and 60%.[45] The Anglo-Irish Agreement has not initiated any serious attempt to deal with such a massive problem. The British government's commitment to 'address the social and economic problems in the most disadvantaged areas of Belfast and other deprived areas'[46] is a predictable type of cosmetic minimalism unchallenged by Charles Haughey's government, itself intent on implementing a similar course of retrenchment in public expenditure and 'market-led' solutions to the Republic's severe economic problems.

The final dismal spasm of social republicanism is thus symbiotically tied to the future of the Thatcherite project. If Thatcherism, even of a moderated sort, survives the present prime minister, then the material conditions for the continuance of the 'long war' will remain, whatever the counter-pulls of political disillusionment and war-weariness in Sinn Féin's heartlands. This would be a tragic outcome. Even some republicans, albeit the most perceptive and politically developed, can acknowledge the possibility of significant reforms draining the sea of ghetto support. There would be some space for optimism if there was any evidence that anyone in the Northern Ireland Office was capable of the following astute evaluation of the economic and social roots of the present conflict made by an imprisoned republican: 'The outburst of Irish nationalism which has developed since the late 1960s would not have been so pronounced were it not for the structural inequality that went unameliorated. I am sure that, theoretically speaking, Irish nationalism would become little more than a residue, taking cultural as opposed to political expression if structural inequality was to disappear and not reemerge.'[47]

The social republicanism of the inter-war period was largely absorbed by the reformism of Fianna Fáil; that of the 1960s was transformed and ultimately subordinated to a strategy of gradualist socialist advance within a politically conservative state – the Irish Republic. The terminal form of this powerful political and ideological tradition is more narrowly rooted in Northern Ireland. There Sinn Féin's use of the decades-old slogan of 'completing the national revolution' serves to conceal from itself and its opponents the fact that it is giving a bitter and disfigured expression to real needs. These are of the Catholic working class for economic, social and political inclusion in a state which, because of a complex, dense and overlapping history, will remain 'British' but with an increasing 'Irish Dimension' in its Northern Ireland extension. Only when these needs are seriously addressed will their repressed and pathological forms of expression be dissipated and the social republican tradition finally be consigned to the history books.

Chronology

1903 The Wyndham Land Act which provides for the buying out of the Irish landlord class by their tenants. The process to be financed by Treasury loans – the origins of the land annuities issue.

1905 The foundation of the Ulster Unionist Council – the first institutional embodiment of the Ulster Unionist movement.

1907 Liverpool born union militant, James Larkin, leads Belfast carters and dockers in major strike.
Formation of Sinn Féin League – from September 1908 called Sinn Féin.
Larkin splits from British-based National Union of Dock Labourers to form the Irish Transport and General Workers' Union.

1909 Foundation of Fianna Eireann.

1912 Third Home Rule Bill introduced in House of Commons. Formation of Irish Labour Party and Trade Union Congress.

1913 Foundation of Ulster Volunteer Force to resist Home Rule. Larkin's Irish Transport and General Workers' Union involved in the Dublin Lockout from August 1913 to January 1914.
Formation of Irish Citizen Army.
Formation of Irish Volunteers.

1916 Easter Rising and subsequent execution of leaders including James Connolly.

1917 Eamonn De Valera elected President of Sinn Féin.

1918 General Election: Sinn Féin 73 seats, Irish Parliamentary Party 6, Unionists 26.

1919 First meeting of Dáil Eireann.
On same day the Irish Volunteers kill two policemen at Soloheadbeg, County Tipperary.
Dáil Eireann declared illegal in September.

1920 Expulsions of Catholics and Socialists from the Belfast shipyards in July mark the beginning of two years of intense violence in which over 450 were killed in the city.
In November the Ulster Special Constabulary is established.
The Government of Ireland Act provides for a Northern Ireland parliament and government.

1921 In July a truce between the British forces and the IRA is established.

December sees the signing of the Anglo-Irish Treaty.

Formation of Communist Party of Ireland in October 1921.

1922 Treaty approved by Dáil Eireann in January by 64 to 57.

April: Anti-Treatyites seize the Four Courts in Dublin.

June: in General Election in Free State the pro-Treaty forces – now Cumann na nGaedheal – are easily victorious.

Attack on Four Courts marks the beginning of the Civil War.

26 August Liam Mellows sends out the first of his *Jail Notes* from Mountjoy Jail.

8 December: Mellows and three other leading republicans executed.

1923 24 May: Frank Aiken orders anti-Treatyites to dump arms.

1926 16 May: Inaugural meeting of Fianna Fáil in La Scala theatre, Dublin.

Peadar O'Donnell launches campaign against Land Annuities in Donegal.

1931 Saor Éire has its first congress in September.

October: Irish bishops issue a Joint Pastoral denouncing Saor Éire as a 'frankly communistic organization'.

Government introduces Public Safety legislation banning twelve organizations including Saor Éire and IRA. Military Tribunals introduced.

1932 9 February: formation of Army Comrades Association.

16 February: Fianna Fáil wins general election and forms a government for the first time.

Withholding of payment of Land Annuities to Britain and beginning of the Economic War.

October: widespread disturbances in Belfast during strike of workers on Outdoor Relief.

1933 Army Comrades Association becomes the National Guard and adopts the wearing of a blue shirt.

In September Cumann na nGaedheal, the Centre Party and the National Guard fuse to form Fine Gael.

1934 Peadar O'Donnell and his supporters leave IRA to

create a Republican Congress. It splits at its first conference in September.

1935 Severe rioting for three weeks in Belfast sparked off by Orange Parade in July.

1936 De Valera's government declares the IRA an illegal organization.

1937 In June De Valera's new constitution approved by a referendum.

1938 Formation of Clann na Talmhan.

1939 January: IRA declares war on Britain and initiates a bombing campaign which culminates in August with murder of five people in explosion in Coventry.
February: first contact between the Abwehr and the IRA.

1940 January: the Dáil passes Emergency Powers Act to deal with the IRA,
August: Sean Russell dies on German U-boat en route to Ireland.

1944 Irish Labour Party splits – reunited in 1950.

1945 Irish TUC splits – not reunited until 1959.

1946 Formation of Clann na Poblachta.

1948 Fianna Fáil loses power for first time since 1932.
New Inter-Party Government takes Ireland out of the Commonwealth and establishes a Republic.

1949 British parliament passes Ireland Act guaranteeing that Northern Ireland will remain within the UK until its parliament decides otherwise.

1951 Census: population of Republic 2,960,593; of Northern Ireland, 1,370,921.

1953 July: Cathal Goulding and John Stephenson arrested and sentenced to eight years for arms raid in Felstead, Essex.

1954 June: successful IRA arms raid on Gough Barracks, Armagh.
October: raid on army barracks in Omagh, County Tyrone leads to capture of eight IRA men.

1955 May: in election for Westminster Sinn Féin candidates get 152,310 votes and two are elected.

1956 12 December 'Operation Harvest' launched by the IRA.

1957 January: Deaths of Feargal O'Hanlon and Sean South in IRA attack on RUC station at Brookeborough, County Fermanagh.
March: General Election in Republic returns Fianna Fáil to power; 4 Sinn Féin TDs elected.
July: De Valera introduces internment in the Republic – it had been in existence in Northern Ireland since December 1956.

1959 The Fianna Fáil government launches the First Programme for Economic Expansion. Lemass replaces De Valera as leader of Fianna Fáil.

1961 Census: Population of Irish Republic, 2,818,341; of Northern Ireland, 1,452,642.

1962 February 26: IRA publicly announces the end of its campaign.

1963 Terence O'Neill becomes prime minister in Northern Ireland in March.

1964 January: Foundation of Campaign for Social Justice in Northern Ireland.
July: Publication of Second Programme for Economic Expansion.
October: Divis Street Riots in Belfast.

1965 January: O'Neill/Lemass meeting in Belfast.
December: Signing of Anglo-Irish Free Trade Agreement.

1966 March: IRA blow up Nelson's Pillar in Dublin's O'Connell Street.

1967 Foundation of Northern Ireland Civil Rights Association in January.

1968 August: First civil rights march from Coalisland to Dungannon.
5 October: RUC attack civil rights marchers in Duke Street, Derry.
Formation of People's Democracy organization by students at Queen's University, Belfast.

1969 January: 'Long March' from Belfast to Derry organized by People's Democracy attacked by militant Protestants; rioting in Derry.
April: Rioting in Derry and RUC invade the Bogside seriously injuring a man who subsequently dies.

28 April: Terence O'Neill resigns and is replaced by his cousin, James Chichester Clark.

12 August: Protestant Apprentice Boys' parade in Derry leads to violence and the 'Battle of the Bogside'.

13 August: Jack Lynch makes TV broadcast attacking the Stormont government and calling for UN to intervene.

14–15 August: serious violence in Belfast, British troops sent in to Derry and Belfast.

December: special IRA convention votes in favour of ending abstentionism and for a National Liberation Front; in response a Provisional Army Council is formed.

1970   11 January: Sinn Féin Árd Fheis votes on abstention and NLF – walkout by group which forms Provisional Sinn Féin.

April: Ian Paisley wins seat in Stormont parliament.

May: Charles Haughey and Neil Blaney are sacked by Jack Lynch and Kevin Boland resigns from government. Blaney and Haughey are arrested and tried on charge of conspiracy to import arms; both are acquitted.

June: Paisley elected to Westminster; return of Conservative government.

July: British army search for arms in Lower Falls leads to riot, 36-hour curfew of the district and 'Battle of Lower Falls' with Official IRA.

August: formation of Social Democratic and Labour Party.

1971   January: serious anti-army riots in Ballymurphy for five days.

6 February: Provisionals kill first British soldier.

23 March: Brian Faulkner replaces Chichester Clark as Unionist prime minister.

April: Provisionals launch a major bombing campaign against commercial targets which intensifies through spring and summer.

9 August: Internment introduced – 342 picked up.

Census: Republic of Ireland, 2,978,248; Northern Ireland, 1,536,065.

1972   30 January: British paratroopers shoot dead 13 civil rights marchers in Derry.

22 February: Official IRA bombing of Paratroop base at Aldershot kills army chaplain and 6 women cleaners.

24 March: resignation of Unionist government and introduction of Direct Rule; William Whitelaw becomes first Secretary of State for Northern Ireland.

15 April: Official IRA leader, Joe McCann, shot dead by British troops while walking unarmed through the Markets area of Belfast.

13 May: referendum in Republic gives a massive majority for membership of the EEC.

20 May: Official IRA in Derry kill William Best, a nineteen year old home on leave from the British army.

29 May: Official IRA declares a ceasefire.

14 June: Whitelaw concedes to Provisional demand for political status for prisoners.

22 June: Provisionals declare a ceasefire.

7 July: 6 leading Provisionals including Gerry Adams are flown to London for a secret meeting with Whitelaw held in house of Paul Channon; meeting is fruitless.

9 July: ceasefire ends.

21 July: 'Bloody Friday'. Provisionals detonate 22 car bombs in Belfast killing 9 civilians and 2 soldiers.

1973   February: Fianna Fáil loses power for first time since 1957 to a coalition of Fine Gael and Labour.

June: elections for a Northern Ireland Assembly – the SDLP get 22% of vote; Sinn Féin campaign for a boycott ignored.

December: Sunningdale Conference leads to formation of a power-sharing government in Belfast.

1974   May: Ulster Workers' Council strike destroys the power-sharing government.

21 November: Provisional bombing campaign in Britain culminates in blowing up of two pubs in Birmingham killing 21 people.

December: formation of the Irish Republican Socialist Party.

1975   January: Provisionals and Northern Ireland Office negotiate a ceasefire.

February: armed conflict between Official IRA and IRSP/INLA in Belfast leads to death of Billy McMillen.
October: Provisionals launch attack on Officials.
November: end of ceasefire.

1976 March: British government announces decision to abolish special category status.
September: Provisional prisoner, Ciaran Nugent refuses to wear prison uniform – the beginning of the 'blanket protest'.

1977 February: Official Sinn Féin becomes Sinn Féin – The Workers' Party.
June: Fianna Fáil win general election.

1978 February: Provisional fire-bombs incinerate eleven people in La Mon restaurant, near Belfast.

1979 27 August: Provisionals blow up Lord Mountbatten's yacht off Mullaghmore, County Sligo killing him and three other people.
On same day a Provisional ambush at Narrow Water, County Down kills 18 soldiers.
December: Charles Haughey becomes leader of Fianna Fáil and prime-minister.

1980 27 October: start of hunger-strike by Provisional prisoners in Maze; called off on 18 December.

1981 1 March: beginning of second hunger strike.
26 March: Bobby Sands elected MP for Fermanagh/ South Tyrone.
5 May: Sands is the first of ten hunger strikers to die.
June: general election in Irish Republic – Fianna Fáil loses power to a Coalition of Fine Gael and Labour. Two hunger-strikers elected as TDs in border consti- tuencies: the SFWP has its first TD elected.
3 October: the hunger strike is called off.

1982 February: general election in Irish Republic returns Fianna Fáil to power: SFWP win three seats.
April: Árd Fheis changes name of Sinn Féin-The Workers' Party to The Workers' Party.
October: elections to Northern Ireland Assembly – Sinn Féin wins 10.1% of the vote; SDLP 18.8%.

1983 March: announcement of New Ireland Forum.
June: Westminster election – Sinn Fein wins 13.4% of

vote to SDLP's 17.9% and Gerry Adams becomes MP for West Belfast.

December: Provisionals car-bomb Harrods killing 8 people.

1984 May: publication of Report of New Ireland Forum.

12 October: Provisionals bomb the Grand Hotel, Brighton in attempt to kill Margaret Thatcher; Thatcher survives but 5 others killed.

1985 May: local government elections in Northern Ireland, Sinn Féin wins 11.4% of vote and 59 seats.

October: Thatcher and Fitzgerald sign Anglo-Irish Agreement at Hillsborough, County Down.

1986 October 31: Sinn Féin Ard Fheis votes to remove abstention from Leinster House from its constitution; Ruairi O'Bradaigh leads a walk-out and establishes Republican Sinn Féin.

1987 February: general election in the Irish Republic – Fianna Fáil returned to power as a minority government; the Workers' Party win 4 seats and 3.8% of the vote – in Dublin with 7.5% of the vote it outpolls the Labour Party; Sinn Féin gets 1.9% of the vote and no seats.

June: British general election – Sinn Féin gets 11.4% of vote and Adams keeps his seat.

November: Provisional IRA bomb at Remembrance Ceremony in Enniskillen, County Fermanagh kills 11 people.

1988 March: 3 unarmed IRA members shot dead by security forces in Gilbraltar.

John Hume and senior members of the SDLP enter into discussions with Gerry Adams and leading Sinn Féiners; the discussions last until September.

October: Home Secretary, Douglas Hurd introduces ban on TV and radio interviews with Sinn Féin – except during elections.

1989 January: at Sinn Féin Ard Fheis Adams criticizes the IRA for an increasing number of 'mistakes' in which civilians have been killed.

May: in Northern Ireland local government elections Sinn Féin wins 11.3% of poll.

June: general election in Irish Republic sees a significant

swing to the left – The Workers' Party win 5% of national vote and 3 new seats giving it seven seats. The Irish Labour Party wins 9.5% of the national vote and 15 seats. In Dublin the WP increases its lead over the Labour Party – 11.4% and six seats, to 9.5% and three seats. Sinn Féin's vote declines to 1.2% and it wins no seats.

European Election in Irish Republic – The Workers' Party wins 7.5% of national vote. In Dublin its president De Rossa wins 15.8% of the vote and wins a seat. The Labour Party wins 9.5% of the national vote and 12.2% of the vote in Dublin where it wins a seat. Sinn Féin wins 2.3% of the national vote – a decline of 2.9% on its performance in the last European election.

European Election in Northern Ireland – Sinn Féin vote slumps to 9.2% of the total – in 1984 it got 13.4% of the total vote.

Notes

Introduction

1   Edward Said, 'Identity, Negation and Violence' in *New Left Review*, 171, September/October 1988, p. 47.
2   See speech of John Hume to the annual conference of the Social Democratic and Labour Party, *Irish Times*, 28 November 1988.
3   ibid.
4   Patrick Bishop and Eamonn Mallie, *The Provisional IRA* (London 1987), p. 359
5   ibid. p. 26.

1: The Origins of Social Republicanism

1   For a very useful analysis of Lalor's significance see Mary Daly, 'James Fintan Lalor and Rural Revolution' in Ciaran Brady (ed). *Worsted in the Game: Losers in Irish History* (Dublin 1989).
2   See 'Socialism and Irish Nationalism' in the edition of Connolly's writings edited by Desmond Ryan, *Socialism and Nationalism* (Dublin 1948), p. 25.
3   Joe Lee, *The Modernisation of Irish Society 1848–1918* (Dublin 1973), p. 151.
4   On Marx see P. Bew, P. Gibbon and H. Patterson, *The State in Northern Ireland* (Manchester 1979), Chapter 1.
5   James Connolly, *The Reconquest of Ireland* (Dublin 1968), pp. 62–63.
6   Paul Bew, 'Sinn Fein, Agrarian Radicalism and the War of Independence 1919–21' in D. G. Boyce (ed.), *The Revolution in Ireland* (London 1988), p. 220.
7   ibid.
8   Charles Townshend, *Political Violence in Ireland* (Oxford 1983), p. 339.
9   Interview with O'Donnell quoted in James Peter McHugh, 'Voices of the Rearguard: A Study of *An Phoblacht*, Irish Republican Thought in the Post Revolutionary Era 1923–

1937', *M.A.*, University College Dublin, 1983, p. 34.

10 Bew, op.cit., pp. 221–222.

11 Michael Hopkinson, *Green against Green: A History of the Irish Civil War* (Dublin 1988), p. 45.

12 ibid.

13 David Fitzpatrick, *Politics and Irish Life 1913–21; Provincial Experience of War and Revolution* (Dublin 1977), p. 207.

14 Hopkinson, op.cit., p. 5.

15 Bew, op.cit., p. 224.

16 E. Rumpf and A. C. Hepburn, *Nationalism and Socialism in Twentieth Century Ireland* (Liverpool 1977), p. 55.

17 James Connolly, op.cit. p. 60.

18 Emmet O'Connor, 'Syndicalism in Ireland 1917– 1923', *PhD* Cambridge 1984, p. 50.

19 Adrian Pimley, 'The Working-Class Movement and the Irish Revolution 1896–1923' in D. G. Boyce, op.cit., p. 210.

20 Dan Brady, *Farm Labourers: Irish Struggle 1900–1976* (Belfast 1988), p. 10.

21 David Fitzpatrick, op.cit., p. 252.

22 Dan Brady, op.cit., p. 55.

23 Emmet O'Connor, op.cit. p. 148.

24 ibid.

25 Hopkinson, op.cit., p. 45.

26 Townshend, op.cit., p. 360.

27 Hopkinson, op.cit., p. 9.

28 ibid., p. 273.

29 P. S. O'Hegarty, *A History of Ireland under the Union* (London 1952), p. 781.

30 Tom Garvin, *Nationalist Revolutionaries in Ireland 1858–1928* (Oxford 1987), p. 131.

31 O'Connor, op.cit. p. 125.

32 Bew, op.cit.

33 All quotes are from C. D. Greaves, *Liam Mellows and the Irish Revolution* (London 1971), pp. 363–368.

34 Townshend, op.cit., p. 363 note 1.

35 Greaves, op.cit., p. 48.

36 R. F. Foster, *Modern Ireland 1600–1972,* (London 1988), p. 286.

37 Greaves, op.cit., p. 155.

38 Quotations from the Irish Communist Organization, *Notes From Mountjoy Jail by Liam Mellows* (London 1965).

39 Rumpf and Hepburn, op.cit., p. 32–the first preference votes were: pro-Treaty 239,193, anti-Treaty 133,864; Labour 132,511; Independents 63,641 and Farmers 51,074.

40 Irish Communist Organization, op.cit.

41 ibid.
42 See for example Des O'Hagan, *The Republican Tradition* (Dublin 1975), p. 2.
43 Quoted in Richard Dunphy, 'Class, Power and the Fianna Fáil Party: A Study of Hegemony in Irish Politics 1923–48', *D. Phil* European University Institute, Florence 1988, p. 60.
44 O'Hagan, op.cit.
45 Dunphy, op.cit., p. 59.
46 Bulmer Hobson, *Ireland Yesterday, Today and Tomorrow* (Tralee 1968), p. 33.
47 Townshend, op.cit., p. 329.
48 Charlotte H. Fallon, *Soul of Fire: A Biography of Mary MacSwiney* (Cork and Dublin 1986), p. 86.
49 All quotations from C. Markievicz, *What Irish Republicans Stand For* (Glasgow, 1923).
50 ibid. and Dunphy, op.cit., p. 54.
51 Markievicz, op.cit.

2: Republicanism in Inter-War Ireland

1 Dorothy Macardle, *The Irish Republic* (London 1968), p. 772.
2 ibid.
3 Hopkinson, op.cit., p. 268.
4 ibid., p. 7.
5 Sinn Fein got 27% of poll and 44 seats, Cumann na nGaedhael got 38.9% of poll and 63 seats: Rumpf and Hepburn, op.cit., p. 88.
6 *An Phoblacht* 22 January 1926, quoted in Richard Dunphy, Class Power and the Fianna Fail Party: A Study of Hegemony in Irish Politics 1923–1948, *D.Phil.* European University Institute, Florence, July 1988, p. 91.
7 J. Bowyer Bell, The Secret Army (London 1972), pp. 70–71.
8 Information on O'Donnell is from Grattan Freyer, *Peadar O'Donnell* (New Jersey 1973), Michael McInerney, *Peadar O'Donnell: Irish Social Rebel* (Dublin 1974) and Uinseann MacEoin, *Survivors* (Dublin 1980).
9 Quoted in McHugh, op. cit., p. 64.
10 Freyer, op.cit., p. 30.
11 McInerney, op.cit., p. 81.
12 MacEoin, op.cit., p. 25.
13 Peadar O'Donnell, *There Will be Another Day* (Dublin 1963), p. 11.
14 Sean O'Faolain, *De Valera* (London 1939), p. 167.

15 Deidre McMahon, *Republicans and Imperialists* (New Haven and London 1984), pp. 38–41.

16 O'Donnell, op.cit., p. 22.

17 *An Phoblacht* 3 October 1931.

18 Greaves, op.cit., p. 313.

19 ibid. p. 364.

20 O'Donnell, op.cit., p. 10.

21 *An Phoblacht*, 12 November 1927.

22 David Howell, *A Lost Left* (Manchester 1986), p. 79.

23 *An Phoblacht*, 25 March 1927.

24 Brian O'Neill, *The War for the Land In Ireland* (London 1933), p. 14.

25 Terence Brown, *Ireland: A Social and Cultural History* (Glasgow 1981), p. 97.

26 *An Phoblacht*, 17 September 1927.

27 *An Phoblacht*, 17 December 1927.

28 *The Nation*, 9 April 1927.

29 When he was acquitted of charges arising out of the Donegal agitation, *The Nation* congratulated him : 'We hope his example will give heart to leaders and people to put new vigour into the fight against the starvation and emigration party of the Free State.' 16 April 1927.

30 Sean Cronin (ed.) *The McGarrity Papers* (Tralee 1972), p. 141.

31 *The Nation*, 9 July 1927.

32 ibid. 3 December 1927.

33 ibid. 28 January 1928.

34 ibid. 24 December 1927.

35 O'Donnell, op.cit. p. 85.

36 *An Phoblacht*, 24 March 1928.

37 O'Donnell, op.cit. p. 79.

38 *An Phoblacht*, 18 February 1928.

39 O'Donnell, op.cit., p. 108.

40 The composition of the provisional organizing committee of the Anti-Tribute League is in the Colonel Maurice Moore *Papers on Land Annuities*, National Library of Ireland 105060. The counties represented were Galway, Clare, Leitrim, Cork and Donegal.

41 *An Phoblacht*, 3 November 1928.

42 Longford and O'Neill, *Eamonn De Valera* (Dublin 1970), p. 261.

43 *The Nation*, 13 July 1929.

44 *The Nation*, 19 October 1929.

45 *The Connaught Telegraph*, 22 February 1930.

46 *An Phoblacht*, 28 June 1928.

47 *The Nation*, 28 January 1928.
48 *Mayo News*, 14 January 1933.
49 ibid.
50 ibid.
51 *Mayo News*, 10 January 1931.
52 *Mayo News*, 6 February 1932.
53 *An Phoblacht*, 29 April 1927.
54 O'Donnell, op.cit., p. 112.
55 ibid. p. 116.
56 *An Phoblacht*, 16 April 1928.
57 J. Bowyer Bell, op.cit. p. 98.
58 T. P. Coogan, *The IRA* (London 1987) expanded edition, p. 85.
59 *An Phoblacht*, 5 January 1929.
60 Commission of Inquiry into Banking, Currency and Credit, *Report P No. 2628*, (Dublin 1938) p. 24.
61 O'Donnell, op.cit. pp. 118–119.
62 ibid., p. 131.
63 Bowyer Bell, op. cit. p. 84.
64 The 1926 estimate is from Bowyer Bell p. 76. The 1929 estimate is from a Department of Justice memorandum which quotes a police estimate of 1,300 officers and 3,500 volunteers, not including Cumann na mBan and Fianna Eireann. State Paper Office, 'Anti-State Activities, April 1929–October 1931' *5864 B*.
65 McHugh, op.cit. p. 175.
66 'Anti-State Activities.' *5844A*.
67 *An Phoblacht*, 5 April 1930. and M. Milotte *Communism in Modern Ireland* (1984), p. 98.
68 'Anti-State Activities.' Memorandum regarding Activities of Certain Organizations, January 1931, *5864B*.
69 *An tOglach* July 1931 included in 5844A. Twomey wrote to McGarrity of 'the extraordinary growth of the volunteer movement' in June 1931, quoted in Richard Dunphy, op.cit., p. 184.
70 Letter from O'Duffy to secretary of Department of Justice 27 July 1931, *5844A*.
71 ibid.
72 *An Phoblacht*, 27 June 1931.
73 See Austen Morgan, 'Connolly and Connollyism: the making of a myth' in *The Irish Review* No. 5 1988.
74 Sean Cronin, *Frank Ryan* (Dublin 1980) p. 34.
75 *An Phoblacht*, 3 October 1931.
76 ibid.
77 He would maintain his republican credentials for a while at

least. Thus the Department of Justice informed De Valera in January 1937 that he was one of two TDs, the other being Dan Breen, and a Senator who were at the burial of an IRA man in Tipperary when six men illegally discharged three volleys of shots over the grave. 'Anti-State Activities' *5864C* 24 January 1937.

78   O'Donnell, op.cit. p. 121.
79   Quoted in Uinseann MacEoin, *Survivors* (Dublin 1980) p. 6.
80   ibid.
81   Dermot Keogh, 'The Red Scare' in J. P. O'Carroll and J. A. Murphy (eds) *De Valera and his Times* (Cork 1983), p. 140.
82   Sean Cronin, *Frank Ryan* (1980), p. 36.
83   It was published as *For or Against the Ranchers? Irish Working Farmers in the Economic War*, (Westport 1932).
84   *Mayo News*, 10 October 1931.
85   Charlotte H. Fallon, *Soul of Fire: A Biography of Mary MacSwiney* (Cork and Dublin 1986), p. 151.
86   *Mayo News* 24 October 1931.
87   McHugh, op.cit. p. 418.
88   ibid. p. 222.
89   *Mayo News*, 17 October 1931.
90   *Mayo News*, 10 October 1931.
91   *The Round Table*, vol.xviii, May 1928.
92   *An Phoblacht*, 19 November 1927.
93   M. A. G. O'Tuathaigh, 'De Valera and Sovereignty' in O'Carroll and Murphy, op.cit., p. 67.
94   Cronin, *The McGarrity Papers*, p. 166.
95   Letter from Fianna Fail to the IRA Army Council in immediate aftermath of 1932 election victory quoted in *ibid*. p. 152.
96   *Irish Times*, 10 January 1937.
97   McHugh, op.cit. p. 80.
98   Cronin, op.cit. p. 152.
99   John Bowman, *De Valera and the Ulster Question* (Oxford 1985), p. 126.
100   Hopkinson, op.cit. p. 34. and Cronin, op.cit. p. 153.
101   Bowman, op.cit. pp. 124–125.
102   MacEoin, op.cit. p. 33.
103   See P. Bew, E. Hazelkorn and H. Patterson, *The Dynamics of Irish Politics*, (London 1989) Chapter 2.
104   *Republican Congress*, 5 May 1934.
105   ibid. and 6 October 1934.
106   George Gilmore, *The Irish Republican Congress* (Cork 1974) enlarged edition.
107   Quoted in ibid., p. 35.

108   ibid. p. 36.
109   O'Donnell, *For or Against the Ranchers?*, p. 5.
110   *Republican Congress* 12 May 1934.
111   ibid. 22 September 1934.
112   ibid. 12 May 1934.
113   *Mayo News* 30 June 1934.
114   *An Phoblacht* 7 July 1934.
115   Gilmore, op.cit. p. 34.
116   ibid., pp. 37–38.
117   Quoted in *Republican News*, 7 June 1975.
118   Freyer, op.cit. p. 36.
119   *An Phoblacht*, 26 November 1927.
120   Brian O'Neill, *The War for the Land in Ireland* (London 1933), p. 14.
121   McHugh, op.cit, p. 208.
122   On the split see Charles McCarthy, *Trade Unions in Ireland 1894–1960* (Dublin 1977).
123   *An Phoblacht* 4 August 1928.
124   ibid., 23 February 1929.
125   ibid., 24 June 1932 quoted in McHugh, op.cit. p. 451.
126   Clare O'Halloran, *Partition and the Limits of Irish Nationalism* (Dublin 1987) p. 42.
127   McHugh, op.cit. p. 449.
128   *An Phoblacht*, 16 July 1932.
129   On Connolly and the Protestant working class see Henry Patterson, *Class Conflict and Sectarianism*, (Belfast 1980)
130   *Republican Congress*, June 23 1934.
131   O'Donnell's description is given in R. Munck and B. Rolston, *Belfast in the Thirties: An Oral History* (Belfast 1987), p. 183.
132   *Republican Congress*, 16 June 1934.
133   Gilmore, op.cit., p. 36.
134   *Republican Congress*, 12 May 1934.
135   *An Phoblacht*, 20 August 1932.
136   *Republican Congress*, 18 August 1934.
137   Quoted in Munck and Rolston, op.cit. p. 184. During the 1932 Outdoor Relief Riots in Belfast, Tommy Geehan, the communist leader of the agitation on levels of Outdoor Relief asked for the protection of the IRA at meetings and marches. The request was refused, to the annoyance of social republicans in Dublin. See Margaret Geehan 'The Activities of the Belfast Revolutionary Workers' Groups' *BA Dissertation*, University of Ulster at Jordanstown, 1988, pp. 28–29.
138   *Republican Congress*, 12 May 1934.
139   ibid., 6 October 1934.

140   ibid., 13 October 1934.

3: In De Valera's Shadow

1   Sean Cronin, *The McGarrity Papers* (Tralee 1972), p. 166.
2   J. Bowyer Bell, op.cit. p. 150 and M. Milotte, *Communism in Modern Ireland* (Dublin and New York 1984), p. 236.
3   T. P. Coogan, op.cit. p. 112.
4   J. Bowyer Bell, op.cit. p. 164.
5   Ronan Fanning, 'De Valera and the IRA 1923–1940' in O'Carroll and Murphy, op.cit. p. 166.
6   Sean Cronin, *Frank Ryan* (Dublin 1980), p. 175.
7   *The Irish Democrat*, 8 May 1937.
8   ibid.
9   M. A. G. O'Tuathaigh, 'De Valera and Sovereignty' in O'Carroll and Murphy, op.cit., p. 70.
10   Coogan, op.cit. and J. A. Murphy, 'The New IRA 1925–62' in T. D. Williams (ed.) *Secret Societies in Ireland* (Dublin and New York 1973), p. 158.
11   Bowyer Bell, op.cit. p. 166.
12   Murphy, op.cit. p. 166.
13   Sean Cronin, *Frank Ryan* (Dublin 1980), pp. 182–190.
14   Interview with Jack Brady.
15   Peter Mair, *The Changing Irish Party System* (London 1987), p. 24 and Rumpf and Hepburn, op.cit. p. 149.
16   see Charles McCarthy, *Trade Unions in Ireland 1894–1960*, (Dublin 1977).
17   Rumpf and Hepburn, op.cit. p. 145.
18   Bowyer Bell op.cit. p. 290.
19   Coogan, op.cit., p. 331.
20   On vocationalism see Joe Lee, 'Aspects of Corporatist Thought
in Ireland: the Commission on Vocational Organization, 1929–43' in Cosgrove and McCartney (eds.) *Studies in Irish History*, (Dublin 1979).
21   see Noel Browne's biography, *Against the Tide* (Dublin 1986).
22   Bowyer Bell, op.cit. p. 292.
23   Coogan, op.cit. p. 330.
24   ibid. p. 332.
25   Brendan Behan, *Borstal Boy* (London 1967), p. 13.
26   ibid., p. 86.
27   Interview with Cathal Goulding and a long and useful interview with Goulding in *The Starry Plough*, the Official Republican paper in Derry, Easter 1972.
28   Richard Dunphy, op.cit. p. 180.

29   Interview with Tomas MacGiolla.
30   ibid.
31   J. A. Murphy, op.cit. p. 162.
32   On Liam Kelly see Michael Farrell, *Northern Ireland: The Orange State* (London 1976), pp. 205–206, 213, and 219–220; Coogan, op.cit. pp. 360–361 and interview with Paddy Joe McClean.
33   Figures from Farrell, op.cit., p. 209. The established pattern in elections in Northern Ireland from the 1920s was for the constitutionalist Nationalist Party to contest elections for the Northern Ireland parliament and for Sinn Féin to contest Westminster elections – Rumpf and Hepburn, op.cit., p. 183–184.
34   Farrell, op.cit., p. 224. The Irish Labour Party began an attempt to organize in Northern Ireland after the decision of the Northern Ireland Labour Party in 1949 to come out clearly in support of the link with Britain. A republican-socialist group then seceded from the NILP and became the basis for the extension of the ILP. Rumpf and Hepburn, op.cit. pp. 190–191.
35   Coogan, op.cit., p. 384.
36   Bowyer Bell, p. 353.
37   The victories were in the border constituencies of Monaghan and Sligo-Leitrim; in adjacent Longford-Westmeath and in the stronghold of traditionalist republicanism of South Kerry. Rumpf and Hepburn, p. 153.
38   Longford and O'Neill, *Eamonn De Valera* (Dublin 1970), p. 445.
39   Farrell, op.cit., p. 216.
40   ibid., p. 218 and Bowyer Bell p. 360.
41   Farrell, op.cit. p. 220.
42   Bowyer Bell, op.cit. p. 392.
43   *Republican Manual of Education: Part Two – Historical* (Dublin nd), p. 34.
44   Interview with Tomas MacGiolla.
45   Bowyer Bell, op.cit. p. 383.
46   Interviews with Francie Donnelly and Sean Garland.
47   Interview with Sean Garland.
48   Interviews with Cathal Goulding and Sean Garland.
49   Interview with Francie Donnelly.
50   Interview with Jim Sullivan.

4: A Limited Reassessment: The IRA After 1962

1   Interviews with Anthony Coughlan, Roy Johnston and Cathal Goulding; see also *Tuairisc: Newsletter of the Wolfe Tone Society* no. 6 June 1966.

2   Liam McMillen, *The Role of the IRA 1962–67* (Dublin 1976), p. 3.

3   Interview with Cathal Goulding.

4   Mallie and Bishop, op.cit., p. 35.

5   C. D. Greaves, *Reminiscences of the Connolly Association* (1978 no place of publication), p. 16.

6   ibid., p. 23.

7   ibid., p. 28.

8   ibid. p. 30 and *Letter* from Anthony Coughlan to Bob Purdie 12 August 1988 concerning Purdie's 'Was the Civil Rights Movement a Republican/Communist conspiracy?' in *Irish Political Studies* vol. 3 1988. Copy of letter courtesy of Anthony Coughlan.

9   Coughlan *letter*.

10 ibid.

11 Greaves, op.cit. p. 31.

12 ibid., p. 32.

13 *Constitution of Wolfe Tone Society* adopted at meeting in Dublin 25 July 1964, courtesy of Anthony Coughlan.

14 *Tuairisc*, no. 6, June 1966.

15 Interviews with Sean Garland and Anthony Coughlan. Coughlan successfully sued the publishers' of Mallie and Bishop for their allegation that he was an IRA member.

16 Roy Johnston, 'Why I quit Sinn Fein' in *Sunday Press*, 23 January 1972.

17 Interview with Goulding.

18 ibid.

19 Cathal Goulding 'The New Strategy of the IRA' in *New Left Review* 64, November/December 1970 p. 51.

20 'Our Ideas' in *Tuairisc* no. 7, 31 August 1966.

21 ibid.

22 ibid.

23 *Constitution of Wolfe Tone Society*.

24 This is discussed at length in Paul Bew and Henry Patterson, *Sean Lemass and the Making Of Modern Ireland* (Dublin 1982).

25 'Our Ideas'.

26 ibid.

27 Sinn Fein, *The Lessons of History*, (Dublin 1970) – first published September 1967.

28 ibid.
29 'Our Ideas.'
30 Sinn Fein, op.cit.
31 The demand to break the link with sterling and repatriate Irish capital abroad was a long-standing one – it featured in submissions to the Irish Banking Commission in the 1930s and was raised again by Clann na Poblachta. It was a central feature in 'Our Ideas'.
32 Sinn Fein, op.cit.
33 Milotte, op.cit. p. 236.
34 'Our Ideas.'
35 ibid.
36 See Bew and Patterson, op.cit., chapter six.
37 *Tuairisc* no. 6, June 1966.
38 Goulding, op.cit. p. 51.
39 *The IRA Speaks in the 1970s* (Dublin 1972), p. 10.
40 Goulding, op.cit. p. 53 and Rosita Sweetman, *On Our Knees: Ireland 1972* (London 1972), p. 142.
41 Sinn Fein, op.cit.
42 ibid.
43 ibid.
44 The document was printed as an appendix to the Inquiry of Lord Scarman, 'Violence and Civil Disturbances in Northern Ireland in 1969', *Report of a Tribunal of Inquiry* (Belfast HMSO, cmnd 556, 1972) vol. 2, p. 45.
45 ibid., p. 46.
46 ibid.
47 ibid., p. 52.
48 ibid., p. 46.
49 ibid., p. 47.
50 ibid.
51 ibid.
52 ibid.
53 Interview with Cathal Goulding.
54 Interview with Sean Garland.
55 Scarman, op.cit. p. 50.
56 Interview with Sean Garland.
57 Interview with Cathal Goulding.
58 ibid.
59. 'The Mind of the IRA', *The Belfast Telegraph*, 16 February 1966.
60 Information on McMillen's role from Sweetman, op.cit., from the pamphlet *Liam McMillen: Separatist, Socialist, Republican* (Dublin 1976) and interviews with Cathal Goulding, Jim

Sullivan, Kevin Smyth and Seamus Lynch.

61 Liam McMillen, *The Role of the IRA 1962– 67* (Dublin 1976), pp. 2 & 10. and P. Beresford, 'The Official IRA and Republican Clubs in Northern Ireland 1968–74', *DPhil*, University of Essex 1975, p. 247.

62 McMillen, op.cit. p. 1.

63 ibid., p. 5.

64 Interviews with Kevin Smyth and Seamus Lynch.

65 McMillen, op.cit. p. 8.

66 ibid., p. 8 and interview with Jim Sullivan.

67 Interview with Cathal Goulding.

68 Interview with Eoghan Harris.

69 Anthony Coughlan, Letter to Bob Purdie.

70 'Our Ideas.'

71 ibid.

72 ibid.

73 ibid.

74 Bob Purdie, op.cit.

75 Cathal Goulding, op.cit. p. 55 and Sean Garland, 'The Lessons of History', *United Irishman*, June 1971.

76 ibid. and *United Irishman*, December 1968.

77 Carol Coulter, 'A View from the South' in Michael Farrell (ed.) *Twenty Years On* (Dingle 1988), p. 108.

78 Michael Gallagher, *The Irish Labour Party in Transition 1957–82* (Manchester and Dublin 1982).

79 See Bew and Patterson op.cit. chapter 6.

80 See Bew, Hazelkorn and Patterson, op.cit., Chapter 4.

81 *The IRA Speaks in the 1970s* (Dublin 1972), pp. 3–6.

82 'Conor Cruise O'Brien and Labour', *United Irishman*, January 1969.

83 ibid.

84 ibid. December 1968.

85 ibid. January 1969.

86 Speech at Bodenstown quoted in *United Irishman*, April 1971.

87 *United Irishman*, January 1969.

88 Beresford, op.cit., pp. 112–114 and interviews with Goulding and Garland.

89 Republican Education Department, *Ireland Today and Some Questions on the Way Forward*, March 1969, p. 5.

90 ibid., p. 4.

91 ibid., p. 5.

92 ibid., p. 15.

93 ibid., p. 8.

94 ibid., p. 15.

95   ibid., p. 20.
96   ibid., p. 20.
97   Beresford, op.cit. p. 114.
98   *United Irishman*, May 1969.
99   *United Irishman*, May 1969.
100 Tomás MacGiolla, *Carrickmore Speech*, (Dublin 1973).
101 ibid.,
102 Mallie and Bishop, op.cit. p. 99.
103 Scarman op.cit. vol. 1 p. 6.
104 ibid.
105 ibid., pp. 21–22.
106 Thus the Unionist prime minister in the Stormont parliament on August 14 1969 'This is not the agitation of a minority seeking by lawful means the assertion of political rights. It is the conspiracy of forces seeking to overthrow a government, democratically elected . . .' quoted in Scarman op.cit., p. 10.
107 McMillen, op.cit. p. 10.
108 ibid., p. 11.
109 Interview with Seamus Lynch.
110 Beresford, op.cit. p. 247.
111 See his interview in Sweetman, op.cit., p. 195 – 'We resisted it tooth and nail. We used to spend hours at meetings trying to come up with ideas and excuses as to why we shouldn't become involved in this type of political activity . . .' and interviews with Jim Sullivan and Cathal Goulding.
112 Interview with Sullivan.
113 Interviews with Seamus Lynch and Jimmy Drumm.
114 Interview with Cathal Goulding.
115 Beresford, op.cit., p. 266 and interviews with Jimmy Drumm, Seamus Lynch and Jim Sullivan.
116 *United Irishman*, October 1969.
117 Scarman, op.cit. vol. 1 p. 12.
118 ibid., p. 9.
119 ibid., pp. 9, 119 & 120.
120 ibid., p. 121.
121 Interview with Seamus Lynch.
122 Gerry Adams, 'A Republican in the Civil Rights Campaign' in M. Farrell (ed.) *Twenty Years On* (Dingle 1968) p. 46.
123 Interviews with Kevin Smyth and Seamus Lynch – Republican Clubs had been formed to get around the northern government's ban on Sinn Fein. Young volunteers like Adams and Lynch were ordered to go to a meeting to elect the first NICRA executive and vote for a list of names given to them in advance

– there was some resistance to being ordered to vote for Communist Party members.

124 printed in full in Scarman, op.cit, vol. 2 pp. 43–44.

125 ibid. vol. 1 pp. 9–10.

126 ibid., p. 14.

127 McMillen, op.cit., p. 11.

128 Scarman, op.cit., pp. 133 & 159.

129 Interview with Jim Sullivan.

130 Scarman, op.cit., p. 14.

131 Interview with Sullivan.

132 Interview with Seamus Lynch.

133 Jack Lynch's speech is quoted in Geraldine Kennedy, 'The Thoughts of Chairman Jack' *Magill*, February 1978, p. 29.

134 *Resistance*, a special issue of the *United Irishman* produced in the aftermath of the August violence reported a speech by Paddy Devlin, NILP MP for the Falls constituency, given at the GPO in Dublin – 'We need guns was Paddy Devlin's unabashed cry – Don't abandon us'.

135 For a balanced analysis of the 'Arms Crisis' see T. R. Dwyer, *Charles Haughey*, (Dublin 1987), pp. 72– 100. For participants' views see Kevin Boland, *Up Dev!* (Dublin n.d.), pp. 142–149 and James Kelly, *Orders for the Captain* (Dublin 1971).

136 The chief civil servant in the Republic's Department of Justice recalled a memorandum which he encouraged his minister to circulate to the government in July 1969. It gave an analysis of the IRA and 'emphasised again that the time had become opportune to drive a wedge between the rural members – the old faithful – and the doctrinaire republicans, mainly based in Dublin, who were sedulously propagating the gospel of a 'Workers' Socialist Republic.' quoted in 'The Berry Papers', *Magill* June 1980, p. 50.

137 Interview with Francie Donnelly and Cathal Goulding.

138 Information is derived from a tape recorded conversation of three leading Officials involved in dealings with Fianna Fáil. The three were Goulding, McMillen and a prominent Belfast Official, Malachy McBurney. The tape, *1970 Discussion*, formed the basis for the anonymous 68 page pamphlet, *Fianna Fáil and the IRA* which was issued in the early 1970s with no place or date of publication. It was on sale for a while in the Official bookshop in Dublin and from their paper sellers. However, it was declared a 'seditious document' and possession of it a criminal offence. Luckily a few copies are still available.

139 Interview with Francie Donnelly.

140 1970 Discussion.
141 Malachy McBurney in ibid.
142 See Beresford, op.cit. pp. 204 and 229.
143 Interview with Jim Sullivan and *1970 Discussion*.
144 Interview with Goulding.
145 Interview with Goulding and *Fianna Fail and the IRA*, p. 24.
146 *1970 Discussion*.
147 James Kelly, op.cit., p. 8 and *Fianna Fail and the IRA*, p. 31.
148 Beresford, op.cit., p. 204.
149 Interview with Seamus Lynch.
150 1970 Discussion and James Kelly, op.cit. p. 19.
151 *Fianna Fail and the IRA*, p. 34.
152 quoted in Conor Cruise O'Brien, *States of Ireland* (London 1972), p. 81.

5: The Officials: Regression and Development 1970–77

1 This account is based on a number of sources – Interviews with Goulding and Garland, *Fianna Fail and the IRA* pp. 51–52, Coogan *The IRA* (London 1987) expanded edition, p. 428 and Bishop and Mallie op.cit. p. 40.
2 'Where Sinn Fein Stands', a statement issued subsequent to a meeting of the Caretaker Executive of Sinn Fein on January 17 1970. It was subsequently reissued in pamphlet form with the addition of a favourable article from the *New Statesman* by David George – 'These are the Provisionals'. (Dublin 1972).
3 'The Walk Out: A Personal View', *United Irishman* February 1970.
4 Interview with Cathal Goulding.
5 Interview with Sean Garland; see also his 'What Sort of Unity', *United Irishman* July 1971.
6 T. P. Coogan, *The IRA* (London 1987) expanded edition p. 429.
7 *United Irishman* January 1970.
8 ibid. April 1970.
9 ibid. March 1971.
10 ibid. April 1971.
11 ibid. February 1971.
12 Interview with Cathal Goulding.
13 Beresford, op.cit. p. 69.
14 Interviews with Jim Sullivan and Kevin Smyth.
15 According to a *United Irishman* estimate in July 1970, the Provisionals took 80% of those actively involved in the various Citizens Defence Committees. It should be noted that some

Provisional leaders were aware of the problems associated with the influx: interview with Jimmy Drumm.

16 Sean Garland, 'Policy, Strategy and Tactics', a lecture given at an internal Sinn Fein conference at Mornington, County Louth on 28th and 29th June 1975.

17 *United Irishman* February 1970.

18 Interview with Kevin Smyth.

19 Interview with Goulding in Sweetman, op.cit. p. 147.

20 *United Irishman* September 1970.

21 ibid.

22 ibid.

23 ibid. March 1970.

24 ibid. September 1970.

25 ibid. May 1970.

26 The role of British government policy in creating the best possible conditions for the development of the Provisionals is dealt with at greater length in P. Bew and H. Patterson, *The British State and the Ulster Crisis*, (London 1985).

27 See an article by Roy Johnston criticising a pamphlet by the People's Democracy leader, Michael Farrell, *The Struggle in the North*. One of his main criticisms of Farrell was the treatment of the Haughey/Blaney, *Voice of the North*, group as 'militantly anti-partitionist' – Johnston commented 'It is not to establish a Fianna Fail republic, it is to draw out the Republican sentiment of people into a civil war situation where it will be smashed so that a federal solution can be imposed by Westminster' *United Irishman* January 1970.

28 Interview with Cathal Goulding.

29 ibid.

30 *United Irishman* April 1970, IRA Easter Statement: 'The IRA is the Army of the People . . . The people must regard it as their own, and not as a remote organisation which is interested in fighting only one facet of British Imperialism, her occupation troops. The people of the 26 Counties must realise that British Imperialism is as strong in their midst. . . .'.

31 Interview with Sullivan.

32 *United Irishman* January 1972.

33 Interview with Kevin Smyth.

34 *United Irishman* September 1971.

35 Beresford op.cit. pp. 504 & 505.

36 See Eamon McCann's *War and an Irish Town* (London 1980) for a sympathetic Trotskyist view of the Derry Officials.

37 Details from Beresford op.cit. pp. 509–510.

38 Roy Johnston, 'Why I quit Sinn Fein' *Sunday Press* 23 January 1972.

39 Interview with Goulding. The Official IRA's own activities in the Irish Republic made some contribution to the problem. Thus in July 1971 it intervened in a long and bitter strike in the Mogul Silver Mines, County Tipperary, against a foreign mining company. A young IRA man, Martin O'Leary, was killed in an unsuccessful attempt to blow up an electricity transformer. At his funeral Goulding provocatively proclaimed 'When their answer to the just demands of the people is lock-out, strike-breaking, evictions . . . our duty is to respond in the language that brings vultures to their senses . . . the language of the bomb and the bullet.' *United Irishman* August 1971. Goulding was charged with incitement to violence but when an RTE tape of the funeral oration was finally handed over to the police it was found to be blank and the charge failed.

40 *United Irishman* April 1972.

41 ibid.

42 The vote in favour was 1,041,890 (83.1%); against, 211,891, (16.9%). Turnout was 70.3%. Michael Gallagher, *The Irish Labour party in Transition 1957–82* (Manchester & Dublin 1982) p. 285 note 53.

43 *United Irishman* June 1972.

44 'What Sort of Unity' *United Irishman* July 1971.

45 Sean Garland, speech at Bodenstown, *United Irishman* July 1972.

46 ibid.

47 Interview with Cathal Goulding.

48 Interview with Seamus Lynch.

49 IRA Easter Statement, *United Irishman* April 1972.

50 Sean Garland, 'Building Revolution', *United Irishman* May 1971. Garland's increasing disenchantment with the civil rights strategy may have reflected in part the influence of the American Trotskyist, Gerry Foley who came to Ireland in 1970 and gravitated towards the Officials. He appears to have influenced Garland's views for a time. See his critique of the political weaknesses of the Officials and the alleged danger that this would leave them open to 'the utopian concept of a long democratic stage ahead as proposed by the dismal hacks of the Northern Ireland Communist party.' Gerry Foley, *Problems of the Irish Revolution: Can the IRA meet the challenge?* (New York 1972) p. 21.

51 *United Irishman* September 1971.

52 Eoin O'Murchu, 'The Workers' Party: Its Evolution and its

Future', *Irish Socialist Review* 1982, p. 20.

53 Interviews with Tomas MacGiolla and Eamon Smullen.

54 O'Murchú op.cit. p. 20 and Margie Bernard, *Daughter of Derry: The Story of Brigid Sheils Makowski* (London 1989) p. 109 – she claims that Garland and Costello submitted a joint document to the Árd Fheis.

55 Beresford op.cit. p. 757.

56 Liam Barr 'The Republican Clubs – The Workers' Party in Mid-Ulster 1974–79', BA Dissertation, Ulster Polytechnic 1980, p. 8.

57 *United Irishman* July 1973.

58 Bew and Patterson, op.cit. p. 124.

59 *United Irishman* July 1973: 'We have a new opportunity to convince the Protestant working class that Republicanism is the only way out of the British created horror.'

60 At one Army Council meeting he proposed the seizure of the Catholic side of the River Foyle in Derry. In 1972 the Provisionals asked for a meeting with representatives of the Official Army Council. Costello was enthusiastic about the meeting's possibilities but when it occurred in a church in Gardiner Street, Dublin it turned out that the Provisionals simply wanted to warn the Officials to keep out of 'their war in the north' – interviews with Goulding and Garland.

61 Sean Garland, 'Policy, Strategy and Tactics' emphasized the need for a National Liberation Front.

62 Beresford op.cit. p. 707,

63 Sinn Féin, *Árd Fheis Report 1973*, p. 6.

64 In May 1974 two members of the South Down/South Armagh IRA were shot dead by British soldiers while attempting to place a landmine 'as retaliation for intimidation and harassment of working class people of Newry.' *United Irishman* June 1974.

65 *The Irish Times* 26 November 1973.

66 For the views of a Costello supporter see Bernard op.cit. p. 114.

67 ibid.

68 *The Irish Times* 26 November 1973 and *United Irishman* December 1973.

69 'He was choking us for the sinews of war' – interview with Cathal Goulding.

70 *United Irishman* July 1972.

71 Beresford, op.cit. p. 767.

72 O'Murchú, op.cit. p. 22.

73 ibid.

74 The documents found their way to the *Belfast Telegraph* which published an edited version of them. 13 November 1973.

75 *Irish Times*, 26 November 1973, Gerry Foley commented on the
    Derry Officials, after the killing of Ranger Best – the local
    youth who had joined the British Army – 'It is true that the
    Derry unit which carried out the execution, is not typical of the
    Official IRA. Among other things, British ultraleftist and
    workerist groups have exercised a more marked influence in
    this area than in other parts of Ireland.' Foley, op.cit. p. 7.

76 MacGiolla urged delegates to support the republican demand
    for withdrawal of British troops. *United Irishman* December
    1973.

77 Interview with one of the members of the Army Council at the
    time.

78 Sinn Fein, Árd Fheis 1974–75 *Internal Clar* (Agenda), various
    branches raised question of why the Extraordinary Árd Fheis
    on the Report had not been held.

79 For a pro-Costello account see Bernard, op.cit. p. 116.

80 Liam Barr, op.cit. p. 12.

81 Interview with Goulding.

82 Interview with Kevin Smyth.

83 Sinn Fein Árd Fheis *Report* 1974–75 p. 2.

84 Statement by Six County Executive of Republican Clubs 14
    November 1975.

85 Bishop and Mallie, op.cit. p. 222.

86 'What better way, the truce leadership thought, to maintain the
    ceasefire but at the same time allow the madmen to let off
    steam, than by allowing them to turn their guns on true
    republicans.' A quote from Official Sinn Fein leaflet, *Provo
    Pogrom* (Belfast 1975).

87 *Peoples Hope* (newsheet of Andersonstown Republican Club)
    February 15 1975 – 'Provo-RUC Deal' and interview with
    Seamus Harrison.

88 Interviews with Seamus Lynch and Kevin Smyth. Also see
    Eddie Rooney, 'From Republican Movement to Workers
    Party: An Ideological Analysis' in C. Curtin (ed) *Culture and
    Ideology in Ireland* (Dublin 1984).

89 Sean Garland, op.cit.

90 Tomas MacGiolla, *The Making of the Irish Revolution: Strategies
    and Tasks*, (Dublin 1976) p. 5.

91 Belfast Republican Clubs *Manifesto* for the Westminster
    Election February 1974.

92 Total deaths in Northern Ireland from the 'Troubles' which
    had climbed from 25 in 1970 to 474 in 1972 dropped to 221 in
    1974 but rose to 244 in 1975 and 296 in 1976. Figures from K.
    Boyle and T. Hadden, *Northern Ireland: A Positive Proposal*

(London 1985) p. 14. The reference to civil war is in a lecture by Des O'Hagan 'Fundamental Policies and Intentions of Organizations involved in the current situation'. Given at internal Sinn Fein conference at Mornington, County Louth, 28 & 29 June 1975.

93 Brian Brennan, 'Sectarianism and Class Politics', lecture at Mornington conference.

94 ibid.

95 Memorandum circulated by Michael O'Riordan, 30 March 1977.

96 The CP was also concerned about the decision of the 1977 Árd Fheis to change name to Sinn Fein The Workers Party and the decision to create the IDYM – 'as a rival to our Communist Connolly Youth Movement'.

97 Typical criticisms can be seen in Vincent Browne, 'The Secret World of the SFWP: Part 2 Political Lobotomy' Magill May 1982 and in O'Murchu, op.cit.

98 The following is based on interview with Eamonn Smullen, on his unpublished paper 'The Workers' Party and the Communist Party – in what ways do they differ' and on O'Murchu, op.cit.

99 see Ray McGuigan 'The Making of a Conspiracy' Magill May 1982.

100 Cormac O'Grada in United Irishman May 1977.

101 Eoghan Harris would admit this but defend it as part of a necessary ideological campaign to shift focus from external to internal sources of division in Ireland – interview with Eoghan Harris.

102 United Irishman May 1977.

103 Research Section of the Department of Economic Affairs, Sinn Fein The Workers Party, The Irish Industrial Revolution, (Dublin 1978) p. 50.

104 United Irishman February 1977.

105 Secretary's/Organizer's Report to Annual General Meeting of Dublin Comhairle Ceanntar, December 21 1973.

106 Organizers' Report to Dublin AGM December 1 1974.

107 ibid.

108 Secretary's/Organizer's Report to 1973 AGM and Reorganization Document 1974.

109 See P. Bew, E. Hazelkorn and H. Patterson, The Dynamics of Irish Politics (London 1989) chapter 4.

110 See in particular Research Section, Department of Economic Affairs, Sinn Fein, The Great Irish Oil and Gas Robbery: A Case Study of Monopoly Capital (Dublin 1974)

111 Eamonn Smullen, 'The Workers' Party and the Communist Party . . .' – 'Our party contributed the bulk of the research material . . . our research contribution was mostly not credited to us.'

112 See Carol Coulter 'How they infiltrated the ITGWU' *Magill* May 1982 – '. . . the main reason for the success of the infiltration process has simply been that the SFWP-inclined candidates were very often by far the most outstanding applicants for positions – most of them have also proved to be highly competent and diligent.'

113 Research Section, Department of Economic Affairs, Sinn Fein, *The Public Sector and the Profit Makers* (Dublin 1975 reprinted 1976).

114 Nationally the Labour Party vote rose from 185,176 (13.7%) to 186,410 (11.75%) but in Dublin its vote dropped from 78,342 (22.3%) to 74,688 (17.5%). In 1969 its Dublin vote had been 93,430 (28.3%) Michael Gallagher op.cit. Appendices 1 & 2.

6: The Provisionals and the Rediscovery of Social Republicanism

1 *Republican News*, 18 June 1977.

2 *Eire Nua: The Economic and Social Thought of Sinn Féin*, (Dublin 1971). The quote from O'Bradaigh is in Christine N. Elias, 'Know your Eire Nua: The New Ulster' *Republican News* 25 June 1973.

3 Bew and Patterson, op.cit. p. 50.

4 Vincent Browne, 'The Provos settle down for a 20 year war', *Magill* August 1982.

5 For a more detailed analysis of the Truce see Bew and Patterson, op.cit. pp. 78–88.

6 Patricia Davidson, 'British Withdrawal: the Economic Case,' *Republican News* 29 May 1976.

7 *Republican News* 18 June 1973.

8 Interview with Jimmy Drumm.

9 Gerry Adams, 'A Republican in the Civil Rights Campaign' in M. Farrell (ed.) *Twenty Years on* (Dingle 1988) p. 47.

10 Paul Arthur, *The People's Democracy* (Belfast 1974) and for conflicting assessments of the PD and 1968 see Ronald Fraser *1968* (London 1988)

11 Interview with Gerry Adams.

12 Peter Arnlis, 'The Nature of Strategy, Politics, Revolution and British Withdrawal' *Republican News* 27 March 1976.

13 ibid.

14 Brownie, 'The Republic: A Reality' *Republican News* 29 November 1975.
15 Brownie, 'Agitate, Educate, Liberate' *Republican News* 22 May 1976.
16 See 'The North – Key to English Influence in Ireland' *Republican News* 23 September 1974 which copies the *Ireland Today* analysis almost word for word.
17 'Why died the sons of Roisin Dubh? Was it greed?' *Republican News* 10 January 1976.
18 'Agitate, Educate, Liberate'.
19 See Peter Mair, 'The Irish Republic and the Anglo-Irish Agreement' in P. Teague (ed) *Beyond the Rhetoric* (London 1988).
20 *Republican News* 29 October 1977.
21 ibid.
22 Richard Davis, *Political Propaganda and the Ulster Troubles: A Mirror Image of Antagonism 1968–82*, unpublished manuscript, University of Tasmania, 1983, pp. 214– 215.
23 'Thoughts on Eire Nua' *Republican News* 5 November 1977.
24 ibid.
25 Bishop and Mallie, op.cit. p. 262.
26 'Agitate, Educate, Liberate' *Republican News* 22 May 1976.
27 *Republican News* 29 October 1977.
28 Peter Dowling, 'Stickies in Trouble' *Republican News* 26 February 1977.
29 ibid.
30 'Now it's official – Stickies accept Orange Rule', *Republican News* 9 April 1977.
31 'Success opens up new challenges: 1978 Review' *An Phoblacht/Republican News (AP/RN)* 27 January 1979.
32 'Struggle on all fronts' *AP/RN* 10 February 1979.
33 'Out of the ashes' *AP/RN* 27 January 1979.
34 'Struggle on all fronts'.
35 'Out of the ashes.'
36 'Not just a Brits Out movement', a speech at Bodenstown, June 1979, reprinted in Gerry Adams, *Signposts to Independence and Socialism*, (Dublin 1988) pp. 23–27.
37 'Active Republicanism' *Republican News* 1 May 1976.
38 'The National Alternative' *Republican News* 3 April 1976.
39 Bew and Patterson, op.cit. p. 93.
40 ibid.
41 The Glover Report is reproduced in full as an appendix to Sean Cronin, *Irish Nationalism: A History of its Roots and Ideology* (Dublin 1980).

42 *AP/RN* 19 May 1979

43 For a detailed analysis of the issues see Liam Clarke, *Broadening the Battlefield*, (Dublin 1987).

44 *Magill* May 1979.

45 'Bernadette and the Politics of H Blocks' in Callaghan's *Irish Quarterly*, vol. 1 no. 1 p. 14.

46 'Sinn Fein Prisoners Conference' *AP/RN* 29 September 1979.

47 'A Tragedy not a Farce' *AP/RN* 2 June 1979.

48 IRA interview *AP/RN* 11 August 1979.

49 Interview with Jimmy Drumm.

50 *Myth and Motherland*, Field Day pamphlet no. 5, Derry 1984, p. 12.

51 See Clarke, op.cit.

52 *AP/RN* 3 February 1983.

53 ibid. 17 March 1983.

54 ibid. 5 May 1983.

55 ibid.

56 'Establishment poll-axed by Sinn Fein vote' *AP/RN* 16 June 1983.

57 'Sinn Fein EEC Challenge' *AP/RN* 3 May 1984.

58 'Steady Progress and an injection of Reality' *AP/RN* 21 June 1984.

59 ibid.

60 See *Magill* July 1983 where Adams called for a refinement of IRA activity while a member of the IRA Army Council called for an escalation.

61 *AP/RN* 21 June 1984.

62 Peter Dowling, 'Dublin Summit opens dangerous option' *AP/RN* 17 January 1981.

63 Danny Morrison, *The Hillsborough Agreement* (Dublin 1986) pp. 8–9.

64 Gerry Adams, *The Politics of Irish Freedom* (Dingle 1986) p. 105.

65 Morrison, op.cit. p. 9.

66 Adams, op.cit. p. 105.

67 *AP/RN* 17 January 1981.

68 Adams, op.cit. p. 154.

69 Gerry Adams, 'A Bus Ride to Independence and Socialism', speech given to Sinn Fein Internal Conference 1986, reprinted in *Signposts to Independence and Socialism*, p. 13.

70 See his 1979 interview: 'There is no Marxist influence within Sinn Fein. I know of no one in Sinn Fein who is a Marxist or who would be influenced by Marxism.' *Hibernia* 25 October 1979.

71 In the autumn of 1980 Seamus Mallon and John McEvoy of the

SDLP had met Morrison and Joe Austin of Sinn Féin for a series of talks. In October 1984, a lack of response from Britain to the Forum Report prompted a prominent SDLP councillor in Belfast, Brian Feeney, to suggest cooperation with Sinn Fein in councils to make Northern Ireland ungovernable. *AP/RN* 11 October 1984.

72 *The Observer* 27 April 1986.
73 *The Guardian* 30 March 1987.
74 The Sinn Fein and SDLP documents were reproduced in the *Irish Times* 19 September 1988.
75 *AP/RN* 5 April 1984.
76 Quotes from Sinn Fein document 'A Strategy for Peace' sent to the SDLP in March 1988, reproduced in full in *Irish Times* 7 September 1988.
77 Bew and Patterson, op.cit. pp. 140–142.
78 *The Guardian* 9 March 1987.
79 *Irish Times* 19 September 1988.
80 ibid. 6 September 1988.
81 *Irish Times* 13 June 1988.
82 *Magill* August 1988.
83 ibid.
84 See Fergus Pyle interview with Adams in *Irish Times* 19 July 1988 and *Magill* August 1988.
85 Peter Mair, op.cit. p. 100.
86 ibid. p. 101.
87 See his speech at Harvard, *Irish Times* 23 April 1988.
88 *Irish Times* 19 September 1988.
89 ibid.
90 *Irish News* 21 June 1988.
91 *An Reabhloid* (The Revolution) Journal of People's Democracy, vol. 1 no. 2 Autumn 1988 p. 12 – A. McIntyre and M. McMullen.
92 *Borderline*, vol. 1 no. 3 Autumn 1986.
93 'Whats on the agenda now is an end to Partition' – Adams interview with Fergus Pyle, *Irish Times* 19 July 1988.
94 'Scenario for a Socialist Republic' *AP/RN* April 1980 reprinted in *Signposts to Independence and Socialism*. pp. 28–31.
95 Gerry Adam's Address, reprinted in *The Politics of Revolution: Main Speeches on 1986 Sinn Fein Árd Fheis* (Dublin 1986) p. 11.
96 ibid. p. 8.
97 ibid. pp. 12–13.
98 ibid.
99 Liam Clarke, op.cit.
100 Adams, op.cit. p. 13.

101 John Ward, 'What is to be done? The struggle in the 26 counties', *Iris: The Republican Magazine*, October 1987.

102 Interview with Gerry Adams.

103 Mair, op.cit. p. 94.

104 ibid. p. 90.

105 ibid.

106 Gerry Adams, *The Politics of Irish Freedom* (Dingle 1986) p. 157.

107 Mair, op.cit. p. 92.

108 Gerry Adams, *A Pathway to Peace* (Cork and Dublin 1989) p. 8.

109 ibid. p. 77

110 ibid. pp. 80–81.

111 ibid. p. 62.

112 Robin Wilson, 'Civilian Unrest' *Fortnight* March 1989.

113 'Peace, War and Understanding', interview with Adams *Magill* August 1988.

114 Gerry Adams, *A Pathway to Peace*, pp. 74–75.

115 'Adams calls on Southern parties' *Irish Times* 13 June 1988.

116 Positions argued by Mairtin O'Muilleoir, Sinn Fein councillor for Andersonstown at a conference of Sinn Fein activists, *Irish Times* 27 June 1988.

117 *Irish Times* 6 March 1989.

118 quoted in *Irish Times* 24 February 1989.

119 In 1985/6 the IRA managed to import over 1,000 Kalashnikov rifles and several tons of Semtex explosive from Libya. Adams, at the 1989 Sinn Fein Árd Fheis quoted an IRA veteran of an earlier campaign – 'If we had the weapons the IRA has now we would have driven the British out of the country.' *Irish Times* 30 January 1989.

120 Eamonn Mallie, 'The Provos Resurgence' *Fortnight* September 1988.

121 Eamonn Mallie 'The Provos: Twenty Years On' *Sunday Press* 5 February 1989.

122 Árd Fheis speech in *Irish Times* 30 January 1989.

123 ibid.

124 Adams interviewed by Mary Holland *The Observer* 19 June 1988.

125 The killing of three Protestants in Coagh, county Tyrone was typical of actions which Adams had to continue to distance himself from see Mary Holland, 'Terrorists hit wrong targets', *Observer* 12 March 1989.

126 Interview with Jimmy Drumm.

127 For example the literature of Mairtin O'Muilleoir, Sinn Fein candidate in Upper Falls in the 1985 Local Government election – 'pledged to use the City Hall structure to highlight

the needs of west Belfast in culture, employment and community resources.'

128 Bill Rolston and Mike Tomlinson, *Unemployment in West Belfast: The Obair Report.* (Belfast 1988)
129 *Irish Times* 27 June 1988.

Conclusion

1 Eamonn McCann, *War and an Irish Town* (2nd edition London 1980), p. 174.
2 ibid.
3 Sean Cronin, *Irish Nationalism: A History of its Roots and Ideology* (London 1988), p. 210.
4 'Northern Ireland: Future Terrorist Trends' in Cronin, op.cit., p. 342.
5 Ed. Moloney, 'Mistaken Strategy' in *Fortnight*, May 1989.
6 Quoted in Bishop and Mallie, op.cit., p. 301.
7 In the 1989 local government elections Sinn Fein's vote remained the same as it had been in previous local government elections in 1985 at 11.3%. However, this disguised a significant loss of support outside Belfast and Derry where in rural areas its vote dropped by about 5%, in part at least a result of IRA 'mistakes' in which a number of civilians were killed. It lost 16 seats. However in Belfast its vote increased by 3.1% on 1985 and it maintained its support in Derry *Irish Times* 20 May 1989 and *Sunday Tribune* 21 May 1989.
8 Sinn Fein, *The Politics of Revolution – Main Speeches and Debates from the 1986 Sinn Fein Ard-Fheis including the Presidential Address of Gerry Adams*, (1986), p. 11.
9 ibid., p. 8.
10 ibid., p. 11.
11 ibid.
12 ibid., p. 22.
13 Cynthia Irvin and Eddie Moxon-Browne, 'Not many floating voters here' in *Fortnight*, May 1989.
14 ibid.
15 Eamonn McCann, 'Republicanism in Crisis' in *Socialist Worker*, July 1988.
16 see the Sinn Fein educational booklet, *Questions of History* (1987), written by 'Irish Republican Prisoners of War' and very clearly influenced by marxism.
17 *Congress 86: Quarterly Journal of Communist Republican Prisoners and their Associates*, vol. I no. 4.
18 Gerry Adams *The Politics of Revolution*, p. 10.

19   'The Language of Revolution' in *Congress 86*, vol. no. 4.

20   Interview with Jimmy Drumm.

21   Michael Farrell, *Northern Ireland: The Orange State* (London 1976). Adams in his writings in Long Kesh referred favourably to Farrell's book.

22   see Sean Cronin and Richard Roche, *Freedom the Wolfe Tone Way* (Tralee 1973), p. 78.

23   Interview with Jimmy Drumm.

24   Gerry Adams, *The Politics of Revolution*, p. 9.

25   quoted in Cronin, op.cit., p. 204.

26   Bew and Patterson, *The British State and the Ulster Crisis*, (London 1985) pp. 118–19.

27   *Irish Times*, 20 May 1989.

28   Results of the February 1987 general election – Irish Labour Party 6.4% of vote and twelve seats, Workers' Party 3.8% and four seats, Niamh Hardiman, *Pay, Politics and Economic Performance in Ireland 1970–1987* (Oxford 1988), p. 232.

29   see the *Presidential Address* of Prionsias De Rossa to 1989 Árd Fheis of Workers' Party and critical response to it by Ellen Hazelkorn and Paul Sweeny in *Making Sense*, May 1989.

30   De Rossa raised the issue of the irredentist Articles 2 & 3 of the Republic's Constitution and even broached the question of the need for a serious debate on the significance of 1916.

31   Interview with Gerry Adams.

32   Adams, *The Politics of Revolution*, p. 11.

33   *An Phoblacht/Republican News*, 6 November 1988.

34   Joe Jackson interview with Danny Morrison in *Hot Press*, 25 August 1988.

35   See note 7.

36   see Liam Clarke, *Broadening the Battlefield: The H Blocks and the Rise of Sinn Fein* (Dublin 1987) p. 240.

37   Peter Murtagh, 'In the shadow of the gunmen', *The Guardian*, 28 January 1989. He interviewed both men and O'Bradaigh argued 'that the bullet and the ballot-box policy of Gerry Adams . . . means that Sinn Fein is slowly but surely accepting the institutions it is pledged to destroy.'

38   Adams, *The Politics of Revolution*, p. 11.

39   Robin Wilson, 'Insecurity Policy' in *Fortnight*, September 1988.

40   'Republicanism Revisited' in *Congress 86*, vol. 1 no. 3.

41   After the Hunger Strikes, Bernadette (Devlin) McAliskey a founder member of the IRSP with Seamus Costello, had given her support to the modernized Sinn Fein: 'The Sinn Fein that came out of the Hunger Strikes was not far from the

organization that Costello envisaged in 1973.' *The Sunday Tribune*, 24 April 1988.

42   Sean Flynn, 'Marxist gunmen of the INLA threaten a resurrection', *The Irish Times*, 18 September 1987.

43   Quoted in leader column of *Fortnight*, September 1988.

44   Bob Rowthorn and Naomi Wayne, *Northern Ireland: The Political Economy of the Conflict* (Cambridge 1988), p. 116.

45   ibid., p. 117.

46   From the review of the Anglo-Irish Agreement published by British and Irish governments and reprinted in full in *The Irish Times*, 25 May 1989.

47   In a letter to the author, 14 December 1988.